THE CISKEI AND TRANSKEI

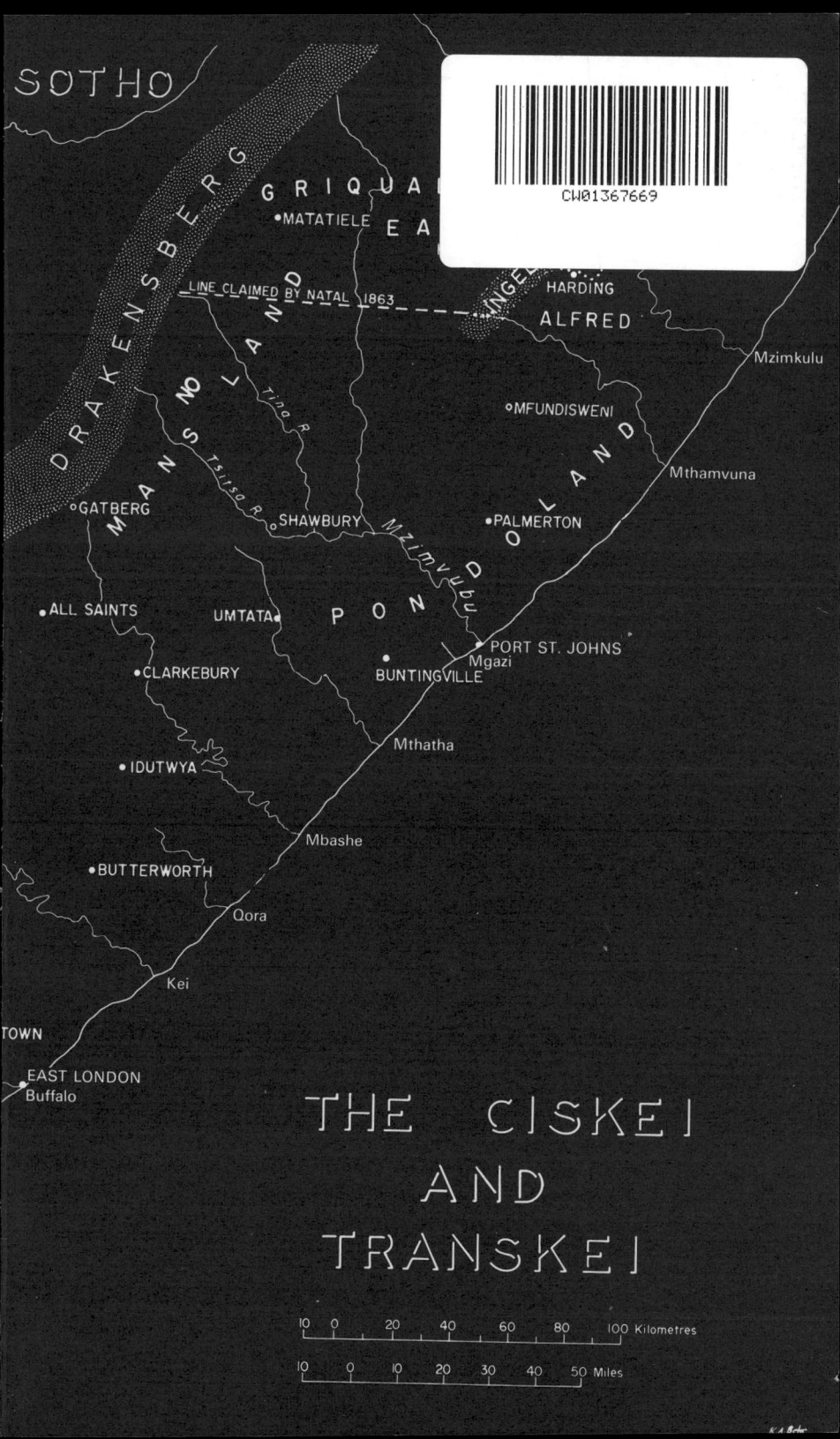

**BEYOND
the CAPE
FRONTIER**

Cape Town.

BEYOND the CAPE FRONTIER

Studies in the History of the Transkei and Ciskei

edited by
Christopher Saunders and
Robin Derricourt

LONGMAN

LONGMAN GROUP LIMITED
London.

*Associated companies, branches and
representatives throughout the world.*

© Copyright Longman Group Ltd. 1974

First published 1974

This book is copyright. Apart from any fair
dealing for the purpose of private study,
research criticism or review, as permitted
under the Copyright Act, no part may be
reproduced by any process without
written permission of the publishers.

Cased edition ISBN 0 582 64587 5
Paper edition ISBN 0 582 64588 3

G & S Ltd.

Contents

Abbreviations vi
List of maps vii
List of plates vii
Acknowledgements viii
Introduction ix

1. Praise Poems as Historical Sources 1
   Jeff Opland (Associate Professor and Head of the Department of English, University of Durban-Westville)

2. Settlement in the Transkei and Ciskei before the Mfecane 39
   Robin Derricourt (Secretary/Inspector, National Monuments Commission, Livingstone, Zambia)

3. Thoughts on the Study of the History of the Cape Eastern Frontier Zone 83
   William M. Freund (Humanities Division, Kirkland College, Clinton, N.Y.)

4. The Mfengu, Self-Defence and the Cape Frontier Wars 101
   Richard A. Moyer (School of Oriental and African Studies, University of London)

5. The Griqua in the Politics of the Eastern Transkei . . 127
   Robert Ross (St. John's College, Cambridge)

6. The Rôle of the Wesleyan Missionaries in Relations between the Mpondo and the Colonial Authorities . . 145
   D. G. L. Cragg (Warden, Livingstone House, Rhodes University, Grahamstown)

7. Natal and the Transkei, to 1879 163
   B. A. le Cordeur (Senior Lecturer in History, University of Cape Town)

8. The Annexation of the Transkei 185
   C. C. Saunders (Lecturer in History, University of Cape Town)

9. African Education and Society in the Nineteenth Century Eastern Cape 199
   Michael Ashley (Lecturer in Education, Rhodes University)

10. Some Fields for Research 213
    Monica Wilson (formerly Professor of Social Anthropology, University of Cape Town)

    Index 231

Abbreviations

AYB	*Archives Year Book for South African History*
D.S.A.B.	*Dictionary of South African Biography*
JAH	*Journal of African History*
M.L.A.	Member of the Legislative Assembly
P.R.O.	Public Record Office (London)
VOC	Vereenigde Nederlandsche Ge-Octroyeerse Oost-Indische Compagnie (United Netherlands Chartered East India Company)

List of Illustrations

List of maps
The Transkei and Ciskei . . . . endpapers
Distribution of Peoples in the Transkei and Ciskei
    1600–1650 73
    1650–1700 74
    1700–1750 75
    1750–1770 76
    1770–1779 77
    1779–1819 78
The Transkeian territories: Peoples (c. 1872) 196
The Transkeian territories: Political Divisions (1880's) and the main road through the territories 196

List of figures
Genealogical Tables 46–7
The Settlement Pattern of Early Cape Nguni
    (a) the village 66
    (b) the clan equivalent 67
    (c) the tribal cluster 68

List of plates
1. A Xhosa imbongi (Mase Attwell Bhuti) . . . opp. 32
   A Xhosa imbongi (Melikhaya Mbutuma) during a performance . . . . opp. 32
2. A Xhosa imbongi (Nelson Title Mabunu) during a performance . . . . opp. 33
3. The Transkei coast . . . . opp. 48
   Homestead in central Transkei . . . . . . opp. 48
   Riverside homestead: the Horseshoe at Ntabankulu . opp. 48
4. San hunter and his quarry (Tsolo District) . . . opp. 49
   San society (Tsolo district) . . . . opp. 49
5. San fishing (Matatiele district) . . . . . . opp. 64
5. Interaction: cattle (with modern imitations) (Engcobo district) . . . . opp. 64
6. Interaction: Horses (Matatiele district) . . . . opp. 65
   Interaction: European ox-wagon with team and driver (Tsolo district) . . . . opp. 65
7. Khoi soldier in the Cape Corps . . . . . . opp. 80
8. Kat River Coloured . . . . opp. 81
9. Charles Brownlee, African administrator and the Cape's first Secretary for Native Affairs (1872–8) . . . opp. 128
10. Dr James Stewart and Lovedale students . . . opp. 129
11. Adam Kok III (1811–75) Griqua kaptyn . . . opp. 144
12. Tiyo Soga (1829–71), African missionary . . . opp. 145

Acknowledgements

The decision to produce this book was taken at a conference on the history of the Transkei and Ciskei held at Rhodes University, Grahamstown, in the first week of February 1973. The conference was made possible thanks to the support of Rhodes University, the Transkei and Ciskei Research Society (TACRESOC) and the Anglo-American Corporation, whose grant also helped to meet the cost of publishing this book. The editors would like to thank these bodies most warmly for their aid. They would also like to thank Professor T. R. H. Davenport, Mrs W. Proctor and the others who assisted in the practical arrangements for the conference, and Professors Colin Webb and Monica Wilson for editorial advice.

Introduction

In the preface to the recently published *Oxford History of South Africa* the editors state their belief that "the central theme of South African history is interaction between peoples of diverse origins, languages, technologies, ideologies and social systems, meeting on South African soil".[1] Acceptance of the importance of interaction, and of the view that South African history is *not* merely the history of the white man in South Africa but is the history of all the peoples of the region, has various consequences. The Great Trek may still be regarded as the central event in South African history but historians can no longer merely follow in the path of the Trek and ignore those areas it by-passed. One such area, ignored for too long, is the Transkei and Ciskei, the land along the south-eastern seaboard of South Africa between the Fish River in the South and the Mzimkulu and Mthamvuna Rivers in the north, the land, as the names Transkei and Ciskei suggest, on either side of the Kei River.[2] Historians are today beginning to see this area as of crucial importance in South African history. This volume is a reflection of this new concern.

The history of the Transkei and Ciskei merits attention for several reasons. There is the significance of the area today. The first "Bantustan" was formed of land east of the Kei. For almost ten years the Transkei was the only "Bantustan" to have been granted limited self-government. Here is the largest area in the Republic of South Africa that did not fall into white hands. If any "Bantustan" is to become independent in the future, it is likely to be the Transkei.[3] To go back into the past, Khoisan people lived for centuries alongside Bantu-speakers on the lands either side of the Kei and historians are beginning to study the relations between these groups.[4] Perhaps the chief importance of the Transkei and Ciskei for historians, however, is that there conflict and co-operation between whites and Bantu-speaking Africans have a longer history than anywhere else in southern Africa. This is the famous "eastern frontier" of the Cape, where for one hundred years white men and black fought each other, but also lived and traded and worked together. At the beginning of the nineteenth century, the Cape's eastern border was the Fish River. Gradually, in the course of the century, the colonial border was shifted eastwards, until eventually all the Ciskei and the Transkei was under Cape rule. In the lands east of the Fish white missionaries first brought western-type education to Africans, and in consequence the first significant educated African elite emerged in this part of southern Africa. In the soil of the eastern Cape frontier lie many of the earliest roots of African nationalism in South Africa.[5]

Until recently, the history of the Transkei and Ciskei has been one of the most neglected areas in South African historiography. True, one classic anthropological work of the 1930s considered change among the Mpondo of the eastern Transkei – Monica Hunter's *Reaction to Conquest*[6] – and C. W. de Kiewiet, probably the greatest of South African historians, turned briefly to the eastern Cape frontier in the 1870s in *The Imperial Factor in South Africa*,[7] but few others besides the occasional thesis writer did serious work on the history of the region. In recent years, however, largely because of the new perspectives that have opened up in South African history, a number of scholars have studied aspects of the history of the Transkei and Ciskei. Not all are historians: they include anthropologists, linguists and archaeologists. Interaction between scholars of different formal academic disciplines has helped give dynamism to the new directions of inquiry that have developed. As has been the case with African studies elsewhere on the continent, such interaction can provide a stimulus to defining problems and deriving a route to answers.

This interaction may also point to the gaps to be filled between disciplines. Formal work on the collection and study of oral tradition is perhaps one such gap. One of the most striking new developments in African studies in the past two decades has been the emphasis placed on the importance of using oral data, collected, sifted and assessed by a series of techniques as disciplined as those of the historian in an archive or the archaeologist at an excavation. Yet in South Africa very few projects have attempted to use oral historical data. Historians have been unwilling to employ an unfamiliar source of evidence. The collection of oral evidence, like anthropological work and other field aspects of research in African areas, has its difficulties in South Africa. There is the need to obtain permits and problems in staying with the community under study. There is the suspicion felt in many areas, both rural and urban, towards a questioning outsider of another ethnic group.

The practical problems of field research, and the importance of obtaining a rounded view of South African history, point to the great need for more black South Africans to work and write in the fields of history and African studies generally. Despite the early writings of black missionary-linked writers, virtually nothing has appeared by black scholars in recent years.[8] The absence of black academic writing on South African history is to the severe detriment of South African academic life in general. The reason for it may be in part the general social situation, and especially the shortage of teachers and texts of quality in the schools and the absence of a significant and positive African studies element in the school syllabus. Knowledge in the humanities is too often seen as data necessary to pass an examination, or obtain a degree, and a degree as a route to a job, often in examination-oriented teaching, which makes the attitude self-perpetuating. There is, too, a fear of writing on topics which may be deemed controversial; this fear is sometimes, but by no means always, justified. It may be that in time the emerging "black consciousness" movement will produce a new interest in the past among Africans. This potential has yet to be fulfilled; to date the new thinking sparked off by this movement has been concentrated mainly in the fields of theology and the arts. It is ardently to be hoped that before long essays on the history of the Transkei and Ciskei will come from the pens of black historians.

By 1972 it seemed to the editors of this volume that the new interest in the history of the Transkei and Ciskei had produced sufficient work to make it worthwhile to call a conference to consider the state of knowledge on the history of the area. As mentioned in the acknowledgements, a conference was held at Rhodes University in Grahamstown in February 1973, at which a number of papers on aspects of the history of the Transkei and Ciskei were discussed. The conference attracted a wide audience of interested persons and contributions came not only from South African scholars but also from outsiders who had done research in South Africa. A somewhat similar conference had taken place in Lusaka, Zambia, in July 1968 on the history of African societies in southern Africa,[9] but the Transkei-Ciskei conference was the first of its kind to be held within the Republic of South Africa. Most of the chapters in this book are revised versions of papers originally presented at the Grahamstown conference.

It was one of the main aims of the conference, as it is of this book, to stimulate further study of the history of the Transkei and Ciskei. This will not be hampered by lack of material from which to work. The contributions to this volume are tentative not so much because we cannot know the answers as because the necessary research has not been done for the answers to be given. Archaeological fieldwork of a systematic kind was not started in the area until 1971, yet already it has been shown that a vast amount of information will be uncovered if it is continued.[10] It is to be hoped that the African authorities in the Transkei and Ciskei will help in the work of recovering the past of the area, and especially perhaps aid in the collection of oral material, which has hardly started. The written sources for the history of the region, which begin with the accounts of shipwrecked sailors on the Transkeian coast in the sixteenth century, are voluminous. From the eighteenth century onwards, a large number of literate travellers crossed the area and wrote of what they saw. In the nineteenth century many missionaries and men involved in African administration left descriptions of their work and the people with whom they lived. The printed official material is extremely rich; to take one example, the recently reprinted report of the Cape Commission on Native Laws and Customs of 1880–83 is a mine of information.[11] There is still a mass of records in the official archives in Pietermaritzburg, Cape Town and London that remain virtually untapped.[12] There are several very valuable collections of private papers, such as the Walter Stanford collection in the Jagger Library of the University of Cape Town. The Cory Library in Grahamstown has a large collection of missionary records on the history of the Transkei and Ciskei, and there is other relevant missionary material at several depositories in London.[13]

The studies in this volume together constitute a preliminary attempt to show what can be learned from some of these various sources of evidence. In the first chapter, Professor Opland looks at praise poems, one example of oral evidence, and discusses them with a view to showing their value to the historian. Then an archaeologist with a keen interest in history examines the early settlement of peoples in the area and draws on a number of different sources to suggest how the Cape Nguni were distributed there before the Mfecane. The 1820s, the "time of troubles" for so much of South Africa, were years of turbulence for the Transkei. Not only did Shaka's armies ravage the northern Transkei and Matiwane lead his Ngwane into Thembu country, but various refugee groups settled south of the Mzimkulu. The survivors of groups broken up and scattered by the Mfecane became known as Mfengu (Fingo).

For a full account of Mfengu history we must wait for Richard Moyer's doctoral dissertation, but in his chapter in this volume he examines an important thread in that history. For more than forty years, in a series of frontier wars, the Mfengu fought with the whites against other black groups. Moyer analyses the nature of this collaboration and points to the benefits the Mfengu derived from it. In his chapter, Robert Ross is concerned with another intrusive group, the Griqua, people of mixed descent who lived north of the Orange River until they decided to cross the Drakensberg and enter the eastern Transkei. From the early 1860s they dominated much of the highlands there. Though called "Nomansland", this area was not uninhabited and Ross discusses relations between the Griqua and the Africans they encountered in the eastern Transkei, as well as relations between the Griqua and their neighbours.

The most important intruders into the Transkei in the nineteenth century were the whites, for they came to rule the whole area. Chapters 6—8 examine aspects of the white impact. Donald Cragg's subject is the way in which the Wesleyan Methodist missionaries helped shape the relations which developed between the Mpondo and the colonial authorities at the Cape, from the establishment of the first mission station in Pondoland in 1830 until the annexation of that part of the Transkei by the Cape in the mid-1890s. The extension of white rule over the Transkei is the main theme of the next two chapters. In the first, Basil le Cordeur looks at this process from the Natal side and asks why Natal's attempts to expand southwards were so unsuccessful. He argues that, although not generally successful, these attempts were nevertheless significant. The second of these chapters is concerned with the way in which the Cape incorporated the Transkeian territories between 1872, when the Cape received responsible government, and 1894, and briefly considers some of the results of the process of incorporation for the Cape Colony as a whole.

At the time the incorporation of the Transkei in the Cape was taking place, some Africans in the Ciskei, who had by the 1870s long been colonial residents, were beginning to receive an advanced western-type education in schools founded by missionaries. Michael Ashley, an educationalist, considers both the rising African demand for education in the last part of the nineteenth century and the white response to that demand. In the middle of the century, whites had welcomed the growth of a westernised African elite. As such an elite began to develop political and economic power, so whites came increasingly to fear competition from blacks and took steps to eliminate such competition. Here is another theme little explored,[14] but an essential part of the background to the present South African situation. All the contributors to this book are very conscious of the gaps that exist in our knowledge of the history of the Transkei and Ciskei.[15] It is fitting that to conclude the volume Professor Monica Wilson, doyen of scholars of the area and herself born and brought up in the Ciskei, points the way to future research.

Note on terminology
Almost every work on South African history comments on the difficulties in reaching an acceptable terminology. Faced with these difficulties and aware that they were unlikely to please everyone, the editors have nevertheless tried to use the most acceptable terms and to employ the correct orthography. Mbashe is used, therefore, rather than Bashee; Khoi and San, not Hottentot and Bushman; and so on. "Khoi/Coloured" reflects ambiguity in the documents.

FOOTNOTES
1 M. Wilson and L. Thompson, eds., *The Oxford History of South Africa* (2 vols. 1969 and 1971) I, v.
2 The name Kei (Xhosa: "Nciba") is probably derived from the Khoi word "gei" (great) (B. Holt, *Place Names in the Transkeian Territories* (Johannesburg 1959) p. 19).
3 It should be noted that this book is concerned with a considerably larger area than the Transkeian and Ciskeian "Bantustans" as presently constituted. In the nineteenth century "Transkei" was often used to refer to the land immediately across (i.e. east of) the Kei; it is used here for the whole area from the Kei to the southern border of Natal.

4 See esp. the pioneering article by G. Harinck, Interaction between Xhosa and Khoi emphasis on the period 1620-1750, in L. Thompson, ed., *African Societies in Southern Africa* (London 1969) and also the chapters by Derricourt and Freund in this volume.
5 See, e.g., D. Williams, African Nationalism in South Africa: Origins and Problems, *JAH* XI, 3 (1970) 371–83.
6 London 1936.
7 London 1937.
8 Besides the polemical work by N. Majeke, *The Role of the Missionaries in Conquest* (Johannesburg 1952).
9 Selected papers presented at that conference, edited by Professor Leonard Thompson, were published under the title *African Societies in Southern Africa*.
10 R. M. Derricourt, Archaeological Survey of the Transkei and Ciskei, *Fort Hare Papers* 5 (1972) 213–22; 5 (1973) 449–55.
11 *Report and Proceedings with Appendices of the Government Commission on Native Laws and Customs* (reprint 2 vols. Cape Town 1968).
12 There is now an archives depot in Umtata; this has little material on the nineteenth century.
13 The most valuable collections in London are those of the Wesleyan Methodist Missionary Society, the London Missionary Society and the Society for the Propagation of the Gospel.
14 C. Bundy, The Emergence and Decline of a South African Peasantry, *African Affairs* 71 (Oct. 1972), is an important, pioneering article.
15 The twentieth century history of the Transkei is treated most fully in G. Carter, T. Karis and N. Stultz, *South Africa's Transkei, The Politics of Domestic Colonialism* (London 1967). A recent general survey of the Ciskei is W. C. Els, *et al., The Ciskei – A Bantu Homeland* (Fort Hare 1971).

1

PRAISE POEMS AS HISTORICAL SOURCES

Jeff Opland

OF all the Nguni traditions of oral poetry the Zulu would seem to have been best served by scholars, since a fair number of books and articles in English on various aspects of the tradition has been published.[1] The *izibongo* of major historical figures such as Shaka, Dingane and Cetshwayo have been printed and translated many times over, with literary and/or historical commentary. Perhaps it is because the three fullest collections of Xhosa *izibongo* — one by Rubusana and two by Ndawo[2] — have never been translated into English that few analyses of Xhosa poetry have appeared.[3] Sooner or later, scholars are going to turn to these invaluable collections as sources of history, and they will find in them much material to work on; more modern collections of *izibongo* may soon be published, and these too may be investigated with profit. Historians will have to consider a number of factors in the evaluation of this material, factors such as the reliability of oral transmission or the problem of feedback.[4] It is with one such factor that I am here concerned, a consideration of whether the oral performance is improvised or memorised.

The study of early western European oral traditions has in this century received considerable impetus from the research of

Milman Parry and Albert Lord into the South Slavic tradition of narrative poetry.[5] This research led Parry and Lord to conclude that oral narrative poetry was improvised, i.e. that the poet creates each poem *in performance* every time he performs. To do this he makes use of a large stock of ready-made metrical phrases which allow him to express on the spur of the moment within the framework of the traditional metre ideas essential to his story. The diction of oral poetry is thus "formulaic," consisting of a high percentage of established formulas and phrases modelled on these formulas, *because* the poet needs such phrases to compose his spontaneous poetry. The details or accuracy of this theory of oral poetry need not concern us here, but what *is* clear from the research of Parry and Lord, and from other studies that followed, is that there exist or existed until recently oral poetic traditions that are primarily improvisational.[6]

When one turns from these studies to examine what has been written about the Xhosa tradition of oral poetry, one is struck by the paucity of references to improvisation as an element.[7] Most authorities apparently consider the Xhosa *izibongo* to be memorised, and many write of the Xhosa tradition as if it were identical to the Zulu;[8] since the Zulu tradition is by all accounts primarily memorial, the implication is clearly that the Xhosa tradition is in this respect quite unlike the South Slavic. My own field work amongst the Xhosa-speaking peoples, however, immediately revealed that improvisation was in fact a prominent element in contemporary *izibongo* sung by the Xhosa tribal poets, *iimbongi*.[9] I propose to consider here the nature of the tradition as regards improvisation or memorisation first as revealed in the collections of Rubusana and Ndawo published in the first third of this century, and second as revealed in the collection I am myself currently assembling. It is hoped that this study may prove of some benefit to scholars who wish to assess the reliability of Xhosa *izibongo* as historical sources.

The Zulu tradition is primarily memorial
The *izibongo* of Zulu chiefs are produced by tribal poets,

izimbongi, and transmitted in a fixed form. Thus Samuelson[10] writes of the "songs and ballads" which the *izimbongi* "hand down to succeeding generations through their successors in office" (p. 254), and Cope writes of the *imbongi* that "An excellent memory is an essential qualification, for he has to memorize not only the praises of the chief but the praises of all his ancestors as well, and he has to memorize them so perfectly that on occasions of tribal importance they pour forth in a continuous stream or torrent" (*Izibongo,* p. 27). These "praises" are, in the terminology of Cope, following Bryant, "short sentences commemorative of notable actions and events in his life" (p. 26), which any man – but particularly a chief – may earn. The "praise" may run into a number of lines forming coherent couplets, triplets or longer stanzas, but the stanzas are not necessarily presented in any coherent order, and their order of presentation may vary from performance to performance. As Cope puts it, "Although the [*imbongi*] may vary the order of the sections or stanzas of the praise-poem, he may not vary the praises themselves. He commits them to memory as he hears them, even if they are meaningless to him, as they sometimes are when they have been handed down for generations" (pp. 27 f.). This latter feature, noted too by other authorities, contributes to the obscurity of the poems; other factors are the concentrated idiom of the diction, the speed of delivery and the elimination of normal intonation (p. 35). P. A. W. Cook[11] has similar observations about the Swazi (another Nguni language) *izibongo:*

> The praises were not recited in an ordinary voice, but were called out at the top of the voice in as rapid a manner as possible. Indeed, so rapidly are these *izibongo* called out that, from habit, those who know them are unable to say them slowly, and to write them down entails countless repetitions. Anyone who is not thoroughly familiar with a *sibongo* cannot possibly understand it, and even to a Swazi it is impossible to understand it the first time he hears it (pp. 183 f.).

Cope supports his observations about the order of stanzas by an illuminating comparison of versions of a poem in praise of Cetshwayo collected by Stuart and by Nyembezi (presumably collected from different poets, though informants are never mentioned), and of two versions of a poem in praise of Hamu collected by Stuart (pp. 35–8). Similar comparisons may be carried out on other published *izibongo*, and they serve to confirm the conclusions of Cope and others who have written on the Zulu tradition. For example, Samuelson has a version of Senzangakhona's *izibongo* (pp. 258 f.), and a comparison with the version collected by Stuart (Cope, pp. 75–81) reveals that a large proportion of lines are common to the two poems, and that the common lines rarely appear in isolation but usually in clusters of from two to four lines. Samuelson's version runs to 79 lines and Stuart's to 93; 44 lines of Samuelson's version (some 55 p.c.) appear in Stuart's version. Each of the three lines in Samuelson's *izibongo* in praise of Ndaba (p. 254) occurs in Stuart's 14-line version (Cope, p. 73). H. M. Ndawo, the Hlubi collector of *izibongo*, must have come across people among the Hlubi and the Bhaca who remembered some Zulu *izibongo*, for he prints in his 1928 collection apocopated versions of the *izibongo* of Shaka, Dingane and Cetshwayo (pp. 37 f.). Of the 19 lines of Shaka's *izibongo* in Ndawo's book, 12 (63 p.c.) appear in Stuart's 450-line version (Cope, pp. 89-117).

Published Xhosa oral poetry seems primarily memorial
What of the Xhosa tradition itself? Three poems are common to the collections of Ndawo and Rubusana, those in praise of the Hlubi chiefs Bhungane, Mhlambiso and Dlomo (Rubusana, pp. 326 f. and Ndawo, pp. 10, 28 and 7 respectively). The 3-line versions of Mhlambiso's *izibongo* are identical except for slight variations that might be the result of the collectors' auditory powers but in any case are of no significance. Rubusana's 5-line version of Dlomo's *izibongo* corresponds almost exactly with (significantly) the first six lines of Ndawo's 41-line version except for dialectal variations or variations attributable to oral diction or consonant with memorial transmissions. All 16 lines of Rubusana's version of Bhungane's *izibongo* occur in Ndawo's 65-line version. There are sufficient slight variations in wording and dialect to suggest that Rubusana

and Ndawo collected from different *iimbongi,* yet the correspondence of Rubusana's lines with Ndawo's is 100 p.c. From this comparison it seems evident that the poems were memorised, and that Cope's observation about the order of "praises" or "stanzas" in Zulu *izibongo* applies equally well to these Xhosa poems. From this evidence it seems clear that in the early years of this century, when Rubusana and Ndawo did their collecting, their Xhosa-speaking informants (whom both identify in their prefaces as *iimbongi*) were, like the Zulu *izimbongi,* primarily memorisers.

One other example will confirm this strong element of memorisation in the Xhosa tradition. Rubusana prints the *izibongo* of the Gcaleka chief Hintsa *(A! Zanzolo!)* as follows:

> NgusoRharhoba, uhlwat' olumadolo lukaKhala,
> Umhle kaNyawoshe, uso-Zanzolo.
> Umbheka ntshiyini bathi uqumbile,
> Udumbhele imilenze, isibi esikhetwayo kweziny' izibi;
> UNondwangu, imbhabalana entsundwana,
> Abayikhuz' ukuhlaba ingekahlabi.
> Nguzigodlwana zemaz' endala,
> Zingahlal' endleleni zilahlekile.

In the course of his history of the Mfengu, K. K. Ncwana[12] prints a 6-line *izibongo* of Hintsa which displays variations from Rubusana's version that may sometimes be the result of oral dictation (e.g. *Nguzigodlwana: Uzigodlwana* and *Zingahlal': Zingalala*) but which are consonant with memorial transmission:

> Uhlwathi lo wakwaGcaleka,
> Uhlwathi olumadolo lukaKhala,
> Umjonga-ntshiyini bath' uqumbile,
> Inkunz' abayikhuz' ukuhlaba ingekahlabi
> Uzigodlwana zemaz' endala,
> Zingalala endleleni yazini kunyembelekile. (p. 39)

The great Rarabe *imbongi* S. E. K. Mqhayi wrote a historical novel set in the times of Hintsa, *Ityala LamaWele.*[13] He introduces Hintsa on p. vii with a 2-line snatch from his *izibongo* that corresponds with line 3 of Rubusana's and Ncwana's versions and lines 6 and 4 respectively:

> Umbheka-ntshiyini bath' uqumbile,
> Inkunz' abayikhuz' ukuhlab' ingekahlabi.

In the course of the novel Mqhayi, who, it must be remembered, was an *imbongi* himself and who was writing a work of fiction, has the *imbongi* utter a 41-line *izibongo* at the end of the trial in which he urges the people to go home, for Zanzolo (Hintsa) says so (lines 4–8):

> Utsho ke yen' uZanzolo.
> Lutsh' uhlwathi lowo kaGcaleka,
> Uzigodlwana zemaz' endala,
> Zingalal' endleleni, yazini kunyembelekile.
> Itsh' inkunz' abayikhuz' ukuhlab' ingekahlabi ...

Later in the same poem (lines 35–7) the *imbongi* returns to the same idea, that Hintsa has spoken:

> Luthethil' ulhwath' olumadolo lukaKhala,
> Uthethil' njongwa-ntshiyini, bath' uqumbile,
> Inkunz' abayikhuz' ukuhlab' ingahlabanga.

It seems clear from a comparison of the versions of Hintsa's *izibongo* printed by Rubusana and Ncwana that the poem was transmitted in a fixed form, and that Mqhayi knew a version of it closer to that of Ncwana's informant than to that of Rubusana's, since both Ncwana and Mqhayi have *inkunzi* (bull) as the subject of the clause *abayikhuz' ukuhlaba ingekahlabi* where Rubusana has *imbabalana entsundwana* (little brown bushbuck) and both Ncwana and Mqhayi have *Zingalal' endleleni yazini kunyembelelike* (They [*zigodlwana*, "the horns"] lie entangled in the path) where Rubusana has *Zingahlal' endleleni zilahlekile* (They stay in the path and are lost). Ncwana may conceivably have taken his version from Mqhayi, though this is unlikely, since Ncwana has the active *Umjonga* (and Rubusana the active *Umbheka,* both meaning the same) where Mqhayi has the passive *njongwa.* Clearly, this *izibongo* of Hintsa underwent oral transmission in a fixed form; I heard illiterate *iimbongi* in the Kentani district in July 1973 using lines from it in their *izibongo.*

The contemporary Xhosa tradition is primarily improvisational

In spite of the above evidence one must be wary of concluding that the Xhosa tradition of *izibongo* in the early years of this century was primarily memorial or that the *imbongi* was a memoriser. All that one can say is that *izibongo* in praise of the chiefs of old were memorised by some *iimbongi,* and that the informants probably recited for Rubusana and Ndawo largely memorised (i.e. verbally fixed) lines. One ought not to assume that a tradition of improvised poetry did not exist, as it could well have done side by side with a tradition of memorised poetry. This in fact is the situation that obtains today, and a study of the contemporary tradition of Xhosa *izibongo* suggests a possible modification of the conclusion that seemed to be indicated from the above study of poems in Rubusana's and Ndawo's collections.

Elsewhere, in a generalised statement on the contemporary Xhosa tradition of poetry, I have suggested that it might be helpful to differentiate four kinds of poets.[14] Firstly, there are the memorisers of poetry : traditional poems referring to Xhosa clans *(iziduko)* are still transmitted today and memorised in a fixed form, especially by the women; men and boys commonly compose *izibongo* in praise of themselves, their age-mates or their cattle which are retained in the mind and recited on suitable (though not necessarily apt) occasions. Secondly, there are the improvisers of poetry, everyday people (especially in the rural areas) who, when particularly inspired, might feel themselves moved to stand up and give expression to their emotion in a spontaneous burst of poetry. Thirdly, there is the *imbongi,* the professional tribal poet who to a large extent composes his poetry in performance, making use of a stock of traditional phrases, expressions and techniques and at times quoting from the traditional memorised *izibongo* when relevant. Finally, there are today the literate Xhosa who are writing their poetry, which may be western or traditional in technique. The *imbongi* is the key figure in the transmission of the *izibongo* of the chiefs; though I shall concentrate on him, it must not be forgotten that he is part of a complex tradition of improvised and memorised poetry, a tradition he probably participated in as a boy before he first had ambitions to become an *imbongi.*[15] It must be remembered too that each *imbongi* is an individual artist, although he plays a part in a common tradition; it is possible therefore to speak of "the *imbongi*" only as a generalisation.

In general, then, the *imbongi* fulfils a complex rôle in society. Intimately associated with a chief, he incites his audiences to loyalty for his chief through the medium of his eulogistic poetry. This poetry usually contains genealogical references, and the *izibongo* are thus partly historical in content and intent. Usually a member of the chief's entourage, the *imbongi* heralds the arrival of the chief, who may be identified from the *izibongo*, at important ceremonies. Since he has licence to criticise the chief tactfully in public with impunity, he serves to moderate excessive behaviour and also acts as the mouthpiece of the people. All these are aspects of the social function of the Xhosa *imbongi*. Qualities the aspirant *imbongi* needs are fluency, knowledge of tribal history and the ability to express the truth as he (and the tribe) sees it. It is essential that his poetry be heard and understood; hence it is rarely produced in an unintelligible babble, but rather in a measured, characteristically guttural manner that merits attention. Furthermore, none of the *iimbongi* I have met has been at a loss to explain the meaning of his poetry: there are in their poetry no allusions obscure to the *iimbongi* themselves.

Few of the Xhosa *iimbongi* I have met prepare a poem in advance, and few of them consciously memorise their poetry. Most of them draw a clear distinction between poets like themselves who are never at a loss for words, and those who are limited in scope. The former are free to refer in their poetry to anything or anyone they see or know about, the latter can go no further than the poems they have learnt by heart. Nelson Mabunu,[16] for example, says
> Some people think perhaps an *imbongi* sits down and studies. That is not the thing: it's an inspiration. When you see something, you know, it's like a preacher in church when he preaches the gospel, you feel touched,

then you feel like saying some words yourself, you know – that's an inspiration. It's nothing else and it can be nothing else. You can judge a recitation, you know, done by school children, I mean by a school child, something that he has learnt and he'll recite. But singing, you know, praises for a chief or anything, it's an inspiration. (114)

Later in the same conversation I was asking Mabunu about the qualifications necessary for an *imbongi*. "You see", he replied, "there is no qualification of *iimbongi*. The qualification is their acceptance, you see, his acceptance *by* the people *as imbongi*."

>**Opland:** So there are no real rules or regulations, this is a sort of question of custom, everybody just does, sort of conforms to the custom?
>
>**Mabunu:** That is the thing. If he is gifted, if he has got that inspiration, then he praises, he sings praises and he is recognised as [an *imbongi*]. There are so many, you know, who just praise or sing praises for a certain thing and it ends there. He cannot sing praises for this and that, this and that, as an accepted *imbongi* [can]. (114)

Naturally enough, if an *imbongi* constantly sings in praise of one particular chief, these poems will tend to verbal stability, especially in lines referring to the physical characteristics of the subject or his past exploits; but as the chief does new things worthy of note, these actions are incorporated into successive performances of the *imbongi's izibongo* in his praise. Thus, in conversation with David Yali-Manisi,[17] who has published two books of his poetry and is working on a third, I asked

>Do you think that the poems that you write, that you've written in your two books are different from the poems that you sing just on the spur of the moment?
>
>**Manisi:** Yes, they are different in this manner: the theme may be the same but the wording is not the same, because every time there is an event I change from the poems I have written. I start from that event, then starting praising the chief from that event –
>
>**Opland:** As new events happen?
>
>**M:** Yes.

O: Yes. Would the technique, the words that you used be the same or would they differ?
M: No, they'd be different.
O: Mm. So each time you sing it'll be different?
M: Yes. Here and there of course. (116)

"Here and there" the words will differ, as the *imbongi* sings of new events or recasts the free narrative of old events; elements common to successive performances would be passages repeated over and again that accordingly tend to stability, and the formulas and formulaic expressions current throughout the tradition.

S. M. Burns-Ncamashe[18] confirmed these observations:
Opland: . . . Do you think [these poets] had composed and memorised certain praises which they would always repeat word for word?
Ncamashe: Well, in some cases they would repeat more or less the same phrases, but with new phrases each time, because usually *izibongo* do include a description of the appearance of a person or a thing, and naturally, since the appearance doesn't change, you'd always refer to a man with that long nose or thin legs and so forth – he'd still have them, you know, a big tummy and so forth. So, in addition to the appearance, then there would be the events that may have taken place which would be included naturally in the subject of the *izibongo*. (236)

Ncamashe produced as an example a 12-line poem in praise of the late Chief Archie Sandile *(A! Velile!),* Paramount Chief of the Rarabe, a poem that I shall return to shortly. If I asked Ncamashe to repeat the poem, would he produce the same words?
Opland: . . . In that little *Velile* that you sang, if you had to sing *now* another *Velile,* you would use sometimes some of the same words, but it would be verbally not an identical poem, would it, although it would be praising the same man? In other words, when you praise you don't memorise, every time you praise you make up what you're saying just while you're saying it?
Ncamashe: You take for example what I have said here. Now what I have said has stuck on to me, because when

Velile was alive that's what I'd often said to him, and it sticks. But I say other things as well. But there are those others which, because of repetition – you see, I was always in contact with Velile as *imbongi yamaRarabe*. I was always with him, whenever I could [be]. So there is this question of, this matter of, words fixing themselves, you know, in a natural, you know, manner, imperceptibly, you see. You find yourself repeating yourself without actually sitting down to memorise this. (236)

Let us take as an example two poems in praise of Chief Sabatha Dalindyebo *(A! Jonguhlanga!)* which Melikhaya Mbutuma[19] produced for me during the same interview.

```
     A! Jonguhlanga!
     A! Jonguhlanga!
     Yinina mntan' enkos'am ungasandijongi nje
     Thole lesilwangangubo sakwaNdyebo
  5  Ngqayi ngqayi yokuqhayisa
     Isilo sam siyoyikeka
     Sihlabe ngophondo phezu kweBumbana
     Zatshw' izizwe zonke zanguqhusa-qhusa
     Kunamhlanje nje madoda ndiyazoyik' izimanga
 10  Nditsho kuwe ke bhelu lentombi yakwaKhonjwayo
     Nditsho kuwe ke mntwan' omhlekazi
     'Nqaba madoda yinqaba
     'Nqab' ithole lerhamba yinqaba
     Nditsho kuwe ke mntan' omhlekazi
 15  Nditsho kuwe k'esibinza ngamkhontw' emazibukweni
     Ukuze kuvel' isilw' esoyikekayo
     Ukuze kuvel' inambulel' isilo saphesheya kolwandle
     Hayi kemadod' umnta' kaSampu madoda
     Hayi ke madod' umntan' esilo madoda
 20  Yintw' eyantywila yaxel' ingqang' esibhakabhakeni
     Yaqhwab' amaphik' ukuze zivuthuluk' iintsiba
     Bakhal' abafazi batshwed' abantwana
     Zakhal' iinkedama zalil' emva kwezindlu
     Zathi kungangi na mntan' omhlekazi
 25  Yeha!
     Yint' eyasuka wazikrazul' iingub' umnta' kaSampu
     Wazikrazula waziqabeka ngodaka
     Ukuz' azile kungekafik' ixesha lokuzila
     Zahlahlamb' iziphath' amandla
```

30 Wothuk' umnta' kaMilo wathi namhlanje konakele
    Zasuk' izilo zaphezu kweNquluqhu zafulathela
    Kwathiwa namhlanje kwenzek' isikiz' ebaThenjini
    Yeyani na le ndaba kwabakokwethu
    Yeyani na le ndaba madoda
35 Kumhla kwenzek' inyala na emahlazwen' ezizweni
    Hayi hayi ke madoda
    Ngxe mntan' omhlekazi ndiyabulisa
    Ngxe mntan' esilo ndiyabulisa
    A! Jonguhlanga!
40 Nde ncam nde ncebelele   (150)

    A! Jonguhlanga!
    A! Jonguhlanga!
    Why are you avoiding my eyes, child of my chief?
    Young son of the vulture chief of Ndyebo,
5   Clay pot, clay pot to be proud of.
    My frightening animal,
    It stabbed with its horn above the Bumbana.
    All the nations started to scatter.
    Today, men, I fear marvels.
10 I refer to you, beautiful son of the daughter of the
        Khonjwayos.
    I refer to you, child of a chief.
    An enigma, men, is an enigma.
    An enigma, the young of a puff adder, is an enigma.
    I refer to you, child of a chief.
15 I refer to you, who stabs with an assegai in the fords,
    So that the feared beast appeared,
    So that the fabulous antelope appeared, the animal from
        across the sea.
    Oh men, the child of Sampu, men.
    Oh men, the child of an animal, men.
20 The thing that dived, like a jackal buzzard in the sky.
    It slapped its wings so that feathers flew out.
    Women cried, children yelled,
    Orphans cried and wept behind houses.
    They said, "What is the matter, child of a chief?"
25 Behold!
    It is the thing that rent its garments, the child of Sampu,
    He tore them and smeared himself with mud,
    So that he mourned before the time for mourning arrived.
    Then the men in authority became excited.

30 The child of Mlilo took fright and said, "Today everything's gone wrong."
Then the animals on top of Nquluqhu turned their backs upon the people.
It was said, "Today a shameful thing has occurred among the Thembus."
What is this thing that has happened among our people?
What is this thing that has happened, men?
35 Is it the first time a disgrace has occurred among the scandals of nations?
Oh no, men!
Pardon me, child of a ruler, I salute you.
Pardon me, child of an animal, I salute you.
A! Jonguhlanga!
40 Nde ncam nde ncebelele!

About half an hour later, after we had listened to his seven-year-old son repeat a poem he had sung for us before Mbutuma produced the above poem, after we had drunk some *amasi* together, and after we had listened to the playback of the above poem, I asked Mbutuma, "What do you think about that poem that you sang now to Sabatha, is it good?"

Mbutuma: It's just a poem, just a poem to encourage him.
Opland: Is it different from other poems that you've sung?
M: If I could praise again, it could be just as different as ever.
O: It would be different again?
M: Just give me again and you will see.
O: It wouldn't be the same?
M: No, no, not at all.
O: Do it again. (148)

Mbutuma took the microphone and immediately produced a second poem:

Ndiboleken' iindlebe madoda ndithethe ngesilo sakokwethu
Ndiboleken' iindlebe magwalandini ndithethe ngesilo sam
Isilo sam simhlophe phakathi
Isilo sikaSampu madoda siyoyikeka
5 Hayi hayi ke madoda
Ndiṭsho ndaqabel' iintaba zoMngqanga
Ndafika zihlunguzela

  Zathi namhlanj' isilo sindoyisile
  Isilo esigqib' amahlath' amakhulu
10 Nditsho kuwe ke mnta' kaSampu
  Ndiboleken' intonga madoda ndihlanganise
  Ndiboleken' intonga mabandl' akokwethu ndigoqe
  Ndigoqel' isilo sam esoyikekayo
  Inqaba madoda yinqaba
15 Yinqab' umnta' kaSampu
  Ndithetha ngengqangantshilili madoda
  Isikhova samathafa kaHala
  Saphaphatheka santlitheka phezu kweentaba zeeNgcobo
  Ukuz' amabandl' akokweth' othuke
20 Iintaba zoMngqanga zindoyisile
  Zindoyisil' iintaba zoMngqanga madoda
  Yinin' ukutheth' izintw' ezingathethwayo
  Masihambeni songen' iintaba zikaGilindoda
  Hlathi likaGilindoda elingenantonga
25 Elithe langenwa ngamadodan' akhuph' iminyololwana
  Hlathi leentaba zoMngqanga liyandoyikisa
  Ziyazul' izizwe ziyangqunga
  Ziyangqunga phezu koMnyolo neGqaga
  Ntab' ezimbin' ezikhweletelenayo
30 Ntaba zoMngqanga ntaba zoMqolo
  Ziyandoyikisa ndakuzondela
  Masihambeni madoda siyokuma phezu koNonisi
  Simvus' uMthikrakra sithi makavuke
  Azokulawul izizwe namhlanje ziyalawuleka
35 Yeyani na le ndaba kwabakokwethu
  Ngxe mntan' okumkan' andenzanga nto
  Thole lerhamba lakokwethu
  A! Jonguhlanga!
  Nde ncam nde ncebelele (152)

  Lend me your ears, men, and let me speak about an animal
    of ours,
  Lend me your ears, men, and let me speak about my
    animal.
  My animal is white inside.
  Sampu's animal, men, is frightening.
5 Oh no, men!
  I say I climbed to the top of the mountains of Mngqanga.
  I found them shaking their heads.
  They said, "Today the animal has defeated me,
  The animal that felled huge forests."

10 I refer to you, child of Sampu.
    Lend me a stick, men, to defend myself.
    Lend me a stick, tribes of my nation, to block the blows.
    I defend myself from my frightening animal.
    An enigma, men, is an enigma.
15 The child of Sampu is an enigma.
    I speak about a real jackal buzzard, men.
    The owl of the plains of Hala,
        It bolted and was tossed onto the top of the mountains of Engcobo,
    So that our tribes took fright.
20 The mountains of Mngqanga have beaten me,
    The mountains of Mngqanga have beaten me, men.
    Why should I speak of unmentionable matters?
    Let us go, we shall enter the mountains of Gilindoda,
    The forest of Gilindoda which has no sticks,
25 Which was entered by men who brought back beautiful sticks.
    The forest of the mountains of Mngqanga frightens me.
    Nations wander about and begin to stir.
    They stir above Mnyolo and Gqaga,
    The two mountains which are jealous of each other.
30 The mountains of Mngqanga and the mountains of Mqolo,
    They frighten me when I gaze at them.
    Let us go, men, and stay on top of Nonisi
    And wake Mthikrakra and say he must be ready
    To come today and rule the nations that are ripe for rule.
35 What is this thing that has happened among our people?
    Pardon me, child of a ruler, I have done nothing,
    Young of the puff adder of ours.
    A! Jonguhlanga!
    Nde ncam nde ncebele!

In spite of Mbutuma's claim that the two poems would be quite different, there are certain verbal similarities. In the following comparison I exclude from consideration the salutation *A! Jonguhlanga!* and the concluding formula *Nde ncam nde ncebelele:* the former is used when any tribesman greets the chief, and would be a standard element of *izibongo* in praise of Chief Sabatha; although I have heard only Mbutuma's son use the same concluding formula in an *izibongo,* most of the *iimbongi* have their own personal way of finishing a performance which may also be traditional (such as *ncincilili, bham dovalele* or *itshw' imbongi*) which they tend to use every time they sing, irrespective of the subject. Apart from these lines common to both the performances under consideration, there are the following whole-line correspondences (lines from text 150 given first): 6 : 3–4; 12 : 14; 33 : 35; 36 : 5. In other words, applying the same criterion for the comparison as was used above for the early Xhosa and the Zulu *izibongo,* repetition of a whole line from performance to performance, only four out of 36 lines (11 p.c.) of text 150 are repeated. There is a far greater correspondence in the incidence of phrases that go to make up a line. Phrasal correspondences are as follows: 13 : 17; 10, 11, 15 : 10; 18, 26 : 10, 15. This list could be extended by a comparison of the two poems with other poems I have recorded from Mbutuma and with the memorised poem Mbutuma's son sang twice during the same interview. Thus, for example, line 4 of text 150 uses the same phrase as is used in a poem Mbutuma sang for me on 19th February 1971: *Ithole lesilwangangubo senz' umhlola* (189). Mbutuma's son used the following lines and phrases in his poem (for which his father claimed he took words from him and added words of his own): *isilo esoyikekayo* (cf. 150, lines 6, 16; 152, line 4), *amadod' akrazul' iingubo* (cf. 150, line 26), *Abafazi benz' isijwil' emva kwezindlu* (cf. 150, lines 22f.), *Yeyani na le ndaba kwabakokwethu* (150, line 33; 152, line 35), *Ngxe mntak' omhlekazi ayenzanga nto* (cf. 150, line 37; 152, line 36), *Ndithetha ngengqangantshilili madoda* (152, line 16), *'Nqaba madoda zinqaba/Thina mnta' kaSampu zinqaba* (cf. 150, lines 12 f.; 152, lines 14 f.). It is clear that a number of lines or phrases that Mbutuma used in his two performances are used regularly by him. Whether consciously memorised or not, these lines or phrases are associated in his mind with *izibongo* in praise of his chief, and they habitually appear in Mbutuma's *izibongo.* These constitute a personal element, whole lines which Mbutuma is particularly fond of, such as lines 6 and 12 f. in text 150, or line 16 in text 152. Now apart from these *personal* lines, there occur more frequently groups of words that might be called *traditional,* in that they are the common property of many poets in the tradition, phrases of general application or usefulness. Thus 150, line 36 and 152, line 5 is a familiar exhortation (not confined to poetry) that occurs at least once elsewhere in my collection, and the phrase *nditsho kuwe* at the start of a line (150, lines 10 f., 14 f.; 152, line 10) is very common in *izibongo*. The use of animal imagery, too, is traditional, so that many chiefs have been referred to, for example, as *ithole lesilo* (cf. 150, lines 4, 13, 19, 38; 152, line 37). These latter phrases tend to form elements of a line rather than a complete line, and as such operate in much the same way as Lord's formulas and formulaic expressions. Indeed, the above analysis reveals much stronger similarities to Lord's description of South Slavic poetry than to descriptions of Zulu *izibongo*. To conclude, from the above (and other) evidence, it is clear that Mbutuma does not produce fixed, memorised *izibongo*; rather, he composes his poems in performance, making use of a stock of ready-made phrases that help him to express what he wants to say. This technique gives him the freedom to comment aptly in poetry on people or actions he is witnessing at the time, with little or no premeditation; his poetry is primarily improvised.

The memorial elements in the Xhosa tradition

The personal lines that an *imbongi* tends to repeat in successive *izibongo* may pass into a common oral tradition and establish a memorial tradition such as that postulated above after the analysis of poems in the collections of Rubusana and Ndawo. In the early 1930s (as far as I can determine), Mqhayi recorded a 72-line poem[20] in praise of the late Paramount Chief Archie Sandile *(A! Velile!)* of the Rarabe:

    A! Velile!
    Ikwekwe kaFaku ezalwa nguNobantu
    Igama layo nguArchie Sandile
    Yeyona nkosi amaNgqika onke selejonge kuyo ngaphesheya nangaphonoshono kweNciba
5 Imbongi yesizwe ithi ngayo
    Yimbishimbishi yingqishingqishi
    Ngumabhinqel' ezantsi ang' ubhinq' isikhaka
    Kant' ubhinq' ibhulukhwe
    Kokw' ezibhulukhwe zimagwagusha

10   Bezifun' ukuya kwezikayise'mkhulu bezifun' ukuya
       kwezikaGonya
     Kulokw' ezikaGonya zimagwashu
     Umntwan' enkos' inzinzilili
     Ngesaphul' abant' ub' ebelekwa
     Kulok' int' ekul' ithwashuza ngokwayo
15   Ikhe yalinga kamb' intlanjana yoMdiza
     Yath' ingambeleka yon' imkhukhulise
     Koko yathwal' inkabi yehashe
     Yayishiy' inzinzilili ngasemva
     Kuze sifike sithabath' iintonga
20   Sibuye nomfo wasemaMbalwini
     Hayi nkosi soyikek' umnta' kaFaku
     Kub' unobugqir' obusegazini
     Uzimisela kwangokwakhe
     Uthi qwab' eliliso xa 'bon' utshaba
25   Athi qwab' eli xa 'bon' isihlobo
     Yintw' engqob' isenqinen' ukusing' eMthatha
     Kub' iphuthum' amaxhoba kaMlawu
     Umacekis' ingcek' abuy' ayiphuthume
     Umaphuthum' ingcek' abuy' ayicekise
30   Umty' omtyenen' osukwe kowawo
     Kub' usukwe ngooyise nooyisemkhulu
     Xa nditshoyo nditheth' uBonisani noGawushigqili
     Hay' umfo kaHolide ngokukwaz' ukusoka
     Aba bakaZaze ngababuzeli
35   Siyamdela thin' umfo kaNikani okaNikani sitsho isisu senkomo
     Ndlela nin' ezi zineentsasa namaqhekeza
     Sikhe sakholwa ngemihla kaZimasile
     Hayi bafo baseBhayi nikwazil' ukusoka
     Nikwazil' ukuyisok' inkosi yenu
40   Seyincinan' indawan' esixakayo
     Asiwabon' amabal' eenkomo zenu
     Mzi waseRhini nowaseKapa nani thina siyanibulela
     Kokw' asiwabon' amabal' eenkomo zenu
     Yingxow' enkul' umfo kaFaku
45   Yingxow' enkul' enemilenze
     Afaka kuy' amadun' akowabo
     Yintw' efunde yafunda yada yayityekeza
     Ndith' asinkos' ukukwaz' ukugweba
     Yamgweb' uMabutho walala ngophothe
50   Yamgweb' uGushiphela yamsakaza
     Ijong' emahlathini x' ikhuph' isigwebo
     Apho balele khon' ooMgolombane ... (161)

A! Velile!
The son of Faku and Nobantu,
His name is Archie Sandile,
To whom Transkei and Ciskei amaNgqika pay homage.
5   The national poet says about him:
He is obese, his step is heavy.
He girds his garment like a skirt around the hips,
And yet it is trousers that he wears.
But they are oversized trousers,
10 Resembling those of his grandfather, resembling those of
        Gonya;
But Gonya's fitted loosely.
The heavily built son of a chief,
Who would be too heavy to be carried,
But he prefers to pace out steadily on his own.
15 The Mdiza rivulet made an attempt
To carry him off and wash him downstream,
But it managed to wash down only his horse
And left the stout one behind.
And so we took our sticks to divine,
20 And we returned with a Mbalu fellow smelt out.
What a revered man, the son of Faku!
For he has supernatural powers in his veins;
He himself can control these powers:
A wink with one eye indicates a foe,
25 And with the other a friend.
He is fleet-footed on the way to Umtata
To recover the spoils of Mlawu.
The one who despises ochre and then falls back on it;
The one who falls back on ochre and then despises it.
30 He is a supple hide rope softened by its owner,
For he has been softened by his fathers and grandfathers;
When I say this I refer to Bonisani and Gawushigqili.
Oh, how well Holiday chooses presents for initiates!
These men of Zaze are dubious givers;
35 We despise this fellow Nikani, for he is mere tripe.
What paths are these, littered with brushwood and pebbles?
We were content during the days of Zimasile.
Men of Port Elizabeth, you have given good presents,
You have given fine presents to your chief.
40 A small matter still puzzles us:
We do not see the colours of your cattle.
People of Grahamstown and Cape Town, we thank you
        too,

>   Although we do not see the colours of your cattle.
>   Faku's son is a huge container,
> 45   A huge container with legs.
>   All his supporters pay him tribute.
>   He is so full of education that he brings it up.
>   He knows very well how to give judgement in law suits:
>   He sentenced Mabutho and knocked him flat,
> 50   He sentenced Gushiphela and tore him to shreds.
>   In giving judgement he faces the forests
>   Where his forefathers, Mgolombane and others, lie buried.

To my knowledge Mqhayi never published an *izibongo* in praise of Velile, although, since Velile was his Paramount Chief, Mqhayi often sang *izibongo* in his praise. As we have noted above, when an *imbongi* sings about one chief regularly, his poems tend to repeat a number of lines, that is they tend to verbal stability to a limited extent; only to a limited extent, because the chief will always be doing things, or new events will occur, that will find expression in the *imbongi*'s poems. Now the few fixed phrases that the *imbongi* may repeat from time to time may well be picked up by others and pass into a common oral tradition, and these phrases may recur in *izibongo* in praise of a particular chief sung by different *iimbongi,* yet each poem of the *imbongi* will be verbally distinct, and different *iimbongi* will for the most part use their own words to describe the same chief. Though some phrases may be common to such *izibongo,* traditional phrases or personal phrases of one *imbongi* that have become generally current, each *imbongi* is an independent commentator; though he may consciously "quote" from another *imbongi,* he sees his subject through his eyes alone. It would be strange, for example, if David Manisi's poem in praise of his Paramount Chief Kaiser Matanzima were identical to that of Melikhaya Mbutuma (the *imbongi* of Sabatha Dalindyebo, Matanzima's political opponent); in fact, all that is common to the poems I have recorded by Manisi and by Mbutuma about Matanzima is the salutation *A! Daliwonga!* In the Zulu tradition the *izibongo* are fixed, and all *izimbongi* reciting the *izibongo* of the same chief would use much the same "praises," though not necessarily in the same order. This is not the case in the Xhosa tradition, at least during the chief's lifetime.

Mqhayi generally repeated line 6 whenever he sang of Velile; in his novel *Ityala LamaWele* the caption (written by Mqhayi) to a photograph of the chief reads
>A! Velile!
>Mbishimbishi! Mbishimbishi!
>Ngqishingqishi! Ndishindishi!

David Manisi, the Thembu *imbongi,* has written a 133-line *izibongo* in praise of Velile that starts
>Mbishi-mbishi! mbushu-mbushu!
>Ngqishi-ngqishi! Ndishi-ndishi!

and has an irregular refrain of the first line and the second line alternately.[21] The only other resemblances between this poem and that of Mqhayi quoted above are Mqhayi's line 7, which appears in Manisi's poem as *Umabinqel' ezants' ang' ubinq' izikhaka,* and Mqhayi's line 12, which appears in Manisi's poem as *Yinzinzilil' umnta' kaFaku,/Yinzinzilili kuba ngumntan' enkosi.* Even Ncamashe, an *imbongi* from the same tribe as Mqhayi, who knew Mqhayi, uses his own words in his *izibongo* for Velile. I have already quoted from an absorbing conversation I had with Ncamashe; on the same occasion we were discussing those recurrent phrases of one *imbongi* that pass into a common tradition of *izibongo* associated with a particular chief. Ncamashe identified these phrases with Cope's definition of Zulu "phrases" and in the course of this discussion he produced his own *izibongo* in praise of Velile:

>**Opland:** ... I want to get more to specific retention of the same words. For example, Cope, in his book on Zulu *izibongo*, says that among the Zulus every man in public life earns praises, that is a sentence, as it were, or phrase, which is attached to him as a result of certain actions, so that if you're very brave in battle I will say "The man who lost an ear in the battle of Amalinde," and I will always, when I praise you, use that specific phrase about you.
>**Ncamashe:** Yes, that is true.
>**O:** Is this true of the Xhosas as well?

N: That is true of the Xhosas as well.
O: So that when you *bonga,* or let's say when Mqhayi *bongas* Velile, he will always say "Mbishimbishi! Ngqishingqishi!"?
N: That is right. And then when the next man *bongas* Velile, he will also use that phrase, but add his own –
O: Which he's heard from Mqhayi?
N: Mqhayi was the first one, then all the others – because that seems to be a kind of title for him, or a permanent name. I also, in the praises of Velile, use it, you see. I'll say a few lines for you, for example. Can I?
O: Yes, please.
N: A! Velile!

    Mbishimbishi yembombosholo
    YakuloMbombo nakuloMbhede
    Wabhukubhukulek' ukubhek' eBholo naseGqolonci
5   MntakaFaku noNobantu
    Ungcith' emdaka yingonyama
    Sona silo siyikumkani yazo zonk' izilo
    Umdak' omkhuthuka yindlovu
    Indlovu yakwaHoho nguVelile Sandile
10 Nt' ethumbu limvanzilili
    Nt' ethumbu linamagumb' okufak' izilo zakowalo
    A! Velile!

    [A! Velile!
    The obese one, all swollen up,
    Of the amaMbombo and the amaMbhede.
    He flops along on the way to Bholo and Gqolonci.
5   The son of Faku and Nobantu.
    The dark tawny one is a lion,
    The animal which is king of all other animals.
    The dark hairless one is an elephant,
    The elephant of Hoho is Velile Sandile,
10 The one whose paunch is firm,
    The one whose paunch has compartments for storing all his animals.
    A! Velile!]

Now there it is. You see now I use the word *imbishimbishi,* because he was often called *imbishimbishi* and when people referred to him they even greeted him with *imbishimbishi:* "Mholo, Mbishimbishi," you see. Mqhayi had given him that title. Now Cope is perfectly right. Soga, for example, was always called *Thol' elimdaka,* Tiyo Soga. Now whoever gave him that, perhaps his father or some of the early Gaikas, whoever referred to him, even if they sang praises on Tiyo Soga, they would always refer to *Thol' elimdaka,* but the first one gave it to him. So Cope is right.

O: Right, but Cope then goes on to say that a praise poem is a whole series of these fixed praises, which are memorised, in other words in a fixed form. So let's say you've done four good things, and I praise you 1–2–3–4, you've got those four "praises." Now when I sing the poem about you then I use just those four and nothing else. In other words, he maintains the whole praise poem, the whole *izibongo*, is memorised, which I don't find among the Xhosas, and I think he's wrong [i.e. his observations about the Zulu tradition do not apply to the Xhosa].

N: Among the Xhosas, those who imitate others may do so. But a praise singer may make use of material that he has heard from others and to it add his own. That's what happens: a line or two may be taken, and it's not stealing, you wouldn't regard that as – if you saw a line in my poem or in Manisi's poem which you knew came from someone else's, now that is because he acknowledges, you know, that that man has described the subject which is common between them, you know, very well, and he feels too he must use the same language, but add his own. (236)

Ncamashe's *izibongo* uses Mqhayi's word *Mbishimbishi* and presents the same genealogical fact that Velile was the son of Faku and Nobantu, but Ncamashe's *izibongo* is verbally distinct from Mqhayi's.

A brief survey of some *izibongo* in praise of Velile will give an indication of the phrases that tended to recur in Mqhayi's *izibongo*. I have in my collection three *izibongo* sung at Velile's funeral.[22] The first two are by the *iimbongi* Billie (223), who knew and on occasion sang at the same functions as Mqhayi, and Hoza (224), who did not know Mqhayi and

23

started acting as an *imbongi* only after Mqhayi's death; both *izibongo* on this occasion have no verbal resemblances to Mqhayi's. The third (225), which I think is sung by the *imbongi* Max Khamile of Middledrift, has only three lines reminiscent of Mqhayi's poem quoted above: *Mbishimbishi* has gone –
>Imkil' indisindisi
>Imkil' imbisimbisi
>Imkil' indisindisi

When I met Billie in 1971 he had not sung for three years, yet he kindly consented to sing an *izibongo* for me. He referred to a number of chiefs, and to Velile in a 19-line passage, starting
>A! Velile!
>Ntw' enkulu kaFaku
>Ntw' enkulu kaGonya
>30 Nditsho ngembishimbishi
>Nditsho ngendishindishi
>Nditsho ngengqishingqishi
>Ubhulukhwe zimazemb' ing' zezikayise
>Ungub' isantanta ing' ekaGonya
>35 Ee! Velile (193)

Apart from the genealogical facts (which many *iimbongi* refer to, in their own words), there is the 3-line echo of Mqhayi's *mbishimbishi*-sequence, as well as the reference to Velile's trousers and to those of his grandfather Gonya. Though Billie's lines 33 f. are verbally distinct from Mqhayi's lines 9 f., the ideas are similar: "His pants have creases like those of his father,/His blanket floats like that of Gonya." Nelson Mabunu is, like Manisi, a Thembu; in a poem he sang in 1963 on the opening of the Transkeian parliament, he referred to Velile and identified him as the one who is called *Mbishimbishi:*
>... A! Velile
>74 Yimbishimbishi ke leyo.[23]

Manisi had travelled amongst the Rarabe to collect material for his book of *izibongo* of the Xhosa chiefs, and he had studied at Lovedale, some thirty miles from Velile's great place; Mabunu had spent his life amongst the Thembu and the Hlubi, yet Mqhayi's tag had reached him. I have referred above to Manisi's poem on Velile; in the same book, in his poem about Chief Kaizer Matanzima, he has the line *Int' efunde yafunda yayityekeza* (p. 28), which recalls line 47 of Mqhayi's poem about Velile. This same line appears in a poem written by Alf Ngani about the chiefs of (South) Africa; three lines refer to Velile:

    Aa, Velile! MntakaSandile, mntakaSoEmma;
    Hlal' ubhekabheka, kub' uyazondw' emLungwini.
    "Int' efunde yafunda yade yayityekeza."[25]

The quotation marks acknowledge Ngani's debt to Mqhayi. From a number of children in the King William's Town and Peddie districts, I have recorded a memorised poem about Velile apparently written by St. John Page Yako, though I have not yet been able to trace the school book from which the children learnt the poem. Yako's poem, which is fairly consistently rendered by the children (boys and girls), has no verbal resemblance to Mqhayi's. On the other hand, the *izibongo* most like Mqhayi's is one sung by Mase Attwell Bhuti, who was born in Middledrift (some fifteen miles from Velile's great place), who knew and heard Mqhayi sing, and who now lives in Langa near Cape Town. The recording, unfortunately, is poor, but, apart from the genealogy, Bhuti refers to the trousers as well as to the escape from drowning.[25]

    Ngumntwan' omabhinqel' ezantsi
    UmntakaFaku
    UmntakaFaku
    Kuba uzalwa ngabantu ababini
    Uzalwa nguFaku noNobantu (2)

Like Mqhayi (line 7), Bhuti says that he is a child who ties his belt low down, he is the son of Faku, the child of two people, Faku and Nobantu (Mqhayi, line 2). A few lines further on, Bhuti refers to the river episode and the consequent search for the culprit:

    Inkabi yehashe
    Yangen' elwandle
    Ukuze sithabath' iintonga
    Ukuze kunukwe umfo wasemaMbalwini (2)

This account bears a fairly close resemblance to Mqhayi's lines 17, 19 and 20: we are told that the horse entered the sea, so divining sticks were taken and a Mbalu fellow was smelt out. There are strong verbal resemblance, but a comparison of the two passages suggests that Bhuti is dependent on Mqhayi and not *vice versa:* Mqhayi's passage about the near-drowning follows coherently from the preceding lines, and leads on to Velile's divining ability, whereas Bhuti's passage has no relation to what precedes or follows. Moreover, Mqhayi's narrative is more detailed: apart from the name of the river, we are told that Velile escaped; Bhuti has the horse entering the sea, and since there is no reference to Velile's having been in any danger the last two lines are obscure and the relation of the horse to Velile puzzling. Clearly, obscurity will increase as the distance between performer and the (eyewitness) source increases.

The poem by Mqhayi quoted above is but one of many versions of the poem Mqhayi sang in his lifetime. It presents his own description of his chief's physical attributes and his personality traits, some good (like his wisdom in passing judgement, lines 20 ff.) and some bad (like his vacillation, lines 28 f.). It expresses Mqhayi's opinion of the relative generosity of various communities judged from the gifts they gave Velile on his initiation. Other poets see Velile differently, and each uses different words to describe him, or refer to different attributes, though his physical stoutness is commonly acknowledged. Each poet's *izibongo* is an individual production. Yet Mqhayi, who sang about Velile often, clearly had a number of lines and phrases which recurred in different *izibongo* in praise of Velile. Obviously the first twenty lines were fairly stable, since they are most frequently "quoted" by other poets, as was line 47. The quoting of lines is traditional. Mqhayi himself did it: the *mbishimbishi* tag which Mqhayi applied to Velile and which came to be associated with the chief, appears in a poem in praise of the Rarabe chief Feni (the son of Tyali, the son of Ngqika) in Rubusana's *Zemk' Inkomo* (p. 255), where Feni is referred to as *Mbishimbishi*. (Although Mqhayi knew Rubusana well, it is not necessary to suppose that Mqhayi took the term from Rubusana's book, as he might well have heard the poem independently in the oral tradition.).

The Zulu *izimbongi* propagate memorised *izibongo*,[26] a comparison of poems found in both Rubusana's and Ndawo's collections would seem to suggest that the Xhosa *iimbongi* did the same. Yet my own research over the past five years reveals that Xhosa *iimbongi* produce *izibongo* that are primarily improvised. Two conclusions seem possible: firstly, that the Xhosa tradition has altered radically during the past fifty years and moved from memorisation to improvisation; and secondly, that present conditions in fact obtained fifty years ago – though between then and now the tradition is affected by new social and political forces – and that early commentators simply failed to note the element of improvisation. My hypothetical reconstruction embraces both alternatives. Prior to the impact of mass media communication and modern transport facilities, the rural Xhosa by and large would live in relatively stable, isolated communities. Their chief would not travel much, so they would hear their *imbongi*'s *izibongo* often. Since the daily life of the chief would be fairly uniform, these *izibongo* would tend strongly to verbal stability, and would regularly incorporate the glorious or notable events of the past; certainly the community would hear certain lines repeated over and again whenever the *imbongi* produced an *izibongo* in praise of the chief. Many tribesmen, without consciously memorising them, could probably repeat a series of such lines, which they could remember even after the chief's death. But the *imbongi's izibongo* would only *tend* to stability during the chief's lifetime, since the chief would always be doing new things; in performance, the *imbongi* might still have the ability to refer spontaneously to strangers or guests or to comment on current events or situations with no verbal preparation, although he would refer to his chief mostly in well-tried phrases (largely personal, but also traditional), as the *imbongi* does at the end of the trial in Mqhayi's *Ityala LamaWele*. After the chief's death, the limitation on the tendency to stability would be removed and to the well-tried phrases few others would be added. These "praises" of deceased chiefs could be handed on in a memorised form by men and women of the chiefdom, to be taken sometimes into the *izibongo* of succeeding generations of *iimbongi*. The contemporary *imbongi*, however, often lives at great distances from the great place, his chief may be involved in politics or lead an active public life, so the *imbongi must* keep on reworking his poetic depiction of the chief. He may find himself performing less frequently than his isolated counterpart – since there are fewer traditional ceremonies amongst the westernised communities – and to widely differing audiences in varying circumstances. Hence the possibility of someone's memorising an extended series of lines from the *imbongo's izibongo* is lessened, and the tradition of memorised *izibongo* in praise of the chiefs tends to die out among the people: in the areas I have worked in, I have not been able to find tribesmen other than *iimbongi* who could produce an *izibongo* in praise of any of their chiefs. The purpose of the contemporary Xhosa *imbongi* is generally to communicate facts or opinions. However puzzled a memoriser might be about what he is repeating, the improviser is consciously shaping his words in performance: I have not met a Xhosa *imbongi* who could not explain what he is saying. To western collectors or scholars, references in the early printed *izibongo* may be obscure, but to the modern *imbongi* and his audience, familiar with the traditional diction and its connotative or suggestive quality, the meaning of the *izibongo* is generally clear.

Improvised and memorised poetry differ in historical value
Now, finally, what is the relevance of this to the historian? The *imbongi* is a specialist in the history of his people and the genealogy of his chiefs. His *izibongo*, accordingly, contain allusions to facts that may be of great interest to historians. The *izibongo* of the chiefs incorporate the history of the group: as A. C. Jordan writes in the seventh article in his series "Towards an African Literature" (see note 3 above),

> The "praises of the chiefs" deal primarily with the happenings in and around the tribe during the reign of a given chief, praising what is worthy and decrying what is unworthy, and even forecasting what is going to happen: rivalries for the chieftainship within the tribe:

> the ordinary social life: alliances and conflicts with neighbouring tribes: military and political triumphs and reverses etc. Thus the tribal poet is a chronicler as well as being a poet. The chief is only the centre of the praise-poem because he is the symbol of the tribe as a whole. (p. 74)

Jordan refers to the historical interest of "the 'praises' composed in the middle of the nineteenth century and after," which present the contemporary attitude to men like Sir Harry Smith, Henry Calderwood and Charles Brownlee. Now the historical interest of such allusions rests heavily on their having been expressed by an eyewitness of the personalities and events, i.e. on their having been composed contemporaneously and transmitted in a fixed (memorised) form. These allusions would not have the same value if they appeared in poetry composed years after the events had occurred by a poet drawing on a free tradition of narrative.[27]

Consider two examples. Bearing in mind the fact that the *imbongi* in general is committed to expressing the truth as he sees it, it should be a matter of some interest to historians that the *izibongo* of Sandile printed by Rubusana refers to Brownlee (as Jordan notes) not as a "friend of the Bantu," as J. H. Soga sees him, but as some one whose motives are suspect: we complain of Brownlee, the *imbongi* says, because he wants to be friendly with the Germans:

> Kub' uTshalisi siyamkhalazela,
> Ufan' ukwazana namaJelimani; (Rubusana, p. 248)

Brownlee looks after Sandile, but the verbs the *imbongi* uses connote the herding of cattle – Brownlee drives him, brings him out, herds him, sends him home:

> NgumntakaNgqik' ogeinwe nguTshalisi,
> Ukhe wamqhuba wamphumeza,
> Ubuye wamnqanda wamgodusa. (p. 249)

Here the opinion of the *imbongi* runs counter to the historian's assessment of Brownlee's motives. Similarly, an *izibongo* I collected from David Yali-Manisi on 20 December 1970 about the cattle killing episode of 1857 presents a view in conflict with the assessment of Nongqause's role current among historians.[28]

Nongqause, in Manisi's poem, should not have been believed by the people:

   Yayilishobo kwaloo nto
   Ukuqalekiswa kwesizwe sikaXhosa
30 Kusuk' umntw' ebhinqile
   Ath' uthethile namanyange
   Uthethe naw' ewabonile
   Azi babeye phi n' abantu balo mhlaba
   Zaziye phi n' izigwakumbesha
35 Zaziye phi n' izidwangube (118)

   That in itself was a sham,
   A curse to the land of Xhosa,
30 For a female to emerge
   And proclaim that she was addressed by the ancestors,
   That she spoke to them in person.
   Where were the people of this land?
   Where were the great men?
35 Where were the dignitaries?

Nongqause's prophecy led to the destruction of the Xhosa, but Manisi's poem exonerates the girl; the downfall of the Xhosa is clearly the result of a vicious plot by the whites, and the archvillain was Sir George Grey, abetted by the missionaries:

   Kwaqal' ingqobhoko sathi samkel' uThixo
   Kanti loo Thixo sithi siyamamkela
130 Le Bhayibhil' izel' inyumnyezi
   Iphethwe yindod' ekhol' ijong' entshonalanga
   Apha ngaphambili ngumqukumbelo
   Ngasemva yil' ntunj' yokuhlal' amabhabhathane
   Kanti kulapho kugangxwe khon' inkanunu
135 Evela phantsi kwendleb' iphum' esilevini
   Kant' iqhawul' iminqambulo kwabanga phambili
   Uthe wakuxakeka k' umhlaba
   Yangena yajojobala
   Yangena yathomalalisa
140 Inj' enkul' into kaGreyi
   Bayawath' ukuyibiza yingang' uJoji
   KaGreyi

       Yath' iyawulungis' umhlaba
       Kanti ngexesha lenyala lesikizi
145 Ibimele mgama yakh' umkhanyo
       Ijong' isiphumo sokufa kwezidumbu
       Abantu bequngquluza bengatyiwa nkanunu
       Kuba babekwaz' ukurhubuluza ngezisu
       Bepheph' inkanunu besiya kumbulali
150 Ncincilili!
       Ncincilili

       It all started with religion, when we said we would accept
          God;
       Yet this God we said we would accept,
130 This Bible is pregnant with abomination.
       It is held by a man whose collar looks westward.
       In the front is the turned over part of the collar,
       At the back is an opening where butterflies stay,
       And that is where a cannon is lodged,
135 Which appears below the ear and comes out at the chin,
       And it shatters the sinews of those in front.
       And when the country was in a plight,
       The cannon penetrated deeply,
       It penetrated and calmed things down.
140 The great dog, the child of Grey,
       Who is called Big George,
       The son of Grey,
       Said he was rearranging the land,
       Yet in this time of shame and scandal
145 He stood apart, and shaded his eyes,
       Watching the result of the piling of corpses.
       People lay stark without any shots fired,
       Because they knew how to crawl on their bellies,
       Avoiding the cannon as they made towards the killer.
150 Ncincilili!
       Ncincilili.

Although the *izibongo* of Sandile printed by Rubusana and Manisi's *izibongo* about Nongqause both present views in conflict with current opinions of historians, the two testimonies do not have the same historical value. As I have suggested above, the *izibongo* which Rubusana published was probably the product of memorial transmission. Apart from slight verbal divergences as a result of this transmission, it is in all likelihood very similar to the poem sung by contemporaries of Sandile himself; accordingly, it may be considered to be an authentic representation of the opinion of a Xhosa tribesman living during the period of Brownlee's influence over Sandile. A memorised *izibongo* may well be obscure and contain allusions no longer intelligible to its transmitter, but the intelligible passages will often provide grist for the historian's mill, since they express the opinion of a man concerned with the history and welfare of his people who lived at the time of the events he describes. Such authentic texts must be for the historian of Africa what medieval manuscripts are for the historian of Europe: valuable, rare, witnesses from a distant time. (Of course, the *imbongi* who lived a century ago had no access to archives or to Brownlee's correspondence, so his opinion must be weighed against the conclusions of the modern researcher.) Manisi's poem, on the other hand was improvised: he had never composed a poem on Nongqause before, and he did it (after 22 seconds of thought) only at my request. Like Sandile's *imbongi* he too is concerned with the historical traditions of his people, but for the material of this *izibongo* he drew on a free oral narrative tradition, and this tradition is subject to far more alteration in time than is a fixed poetic tradition. Historical traditions may well be altered for political reasons. Current Xhosa tradition would blame the Whites for the cattle killing; to support this view Manisi (or his informants) attempts to show how transparent the "prophecy" was. Monica Wilson has drawn my attention to the fact that Manisi is incorrect when he claims that the ancestors would not speak to a mere girl; but this distorted representation of traditional belief makes Manisi's poem all the more interesting, since it provides an illustration of the distortion of traditional belief for political reasons. This *izibongo*, impressive as a work of literature, is of limited value to the historian; the attitudes it expresses are those of a Xhosa tribesman living 120 years after the events he describes and drawing on a free oral tradition.

The historian of the Transkei and the Ciskei must come to

A Xhosa imbongi *(Mase Attwell Bhuti)*

photo: J. Opland

A Xhosa imbongi *(Melikhaya Mbutuma) during a performance*

photo (taken by R. Moyer): J. Opland

PLATE 1

▲ *A Xhosa* imbongi *(Nelson Title Mabunu) during a performance*

photo: J. Opland

PLATE 2

appreciate the value of learning the Xhosa language so that he may gather the opinions of the Xhosa themselves about their own history, opinions expressed in vernacular writings or by oral informants. When the historian comes to the *izibongo*, those receptacles of the history of the Xhosa-speaking peoples, he should in his assessment of their testimony consider amongst other factors the nature of their propagation, for the improvised and memorised *izibongo* differ in value as historical sources.

FOOTNOTES

1 See for example E. W. Grant, The *izibongo* of the Zulu Chiefs, *Bantu Studies* 3 (1927-9), 205-44; B. W. Vilakazi, The Conception and Development of Poetry in Zulu, *Bantu Studies* 12 (1938), 105-34; C. L. S. Nyembezi, The Historical Background to the *izibongo* of the Zulu Military Age, *African Studies* 7 (1948), 110-25, 157-74; David Rycroft, Melodic Features in Zulu Eulogistic Recitation, *African Language Studies* 1 (1960), 60-78; Raymond Kunene, An Analytical Survey of Zulu Poetry both Traditional and Modern (M.A., University of Natal 1961); David Rycroft, Zulu and Xhosa Praise Poetry and Song, *African Music* 3 (1962), 79-85; Trevor Cope, ed., *Izibongo: Zulu Praise-Poems* (Oxford 1968).
2 W. B. Rubusana, ed., *Zemk' Iinkomo, Magwalandini* (London 1906, 2nd ed. 1911); H. M. Ndawo, ed., *Izibongo Zenkosi Zama-Hlubi NezamaBàca* (Marianhill 1928); H. M. Ndawo, ed., *Iziduko Zama-Hlubi* (Lovedale 1939).
3 See A. C. Jordan, Towards an African Literature: II Traditional Poetry, *Africa South* 2 (1957), 97-105; A. C. Jordan, Towards an African Literature: VII Poetry and the New Order, *Africa South* 3 (1959), 74-9 (Jordan's excellent series of twelve articles has recently been published in full as *Towards an African Literature: The Emergence of Literary Form in Xhosa* (Berkeley 1973); Archie Mafeje, The Rôle of the Bard in a Contemporary African Community, *Journal of African Languages* 6 (1967), 193-223; J. Opland, Two Xhosa Oral Poems, *Papers in African Languages 1970* (School of African Studies, University of Cape Town), pp. 86-98. Another article of Mafeje's contains much incidental information about the performance of Xhosa poetry, A Chief visits Town, *Journal of Local Administration Overseas*, 2 (1963), 88-99; and there are two valuable statements in Xhosa: The introduction to L. M. S. Ngcwabe's *Khala Zome* (Johannesburg n.d.) and Miss D. N. Jafta's introduction to Michael

Huna, *ULindipasi* (Cape Town 1966). For convenience, since I am concerned with literature and not ethnology, I use the term "Xhosa" for "Xhosa-speaking people" throughout. The Xhosa noun *izibongo* is grammatically plural, but is used to denote one or more "praise poems", a practice followed in this chapter.

4 On the former, see J. Vansina, *Oral Tradition* (London 1965); on the latter, a useful article that has appeared recently is David P. Henige, The Problem of Feedback in Oral Tradition: Four Examples from the Fante Coastlands, *JAH* 14 (1973), 223–35. Vansina's *Oral Tradition* has recently appeared in a paperback edition (Aylesbury 1973) in which the preface contains a number of modifications and qualifications of the original text (pp. xiii f.).

5 The most convenient approaches to the work of these two scholars are Adam Parry, ed., *The Making of Homeric Verse: The Collected Papers of Milman Parry* (Oxford 1970) and A. B. Lord, *The Singer of Tales* (Cambridge Mass. 1960).

6 The term is taken from Alan Jabbour, Memorial Transmission in Old English Poetry, *The Chaucer Review* 3 (1969), 174–90. His classification of oral traditions with respect to the character of transmission merits quotation in full:

> If we discover that in a certain oral poetical tradition the variants of a song are related only in subject-matter and have no discernible history of word-for-word or phrase-by-phrase transmission, we may conclude that the tradition is improvisational. It would, however, be more than likely that passages would crop up here and there with a considerable number of verbal parallels, especially in separate renditions by the same singer, renditions from father and son or teacher and pupil, and renditions from the same locality. Such cases would require us to qualify our description, using the term "primarily improvisational" to show our recognition that memorial transmission is also taking place. If, on the other hand, we discover that in a certain tradition the variants of a song show a history of word-for-word or phrase-by-phrase oral transmission from a known or presumed archetype, we may describe the tradition as memorial. But considerable variation would almost certainly appear in the several texts, such as omission, addition, interpolation from other songs, stylizing, formulizing, or the like. These improvisational traits would compel us to call the tradition "primarily memorial" (p. 178).

7 Albert Kropf defines an *imbongi* as "The poet who praises; an improvisator" and the verb *ukubonga* as "To praise, extol loudly and impromptu by songs or orations..." in his *A Kafir-English Dictionary*, 2nd ed., ed. Robert Godfrey (Lovedale 1915); and composition on the spur of the moment is implicit in the description of the activities of the *imbongi* in Mafeje's 1963 article

(see note 3 above), in which Mafeje explicitly says in a footnote that the "distinctive feature" of an *imbongi* "is that he can recite poems without having prepared them beforehand" (p. 91).

8 Works which treat the Nguni or "Bantu" tradition in general are G. P. Lestrade, European influences upon the development of Bantu Language and Literature *in* I. Schapera, ed., *Western Civilization and the Natives of South Africa* (London 1934); G. P. Lestrade, Bantu Praise-poems, *The Critic* 4 (1935), 1–10; G. P. Lestrade, Traditional Literature *in* I. Schapera, ed., *The Bantu-speaking Tribes of South Africa* (Cape Town 1937); B. W. Vilakazi, The Oral and Written Literature in Nguni (Ph.D., University of the Witwatersrand 1945); R. H. W. Shepherd, Bantu Literature, *Standpunte* 28 (1953), 44–54; P. D. Beuchat, *Do the Bantu have a Literature?* (Institute for the Study of Man in Africa, Paper No. 7 1962); R. Finnegan, *Oral Literature in Africa* (Oxford 1970), pp. 111–46.

9 At various times from August 1969 to the present I have worked in Cape Town, the Transkei and the Ciskei with Mfengu, Rarabe (i.e. Ngqika and Gcaleka), Thembu, Hlubi and Bhaca poets. I gratefully acknowledge the assistance afforded by the award of Lestrade Scholarships in 1970 and 1971, without which this field work would not have been possible. Numbers in round brackets following quotations from my field recordings in the present article refer to the catalogue of my collection of tapes; copies of many of these tapes are housed at the Center for the Study of Oral Literature at Harvard University.

10 R. C. Samuelson, *Long, Long Ago* (Durban 1929). I am grateful to Mr Charles Boyd for lending me his copy of this book.

11 P. A. W. Cook, History and *Izibongo* of the Swazi Chiefs, *Bantu Studies*, 5 (1931), 181–201.

12 *Amanqakwana ngeminombo yesizwe zase-Mbo* (Lovedale 1953).

13 First published at Lovedale in 1914, second (enlarged) edition 1931. My quotations are from the latter edition, since the latest edition in the revised orthography is (inexcusably) abridged.

14 *Imbongi nezibongo:* The Xhosa tribal poet and the contemporary poetic tradition, an article not yet published.

15 In his autobiography *UMqhayi waseNtabozuko* (Lovedale 1939), revised ed. 1964, Mqhayi says that as a boy in Kentani he used to sing praises of the cattle he was herding, of dogs and of other boys, and that many boys did this (p. 66). Later (p. 79) he quotes a poem that another boy used to sing in praise of him.

16 A Thembu *imbongi* from Queenstown. The conversation was held in his home on 20 December 1970.

17 A Thembu *imbongi* from the Khundulu location near Queenstown. The conversation was held outside his home on 20 December 1970.

18 A Rarabe *imbongi* who is now Minister of Education in the Ciskeian Legislative Assembly. The conversation was held at the University of Fort Hare in Alice on 9 July 1971.

19 A Thembu *imbongi* from the Egoso location near Engcobo in the

Transkei, who is the *imbongi* referred to in Mafeje's two articles (see note 3 above). The conversation was held in Mbutuma's home on 9 January 1971.
20 I am grateful to Mr R. Schwarz and members of the staff of the Radio Bantu studios in King William's Town for their help and cooperation in the transcription of the poem from the 78 r.p.m. shellac disc in the Radio Bantu collection.
21 *Izibongo zeenkosi zamaXhosa* (Lovedale 1952), pp. 48–52.
22 Copies of these invaluable tapes, recorded before I started my field work, were kindly given to me by Prof. H. W. Pahl.
23 This recording is housed in the archives of Radio Bantu in King William's Town; again, I am grateful to Mr Schwarz and members of his staff.
24 Alf. Z. Ngani, *Intlaba-Mkhosi* (Lovedale 1965), p. 36.
25 This was the first *izibongo* I ever heard; I am grateful to Mr R. M. Tobias for letting me have his tape recording of the performance.
26 However, Prof. Cope has kindly drawn my attention to the fact that all publications on the Zulu tradition to date deal with the *izibongo* of deceased chiefs or heroes; to his knowledge no one has done – or is doing – research on Zulu *izibongo* of living chiefs. In an earlier article, *Scop* and *Imbongi:* Anglo-Saxon and Bantu oral poets, *English Studies in Africa,* 14 (1971), 161–78, I wrote:
> Cope would make a distinction between the praise poem sung by an ordinary tribesman and that sung by an *imbongi*. But we must go further: we must distinguish between the praise poem sung by an *imbongi* in honour of a chief long dead and that sung by an *imbongi* in honour of a chief during that chief's lifetime. The former will tend to be a mere repetition of recollected praises, the length of the poem directly proportional to the stature of the chief and inversely proportional to the time elapsed since his death. The latter will be far less fixed in content and will vary according to the context of the performance. The praise song of a long dead chief tends to stability in form and content; the praise song uttered on the spur of the moment by an *imbongi* inspired by the presence of his chief or eager to incite his audience to loyalty for the chief bears the individual stamp of the singer: it is, in Lord's sense of the term, an oral poem. (p. 172)

Research on contemporary Zulu *izibongo* in praise of living chiefs may in fact reveal an element of improvisation in the Zulu tradition such as exists in the Xhosa tradition.
27 The terms "fixed" and "free" are those used by Vansina: "From the formal point of view, it is possible to distinguish between two types of traditions: those which have a fixed form and are learnt by heart and transmitted as they stand, and those which are free in form and not learnt by heart and which everyone transmits in his own way" (*Oral Tradition,* pp. 22f.); see further pp. 120–9. It should be clear

from what I have said above that "improvised" poetry is not strictly "free" in form, since it makes use of a common stock of ready-made phrases.
28 See, for example, the discussion in Monica Wilson and Leonard Thompson, eds., *The Oxford History of South Africa* I (Oxford 1969) 257ff.

2

SETTLEMENT IN THE TRANSKEI AND CISKEI BEFORE THE MFECANE

Robin Derricourt

THE Cape Nguni, the Xhosa-speaking people of the Transkei and Ciskei, have been one of the most discussed of the South African Bantu-speaking groups. Much of the documentation and popular tradition about the Cape Nguni dates, however, from the period when these communities had already undergone a series of major changes and were living in a context much altered from their traditional organisation. Many of these changes took place in the period 1820–1830. I examine here aspects of the pattern of settlement prior to this time.

The influences of change were felt by all the pre-1820 Cape Nguni tribal clusters, the Xhosa, Thembu, Bomvana, Mpondomise and Mpondo.[1] They were felt the more intensely because of the bottleneck context of the communities, enclosed by the Drakensberg on the north and the Indian Ocean on the southeast. From the east and northeast, the incursions in the 1820s of the Mfengu and other refugees of the Mfecane, communities of Natal Nguni displaced directly or indirectly by the military activities of Shaka's Zulu impis, produced waves to affect not only the Transkeian and Ciskeian peoples, but the colony too, for some decades. The immigrant populations were variously dispersed from among the Mpondo westwards. They disturbed the settlement pattern of the Mpondomise and their pressure led, for example, to the Thembu fission and the migration of emigrant Thembu northwards and westwards.[2]

The greatest pressure from the west was felt by the Ngqika section of the Xhosa when the Tyhume and Keiskamma Rivers were defined by Somerset as the boundary of the Cape Colony in 1819. This changed the settlement pattern, at least of the western Xhosa, into one of over-population and inadequate pasture.[3] The eastern colonial frontier was further strengthened by the settlement in 1820 of several thousand English settlers.

More subtle innovations occurred in the same decade. The establishment of Fort Willshire on the Keiskamma in 1824 for trade with the Xhosa created a boom in what had been for more than a century illicit exchange. By 1830 some twelve hundred to fifteen hundred Xhosa came to trade each week as large quantities of glass and metal objects were exchanged for hides, ivory and other goods.[4] Missionaries, almost continually from 1816, and a printing press at Lovedale from 1822, accelerated the process of change in many fields.[5]

Any study of settlement and economic patterns among the Cape Nguni must clearly distinguish between data on the period before 1820 and the much more plentiful data on the period from 1820 onwards.

Sources
For information on the Cape Nguni before 1820 we must look to archaeology, oral tradition and written records for the period. Linguistic studies have aided in the construction of relationships between Bantu-speakers and Khoi but so far have contributed only to a limited extent to the history of other Transkeian events.

Archaeological work by the author has indicated the presence of Cape Nguni agriculturalists as they affected Late

Stone Age hunters and has suggested a widespread pattern of coastal exploitation by Iron Age groups related to Natal Nguni. The survival of evidence from inland settlement sites has, however, been poor and contributes little to our knowledge of the early Cape Nguni.

Primary written sources can be grouped by period into three main divisions.[6] For the period from 1552 to c. 1700 we have only the accounts of people shipwrecked on the coast and of their travels to safety. There are six Portuguese shipwrecks of relevance between 1552 and 1647 and for 1686–8 the accounts of the survivors of the *Stavenisse* and the crew of the *Centaurus* and *Noord*, which searched for survivors.[7]

In the 18th century an increasing pattern of ivory trade and hunting expeditions to the territory of the Cape Nguni developed from the Colony.[8] Records of these are scant, the trade was not officially encouraged, the traders were not likely to record their activities in writing, and it is indeed hard to judge the extent of these expeditions beyond the boundaries of the Colony. They seem to have occurred from before the beginning of the century. In 1702 Xhosa hunters were met at what is now Somerset East.[9] Theal describes the English galley, *Clapham*, trading on the coast somewhere south of Delagoa Bay, offering beads and copper rings for ivory, in 1714. Elephant hunters penetrated into the Transkei beyond Thembuland in 1736 and Collins met a man who had been a hunter there in 1738. This trade seems to have increased in the Ciskei until the period of open conflict between colonists and Nguni, and trading seems to have been regular in the 1770s.[10]

In the period prior to the outbreak of the first frontier war in 1779, few travellers beyond the eastern border of the colony wrote up their experiences. Ensign Beutler went on an official expedition of exploration into the Transkei as far as the Qora River in 1752. In 1772 Thunberg travelled to the Gamtoos River and encountered there Xhosa who had crossed to the west of the Fish River. Sparrman reached the Great Fish River in 1775 and penetrated beyond the Kroomie near the Koonap. In 1778 Van Plettenberg went to the Fish River and the following year, the year of the outbreak of hostilities, Paterson went on a journey across the Fish and penetrated further than these recent predecessors, almost reaching the Keiskamma. From these travellers and from official reports a good picture is gained of aspects of the Ciskei, and Xhosa penetration west of the Fish.[11] Traditional histories were not collected, for none of the travellers spent any significant time with Xhosa themselves.

During the forty years from 1779 to 1819, when conflict between the Dutch frontiersmen and the Xhosa emerged as a dominant theme in the politics of Cape governments, written sources expand. A score of travellers' accounts mentioning the Xhosa in this period are known, but many of these take their information from hearsay or repeat the contents of earlier publications. The conflict situation discouraged adventurers into "Kaffraria" except on official government service and negotiations.

Among those who described their own travels across the Fish during this period were Le Vaillant and Lichtenstein. They were followed by Barrow, who went beyond the Keiskamma. Janssens, Paravicini and D. G. van Reenen, three participants in the 1803 negotiations with Ngqika, are additional sources. Collins, who visited Hintsa in 1809, was the only writer to cross the River Kei. Alberti's account of the Xhosa is the most thorough and he and Lichtenstein give genealogical information of Xhosa chiefs. These writers in general provide useful contemporary information on areas beyond those in which they travelled.[12] From 1799 to 1800 Van Der Kemp worked for the London Missionary Society, mainly in the central Ciskei, and travelled along the Keiskamma and on the coast.[13]

In this period occurred the shipwreck of the *Hercules* on the Ciskei coast, but Theal assessed the account of the survivors' journey as very inaccurate and of no value.[14] The more important event was the wreck of the *Grosvenor* on the Transkei coast in 1782 and Jacob van Reenen's expedition of 1790–91 to search for survivors.[15] Invaluable data is given on the country beyond that in which normal European travel for trading, hunting and enquiry took place at that time.

Traditions
The effect on the Cape Nguni of the Mfengu and parallel migrations appears more impressive than most previous events and processes. As a result, collections of traditions since this time often have a boundary with these events. The arrival of missionaries and of the printed word in the 1820s and 1830s was a further disruptive influence on oral tradition, and the process of feedback from publications into tradition has consequently been more serious than amongst most other African societies. In considering the validity of traditions, what is important is to consider the context and particularly the date of their collection and not merely to accept fuller but later collections of data.

Cape Nguni traditions centre on chiefs and their followers, with some geographical reference to burial places. Very little recorded tradition mentions social, economic, technological or settlement pattern changes. Traditions dealing with the Cape Nguni prior to 1820 are fullest when discussing the Xhosa tribal cluster after 1775: the fission of the cluster, the political intrigues and conflicts.

Only three sets of traditional information of the type I have described were actually collected before 1820, although in 1809, Collins, coming to the Stormberg, reported hearsay on Xhosa and Gonaqua. Alberti in 1803–6 collected genealogies of the Xhosa tribe cluster back to Phalo. Henry Lichtenstein at the same period, but published only in 1811, presented the genealogy back to Togu, six generations before Ngqika, but managed to make two major errors in what must have been recent history, placing Phalo as brother instead of father of Gcaleka and, even stranger, Ndlambe as brother instead of uncle of Ngqika. This doubtless reflects the political prejudices of his informants. Yet John Brownlee, working as a missionary from 1820 and writing with more detail of fission and settlement also gives the same, but expanded genealogy with the same errors.[16]

W. Shepstone, working from c. 1824, collected a genealogy of all the Cape Nguni groups, linking them in a single family; this agrees in its later details with Alberti.[17] Another version of the Cape Nguni genealogy, said for the earlier generations to derive from Shepstone, was said to have been collected in 1833 among the Mpondo and their neighbours. It differs from the first list of Shepstone's in a number of places in order and spelling, with some new names. It was edited by B. Nicholson, who added the later names, and it is not clear to what extent he made other alterations.[18] In 1837 Justus published a somewhat different genealogy of the Xhosa in his polemical work,[19] but we do not know the source for this. A further set of oral traditions related by John Knox Bokwe and published in 1889,[20] deal with the Xhosa and, in particular, their relations with the Gonaqua. The only other 19th century survey of traditions is contained in the report of the 1883 Commission on Native Laws and Customs.[21] The first full recording of oral data is presented in the two versions of the history of the Mpondomise collected in or just before 1881 from senior tribal members and reproduced *verbatim*. These deal with chiefs, their movements and political events. One, from a man called Vele, contains references to Langalibalele, the fleeing Natal chief. References to Christian missions suggest Vele was a man with outward contacts which may have affected the nature and reliability of his story. There are contradictions and inconsistencies in several places in his testimony: the number of chiefs, the movement of Mpondo and the Great House succession. The post-Mfecane events are the main interest of this account as the informant was a participant. The second collection of Mpondomise traditions from senior members of the tribe is probably more reliable; it was collected by the interpreter to the magistrate in Tsolo. The genealogies differ in the two accounts.

Popular historical writings in Xhosa appear early in this century with stories relating mainly to the later history.[22] These played a role in the work of J. H. Soga.

Most recent authors have looked for the picture of Cape Nguni history to John Henderson Soga and his work *The South-Eastern Bantu,* completed in 1928–1930. This was a remarkable achievement in many ways and a volume of great interest. Soga has gained a high status as an oracle on his people and these views need assessment. Soga himself, son of the distinguished and highly educated Xhosa clergyman, Tiyo Soga, and a Scottish mother, was similarly educated in Europe and married to a Scottish wife. His cultural background placed him far closer to his predecessors among missionaries and administrators in the collection of oral traditions than to the originators of these traditions themselves, although he would not have shared language uncertainties. Soga worked in an area of Cape Nguni settlement, Elliotdale, from 1904 and it must have been here in the midst of Bomvanaland that most of his oral collecting was done. His book relies heavily on published works, yet his bibliography mentions neither Maclean, Godlonton, Alberti, Lichtenstein nor the Cape of Good Hope *Report,* except where it is quoted by Brownlee.[23] Soga seems to have leant heavily on Theal, whose views he frequently repeats, and he uses also the volumes of vernacular stories. His uncritical approach to white authors allows him to repeat the myths of Bantu origins – including a digression on the descent of Ham – on misleading and unfortunate lines. He accepts conventional views on Zimbabwe and Theal's views on Abambo migrations.

This is not to decry the remarkable achievement of Soga as man, missionary and author. As has been suggested by Shula Marks for Bryant on the Natal Nguni,[24] however, Soga's work needs to be assessed far more critically than has been the case and together with the earlier collections of oral data mentioned here, rather than be given adulatory repetition.

GENEALOGY OF CAPE NGUNI
FOLLOWING 19TH CENTURY SOURCES

Following Maclean 1858 (except some spellings). Variants as (Palo) from Shepstone in Godlonton 1835; variants as Palo from Cape of Good Hope Commission 1883. Eponymous founder in square. Not all variants in spelling are given. Gladwin additions for Mpondomise as [2 additions].

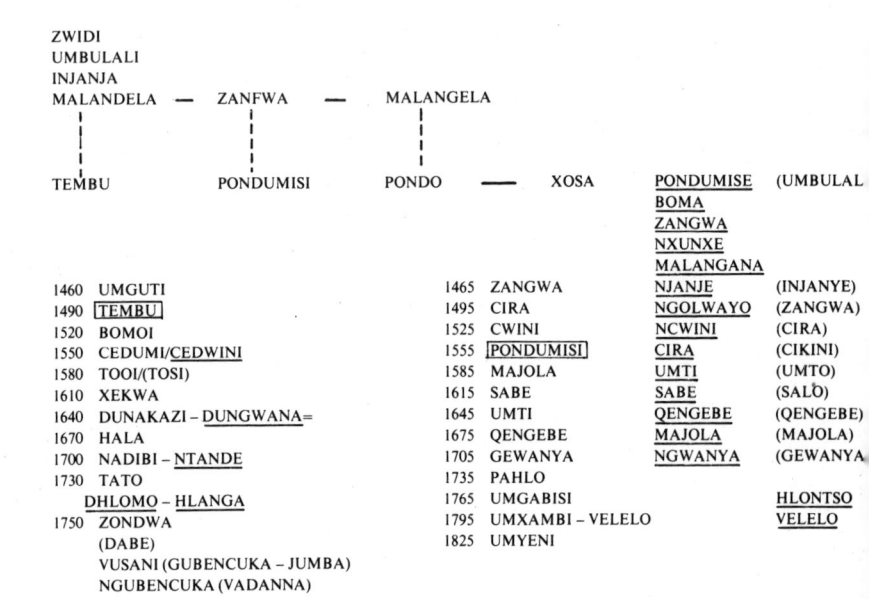

```
ZWIDI
UMBULALI
INJANJA
MALANDELA  —  ZANFWA  —  MALANGELA
    |                |             |
    |                |             |
TEMBU           PONDUMISI      PONDO  ——  XOSA      PONDUMISE   (UMBULAL
                                                    BOMA
                                                    ZANGWA
                                                    NXUNXE
                                                    MALANGANA
1460  UMGUTI                         1465  ZANGWA   NJANJE      (INJANYE)
1490  [TEMBU]                        1495  CIRA     NGOLWAYO    (ZANGWA)
1520  BOMOI                          1525  CWINI    NCWINI      (CIRA)
1550  CEDUMI/CEDWINI                 1555  [PONDUMISI] CIRA     (CIKINI)
1580  TOOI/(TOSI)                    1585  MAJOLA   UMTI        (UMTO)
1610  XEKWA                          1615  SABE     SABE        (SALO)
1640  DUNAKAZI – DUNGWANA=           1645  UMTI     QENGEBE     (QENGEBE)
1670  HALA                           1675  QENGEBE  MAJOLA      (MAJOLA)
1700  NADIBI – NTANDE                1705  GEWANYA  NGWANYA     (GEWANYA
1730  TATO                           1735  PAHLO
      DHLOMO – HLANGA                1765  UMGABISI             HLONTSO
1750  ZONDWA                         1795  UMXAMBI – VELELO     VELELO
      (DABE)                         1825  UMYENI
      VUSANI (GUBENCUKA – JUMBA)
      NGUBENCUKA (VADANNA)
```

46

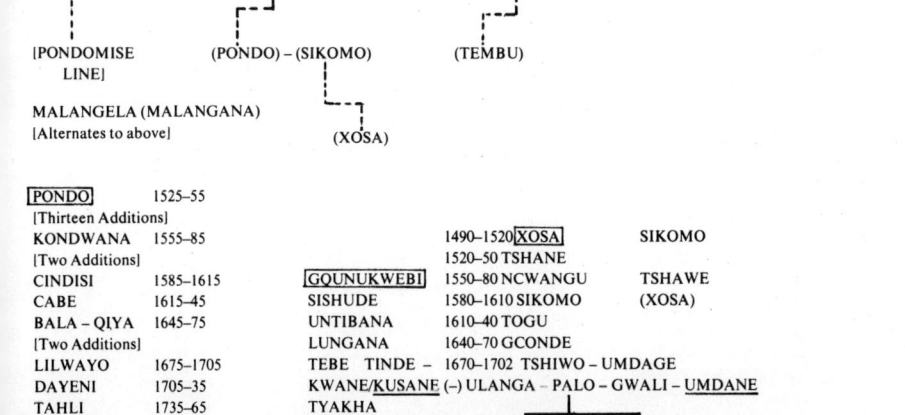

```
(ZWEDI)
(UMBULALI)    —    (MALANGANA)    —    (MALANDELA)
    |                  |--.                    |--.
    |                  |  |                    |  |
[PONDOMISE         (PONDO) – (SIKOMO)       (TEMBU)
 LINE]
                              |-----7
MALANGELA (MALANGANA)         |   |
[Alternates to above]        (XOSA)
```

PONDO	1525–55			
[Thirteen Additions]				
KONDWANA	1555–85		1490–1520 **XOSA**	SIKOMO
[Two Additions]			1520–50 TSHANE	
CINDISI	1585–1615	**GQUNUKWEBI**	1550–80 NCWANGU	TSHAWE
CABE	1615–45	SISHUDE	1580–1610 SIKOMO	(XOSA)
BALA – QIYA	1645–75	UNTIBANA	1610–40 TOGU	
[Two Additions]		LUNGANA	1640–70 GCONDE	
LILWAYO	1675–1705	TEBE TINDE –	1670–1702 TSHIWO – UMDAGE	
DAYENI	1705–35	KWANE/KUSANE	(–) ULANGA – PALO – GWALI – UMDANE
TAHLI	1735–65	TYAKHA		
NYANZA	1765–95	TSHAKA ULANGE – GCALEKA RARABE		
QUNQUSHE	1795–1824	CUNGWA	KHAWUTA	
FAKU	1824–67	PATO	HINTSA	

```
                                    UMLAU   NUKWA   NDMLAMBE
                                    NGQIKA                CEBO
```

This is particularly true of his genealogies: a genealogy of the early or middle 19th century is far more likely to be accurate than one collected early in the 20th century and should be preferred. Data of Soga's contradicting well-documented early material should be held in suspense, though he does provide valuable additional information. In genealogical tables given here (pp. 46–7), I follow the 19th century genealogies and use Soga only where indicated. Since Soga, genealogical information has been published on the Bomvana, the Thembu and the Xhosa, and further details on the Lungu and Tshomane clans.[25]

San

Consideration of the distribution of Cape Nguni before 1820 requires also a consideration of the distribution of their neighbours, the San (Bushmen) and Khoi (Hottentots). Archaeologically, the distribution of Late Stone Age hunters who may be seen as ancestral to the San is attested in all areas of the Transkei and Ciskei. Weak in organisation, however, they fell an easy prey to expanding pastoralists and agriculturalists. Rock art, as well as this author's excavations at Oakleigh Farm, Queenstown, confirms a pattern of stock theft which was part of the adaptation and, finally, resistance of the San to their loss of territory.[26]

The San of the area east of the Fish are known in documentary and oral sources from the 17th century. Survivors of the wreck of the *Stavenisse* mention "Batuas" west of the Xhosa, doubtless baTwa or San, saying that some travellers were put to death by them. People in this area were said to have bows and arrows. Other survivors named the "Makanaena" as the enemies of the Xhosa, using bows and arrows, stealing cattle and murdering people.[27] The stock theft pattern seems to have already begun. These San may have been living, at least partly, between Xhosa and Gonaqua. They may have been the same people as those met hunting and collecting between these two clusters by the survivors of the *São João Baptista* in 1622 in the eastern Ciskei.

▲ 1. The Transkei coast

▼ 2. Homestead in central Transkei

▼ 3. Riverside homestead; the Horseshoe at Ntabankulu

PLATE 3

▲ 4. San hunter and his quarry (Tsolo district)

▼ 5. San society (Tsolo district)

In 1775-6 Sparrman reported San on the Fish River and across to the River Tsomo, which was the border of "another nation". Some were reported to have cattle, perhaps stolen, and kept, if not actually bred. In 1775 San were reported the only inhabitants of an area which seems to represent the Winterberg and Amathole range and about the same time they were said to be traversing Kaffraria.[28] Shortly afterwards, Lichtenstein recorded hostility between Xhosa and San.[29] In 1790 San were seen between the two Kei rivers and in 1803 Van Reenen reported that there were yellow-skinned, but long-haired people called "Matola" north of the Thembu.[30] Collins noted San in the Queenstown district at Schaap Kraal in 1809. In the rest of our area, the pattern of 1820 would seem to be of San hunting and raiding stock from the north of the Amathole and the upper part of the Kei, extending across to the mountainous northwest area of the Transkei. In 1813 Campbell met a Xhosa family which claimed to have suffered San depredation on the Seacow River.[31]

Thereafter, pressures increased on San territory. The emigrant Thembu swept to the north and west of the Xhosa, while settlers moved up to the northeast Cape from the other side. The number of San killed by white commandos and the pattern of the conflict in this area remains to be studied.

Certain San bands' movements in the area can be traced. Stow describes the band under Madura moving from the Klipplaat and Upper Swart Kei in c. 1835 to Glen Grey in 1849 with a following of 300 people and continuing about 1850 to the White Kei at St. Mark's, going finally into the Drakensberg. Mada'kane dominated the Swart Kei in the 19th century, where he was attacked by Thembu, Xhosa and white settlers. His brother, still painting, was drawn by Stow in 1869. The following year, Madolo's cave in the Swart Kei was still being used annually by mobile San, who were probably the last in the area.[32]

In the Transkei, the widespread archaeological distribution

of the Late Stone Age is probably confirmed by the existence of names of San origin.[33] In 1782 survivors of the wreck of the *Grosvenor* on the Pondoland coast were warned not to travel inland as San were there. The relations between Nguni and San were not always antagonistic. Statements that the Tambookies (Thembu), especially to the northwest of the area, were yellower than most of the Nguni may suggest a long history of inter-breeding.[34] A Thembu man interviewed by Stanford had lived with a San group in the middle of the last century in the headwaters of the Mbashe and Mzimvubu basins, raiding for cattle.[35] This group retreated in 1858 to the sources of the Mzimvubu. Madura's group had similarly been of mixed descent in 1849. Mpondomise chiefs praised San as rainmakers and used them in clientship in this role, paying them with cattle and crops. In 1886 a San family was still living among the Mpondomise, and one of this family had been painting until shortly before that date; indeed, the last San in the area was said to have died in 1913.[36] The rock art of the hills at Tsolo indicates cattle as well as an ox wagon (see plate 6).

The headwaters of the Mzimvubu in East Griqualand is an area which has received intensive study of its Late Stone Age rock art and, to some extent, its Late Stone Age cultural sequence. The evidence is that it was of major importance through the Late Stone Age, relating in its art styles to the Natal Drakensberg and in elements to eastern Lesotho. Despite two sources of Mpondomise tradition, no evidence has emerged in the rock art or archaeology for an Iron Age settlement in the area prior to the 19th century. Certainly for the earliest 19th century it was an important base of San hunters and cattle raiders[37] and the pressure from several sources on these led to the concept of it as a "nomansland" to be invaded by Griqua, Sotho and others. San based in East Griqualand and further down the Mzimvubu were raiding the Bhaca in 1852; they raided Faku and the Mpondo, and by trade or theft obtained European objects. A San reoccupation of East Griqualand after an early Nguni occupation seems unlikely and the area was probably always of key importance and finally a retreat area for hunter-gatherers before their final move into eastern Lesotho.

Khoi (Gonaqua)
My concern here is with the occupation of the area east of the Fish by pastoralists and the nature of their interaction with their neighbours.[38] The term "Gonaqua" is used regularly by writers and travellers for the easternmost group of pastoralists and the question of the nature and position of the eastern border of the Gonaqua becomes that of the western border of the Xhosa, at least from the 18th century. By tradition, the Gonaqua came east into the area.[39] My archaeological work has suggested that pastoralists may have been present on the middle Keiskamma in the Ciskei by the 11th century A.D. By 1622, pastoralists using assegais and valuing metal were on the coast at a point conventionally considered just west of the Keiskamma River.

It took the large, slow party of survivors from the wrecked *São João Baptista* over a month to trek eastwards along the coast between pastoralist settlements and the first villages of cultivators. They met individual hunters and gatherers who could have been, from their descriptions, Khoi, San or Xhosa. The presence of assegais and knowledge of iron amongst the pastoralists suggests that these groups were already in contact with the Nguni; in 1686 trade of dagga (cannabis) for copper with the Xhosa was attested by the survivors of the shipwrecked *Stavenisse*.

Traditions, too, give valuable information. Collins records a tradition from a Gonaqua informant that they reached the territory of the Xhosa in the chieftainship of Tshiwo and, after a conflict involving loss of human life and cattle, returned to the area of the Great Fish, others going to the north. Elements of the same tradition are found with the Xhosa. J. Brownlee recorded that the Gonaqua were mainly on the Ciskeian coast and inland along the Buffalo River and the Keiskamma to its source at the time of Togu, grandfather of Tshiwo, in the early 17th century. The later Gonaqua, under Kohla, lived between the Fish and Bushmans

Rivers. Both traditions seem, however, to refer to the Gqunukhwebe rather than the Gonaqua. The Gqunukhwebe are recognised as a mixture in some sense between Gonaqua and Xhosa, and have emerged as a group within the Xhosa tribal cluster. The genealogies give four generations back from Cungwe (Congo) to Kwane (Kusane), who is said to have been a chief councillor of Tshiwo or, by Shepstone, the brother of Tshiwo's son, Phalo. In either case, fission would appear attributable to the reign of Tshiwo, which I suggest was in the late 17th century. It may have been the western group from this fission which met the hunting party at what is now Somerset East in 1702. Stories concerning this fission presented by Soga suggest that the Gqunukhwebe had their origin in a merger of Kwane's followers with Gonaqua.[40]

Khoi place-names are known to occur to the east of the Kei and it seems possible, therefore, that their area of exploitation reached at least this far.[41] It has even been suggested that it reached as far as the Mzimvubu. A long period of interaction is attested by the linguistic evidence and a period before 1450 is suggested.[42] A Gqunukhwebe genealogy allows the early 16th century for the obscure figure, Gqunukhwebe himself, who may thus be a point for the emergence of closely linked Xhosa and Khoi.[43] In interpreting early Gonaqua settlement, we must differentiate areas of habitation and pasturage from the far wider hunting territories and note that coastal and inland distribution west to east may have been very different.

In 1736 the Gonaqua proper were west of the Xhosa, but east of the Fish, under Babbelaan.[44] In 1752 Beutler reported them settled between the Fish and Keiskamma, but many further east in a client relationship to the Xhosa. The Keiskamma remained the boundary until c. 1775, according to Ngqika as reported by Napier.

Further information for the latter 18th century indicates the results of pressure of colonists and Xhosa on the Gonaqua. In 1772 Gonaqua were settled patchily along the

Gamtoos River and along the east of the Van Staden's River in 1776. By 1777 the Fish divided the Gonaqua from Xhosa.[45] Ruyter's homestead was at the Fish mouth in 1775 and in 1779 there were claims that the Xhosa raided east in reaction to Gonaqua raids. The Gonaqua were thus impossibly caught between two groups. Having been driven east from the suurveld by colonists, they were given protection by Rarabe, but were forced out of the area after the Ndlambe revolt, apparently to disperse. Another tradition relates that as the Xhosa advanced through the Transkei westwards, Khoi advanced to their right (i.e. close and parallel to the Drakensberg).[46] This would correspond to the report of Thembu with Khoi elements and perhaps to the early presence of sheep in our excavations at Queenstown, but there is little further context to allow us to evaluate the story.

Cape Nguni history from the traditions
Five tribal clusters have been distinguished for the period before the Mfecane: Xhosa, Thembu, Mpondo, Mpondomise and Bomvana. Within these tribal divisions, the individual tribes are named, for the most part, from members of the chiefly line of the cluster who led the fission movements which increased mainly from the beginning of the 19th century. Most tribes may thus be "linked" genealogically. Other non-related tribes belong within the cluster by recognising the paramount over their own chief. The tribe is essentially a political organisation and outsiders may belong within it. This is particularly so with exogamous marriage. Van Warmelo, however, recognises and lists blocks of individuals attributed to one tribal cluster, but subject to another as chief.[47]

I here present and attempt to collate the genealogies of these Cape Tribes Proper as collected in the 19th century. For periods in which there is no date from documentary sources, a reign is taken as being 30 years, an estimate used commonly in other studies. It is valid over a lower date in the Cape Nguni context since the heir to a chieftainship would come, not from the first wife taken, but from a senior wife in a later marriage. In calculating reigns by 30 year modules one must apply the calculation to Great House heirs only and ignore regents.

Although Soga's *South-Eastern Bantu* is the most commonly used source on the movement and position of Nguni groups, it provides little new information, beyond the genealogies, on the actual movements of tribal clusters before 1820. Soga follows Theal in linking Abambo movements of Southern Africa and this has been convincingly criticised by Monica Wilson.[48] Soga's other arguments for the period under discussion use three main pieces of evidence: references to the origin of tribes at the Dedesi stream; the supposed identification of Togu in 1686; and chiefs' graves.

Soga's claims for an origin of the different Cape Nguni groups are quite clearly taken from Brownlee's historical records, themselves reprinted from the Cape of Good Hope *Report* of 1883. The sole evidence comes from Mpondomise informants: the somewhat inconsistent report of Vele, son of Mziziba, and of the regent, Mabasa. The former puts the origins of the Mpondomise at the Dedesi River and locates this where Langalibelele crossed the Drakensberg. This would be at the head of the Bushman's River Pass near Giant's Castle in Natal and not in the Mzimvubu basin at all. The other tribes of the Cape Nguni, the Xhosa and the Togu, the Thembu and the Hala are said to have been there at the same time, which is clearly not possible from a chronological point of view. In the second version, the Mpondomise are said to have lived at "the sources of the Mzimvubu called the Dedesi", but also called the Eluhlangeni "which means a large lake". Soga tested this report in 1926 by searching the upper regions of the Mzimvubu for the Dedesi, but this name was unknown[49]; others have sought it with similar lack of success.

The area in question, from East Griqualand and the Underberg district to Giant's Castle, is, however, a well known region archaeologically. For reasons discussed earlier in this chapter, it seems unlikely that there was Nguni settlement between the prehistoric Late Stone Age occupation and the San occupation of the early 19th century. The painted rock shelters do not hold evidence of Iron Age activity prior to stone walling of Sotho type which entered the area in the middle of the 19th century. On all grounds, settled occupation of the area by Nguni people in any period prior to 1820 is very improbable, although the passage of Mpondomise or other groups from Natal into the Transkei *via* a route close to the Drakensberg is feasible.

An alternative set of information on the origins of some Cape Nguni groups remains. *Eluhlangeni*, mentioned above for the Mpondomise, is the locative of the form *uhlanga* reported by Maclean as the origin of the first chief. The translation in the former case, "the lake", is unconfirmed and probably in error. Maclean translated *uhlanga* as "cave" or "reed". However, Alberti gives the myth in more detail, relating the origin of all life from the cave referred to and this is confirmed by Ayliff, who speaks of a cavern *in the east* from which all life came.[50]

Both Zulu and Xhosa have dialectal differences using both *uhlanga* and *umlanga*. Kropf distinguished the use in Xhosa of *uhlanga* as the place or hole from which living beings came forth or a stalk of kaffircorn or maize.[51] *Umhlanga*, probably introduced in this form by Mfengu, was a reed or the original stem or stock of these people. From these sources, it comes to mean a nation, race or people; the latter use of *uhlanga* is the only one in Xhosa today, mission activity being presumably responsible for the end of the myth of an origin from *uhlanga*. *Umhlanga* is used today for a wild grass in Xhosa.[52] In Zulu *uhlanga* has the basic meanings of "a stalk of grain", "a reed" or "original stem or stock of the tribe or people". It also means "a reed" or "reedy place".[53] A logical parallel between the concept of a reed and the concept of a line or stock of descent seems feasible and may exclude us from linking a place of origin with real reeds. There is, however, a remnant indication of a belief in a place or hole (cf. a cave) from which life originated, but this tells us little of the specific origin of Nguni groups beyond the Ayliff reference of "to the east".

Steedman records a Xhosa tradition that the first chief came from a cave called *uDaliwe* to the eastward.[54] While the cave image repeats the former story, *uDaliwe* merely has the meaning "being created" and may represent a misunderstanding by the collector.

Movement of Cape Nguni from Natal rather than inland around the Drakensberg would correspond to the archaeological evidence, where coastal pottery from the Transkei can be linked with preZulu pottery from iron working people in Natal. Such Natal links are borne out by the trade routes reported by the early travellers and linguistic similarities extending this to Swaziland. A further link is the recurrence of the name "Malangana" early in the genealogies and the fact that the same name was encountered in the 16th century in Natal by shipwrecked sailors.

Harinck has argued carefully against accepting Theal's date of 1686 for Togu, noting the original form of the name as given by *Stavenisse* survivors as Tokhe, Sotopa or Sessi. He argues that this is more probably Tahle, Faku's grandfather in the Mpondo line.[55] This lengthens Mpondo reigns a little too much, but accepting Togu would compress them too much. Since Phalo's son, Gcaleka, had his own homesteads in 1752,[56] Soga's date of 1702 for Phalo's birth is probably approximately correct. If Phalo was born after his father's death in that year, as Soga suggests, the reigns of Togu, Gconde and Tshiwo could not easily be accommodated in 16 years.

Other traditional data deals with chiefs' graves and movements. In considering these, we must note three points: firstly, the chief's great place would probably be in the middle of the village territories of his subject people; secondly, the hunting territory would extend beyond the area of villages in all directions; thirdly, fissive groups of the cluster would move, as noted in the fuller traditions, beyond the hunting and collecting territory of the core groups, and in most cases this would be in a westerly direction. Settlement of a tribal cluster would extend widely, away from the chief's great place, as with Phalo in 1752, whose territory extended from the Keiskamma to the Kei and whose own great place was in the middle.

For the Xhosa lineage we have information collected in the 19th century and mostly not repeated in Soga. Soga suggests that Ngcwangu (1550–1580) was buried near the Mzimvubu. Sikomo is the first figure mentioned to the west; his dates would be 1580–1610 in most lists (1520–1550 from the earliest published. He was said by Soga to have been buried at Cumgce, Buntingville, just east of the Mthatha, but, in contradiction, Soga also gives his place of death and burial at Ntabankulu, west of the Mzimvubu. This tradition seems lost locally in what is now a Mpondo area.

According to Kropf, Togu's reign (1610–1640) was a period of interaction of Xhosa and Khoi. By traditions collected by J. Brownlee in the 1820s it was the time of the first Xhosa settlement on the Kei, though, as stated, Togu would not be expected to have his own great place there. From the shipwreck records, there was certainly Nguni settlement west of the Mthatha, but Soga gives Togu's grave at Qokana in Ngqeleni east of the Mthatha, while the Mpondomise traditions put him as moving from the Dedesi to Ncocora. These records are at variance with the other earlier collected data.

In Gconde's reign (1640-1670), according to the earlier collected traditions, his brothers removed themselves across the Kei to settle in the area between the Buffalo and the Chalumna, perhaps beginning the process of pressure on Gonaqua territory.[57] Also in this reign movements of fissive groups to the Somerset East area and the suurveld between the Sundays River and the Fish River took place. The size of such groups and the degree of mixture with Khoi cannot be estimated. While one is hesitant to assume significant or permanent settlement west of the Fish at this time, there is no evidence to contradict it in the historical sources. Gconde is said by Soga to have been buried at Cumgce (Buntingville), but there is no sign of a grave or local tradition surviving to-day.

There are traditions that in Tshiwo's time (1670-1702) further fission took place, with Gando fleeing west of the Fish to the Somerset East area, but later settling between the Kobonqaba (just east of the Kei) and the kraals of the Khoi chief, Hintsati. Survivors of the *Stavenisse* reported hospitality from a Xhosa chief, Magamma, at this time, but the names are not a good fit. The same source reports other groups of Xhosa settling west of the Kei in this reign. Tshiwo is said by Soga to have been buried in Ngcwanguba Forest just west of the Mthatha and to have had territory between the Mthatha and the Mbashe. Although this burial site and nearby grain pits have been visited by the author and are clearly of some antiquity, the identification as the grave of Tshiwo need not be correct.

Phalo or Palo (1702–75) is better known and was encountered in 1736 by Hubner's party, who were killed west of the Kei. His great place was near the Amathole in 1752.[58] During Mdangi's regentship, a further flight of groups to today's Somerset East area took place and in 1715 the Ntinde settled between the Buffalo and Keiskamma, with Gqunukhwebe on the coast.[59] The quarrel between Rarabe and Gcaleka took place in this reign when Rarabe crossed the Kei to make a homestead at Izele, Kingwilliamstown, and Phalo followed.

Phalo was, however, buried at Tshomane, east of the Kei, and Rarabe was also buried overlooking the Kei.[60] If such a pattern of burial in the east of a chief's territory occurred earlier, it could fit both Soga's claims for burial locations and the earlier evidence. Rarabe was said by Paterson in 1779 to have moved 100 miles north of Gcaleka's son, Khawuta, i.e. west of the Kei, for Khawuta's chief homestead lay between the Keiskamma and the Fish. On the death of

Phalo, in c. 1775, Rarabe migrated west to the Keiskamma, according to Brownlee, though Collins maintains he went to the area between the White Kei and the Tsomo Rivers.[61]

By 1809 Khawuta's son, Hintsa, was west of the Kei and the Thembu were pushed back to the Mbashe. Soga mentions conflict between Rarabe and the Thembu in 1770, which the latter lost. To what extent this involved war rather than merely a realignment of forces is unknown, but travellers observed devastated homesteads.

The Thembu are problematic, as the genealogy Soga gives varies on a number of points from those of Brownlee and the Cape *Report* of 1883. Soga puts Nxego (c. 1640) buried at Msana on the Mbashe, his son Mlanga (c. 1640) probably buried at Nkanga in Willowvale and Talo (c. 1730) at Mkulu east of the Mbashe River. Zondwa (c. 1750) was placed at Dawabe in Mqanduli, Ndabe (c. 1780) at Mtentu on the east of the Mbashe. All this fits in well with the historical data.

The Bomvana genealogies were collected separately, but contemporaneously, by Soga and Cook. Both would take the eponymous founder, Bomva, back to 1520, using a 30 year module. Cook gives their arrival as refugees from Natal to the Mpondo in the reign of Dubandlela (1670–1700 in Cook's list, 1610–40 in Soga's). This was said to be under the Bomvana Njilo, which would slightly raise Bomvu's date. The possible meeting in 1790 of Gambushe on the Mgazi would be the correct time by Cook's genealogy, but one generation out by Soga's. The Bomvana are said to have moved to the present area in the early 19th century.

The Mpondomise genealogies conflict. Soga's list would put the eponymous founder at 1495. Information on places of burial is given, however, in the the Cape *Report* of 1883. Working back from Umyeki (Myeki), c. 1825, and using a 30 year module, Malangana, said to have been at the Dedesi, would be c. 1465, Ntose 1525 (or 1495), dying at the Rhode; Ncwini 1555 (or 1495 or 1525), dying at Lotana in

Qumbu, with homesteads on the Mthatha, Tsitsa, Tina, Kinira and Mzimvubu Rivers; Cira at 1585 (or 1525), Umte 1615 (or 1685 or 1645) and Mgcambi 1645 (or 1615). Their successors Majolo, Palo and Sontlo (1675, 1705, 1735) were said to be buried at the Tina River. Mgabisi occupied the Tsitsa and Tsolo districts (1765). Mgcambi was at Qanga (1795); Myeki (1825) fled to the Mzimvubu. Lotana is now Mpondomise, but the inhabitants know of no grave sites or early great places. According to this author's local informants, Mhlontlo took the area from the Mpondo and it is possible that the mention of the place in the 1883 genealogy is a justification of the succession of settlement.

While Vele's account in the 1883 *Report* gives the graves as above, that of the regent, Madusi, is more feasible and correlates better with the account of the Mpondomise by the survivors of the *Stavenisse*. This account suggests that the Mpondomise moved from the Dedesi or *Eluhlangeni* to the Mzimvubu (position unstated), where they remained until Mgabisi (c. 1765) moved into the Tsitsa and Tsolo river basins.

The fifth tribal cluster in the Transkei prior to the Mfecane was the Mpondo one. Though Harinck puts Tahle at 1686, using the *Stavenisse* survivors' reports, this suggestion is unconfirmed and I prefer 1735–65. Most early reports mention chiefs without a position in the genealogy. Information on graves puts Msiza (1525–55 in Soga) in Natal, Ncindise (1555–85 in Soga, 1585–1615 in others) east of the Mthamvuna in Natal, Cabe (1585–1615 in Soga, or 1615–45) possibly at Bumazi, and Tahle (1735–65) in the Transkei east of the Mzimvubu.[62] According to Brownlee,[63] it was under Tahle that the Mpondo settled on the south bank of the Mzimvubu, while the Xesibe settled on the border; Ngqunguba, according to Soga (and dating 1775–c. 1820), was killed on the Dwangwano. The Mpondomise informants of 1883 claimed that the Mpondo crossed the Mzimvubu before the Mpondomise, but that the Xhosa and Thembu came after them.

Pre-trading period: distribution of groups
The records of shipwrecks, though in many cases excellent historical documents, are least certain in the geographical location of the features encountered. The identification of places advanced casually by Theal has tended to gain acceptance with little further consideration. Boxer[64] and others have offered interpretations, but none of the texts have been subject to the same scrutiny that Forbes and Kirby applied to later travellers. The inaccuracy of early map readings and misidentification of river names from maps causes further uncertainty. On the maps accompanying this chapter I have attempted to suggest the most probable distribution of groups from this data.

The *São João* was wrecked in 1552 at a place the survivors estimated at 100 leagues or c. 300 miles along the coast south of the Pongola. Theal's identification of this was "to the northeast of the Mzimvubu". The *São Bento* wreck in 1554 is similarly difficult to place, but is probably on the Transkei coast.[65] The survivors traversed the coast and found it thinly populated.

The *Santo Alberto* (1589) is a far better account, a remarkably detailed description of an inland journey.[66] Theal thought the landing was at Hole-in-the-Wall east of the Mbashe River, but, even if the readings were out, the shipwrecked survivors' estimate that they were travelling N.N.E. must have been close to accurate. They were to see the Drakensberg and veer away from it, and such a route would be due north from Hole-in-the-Wall. A position further southwest on the coast is altogether more consistent with several aspects of their report, closer to their reading and fits the map better. One area of key interest is the uninhabited area encountered as they approached the Drakensberg and, veering east, found the Mzimkulu. The uninhabited area would seem to have been the "nomansland" of East Griqualand, which they crossed in 14 days. The richest and most fertile area would seem to have been east of the Mzimkulu. Using their information on direction and major rivers crossed, areas of concentrated settlement seem to have lain in the Tsolo and Mthatha districts, from the Tsitsa River across the Mthatha, but not to the Mbashe; an uninhabited area in the Mbashe Valley; and a more inhabited area, another cluster, westwards to the coast in the western Transkei, if not crossing the Kei itself.

The *São João Baptista* was wrecked further west than the others, in 1622. The landing spot seems to have been somewhere on the Ciskei coast and here yellow-skinned pastoralists were encountered. This corresponds to the Gonaqua distribution in traditions. After a difficult journey eastwards along the coast, the survivors came to Nguni coastal settlements, probably in the western Transkei.

The *Nossa Senhora de Belem* was shipwrecked in 1635, probably near the Qora Mouth, although Theal considered the wreck to have been north of the Mzimvubu.[67] The people of the *Sacramento* of 1645 seem to have landed in the Khoi area of the Ciskei and after a march east to have encountered Nguni.

The *Stavenisse* was assumed by Theal to have been wrecked on the southern Natal coast. Several survivors set off south and were collected at a point interpreted as close to the Buffalo River. The sequence of peoples met in travels from the wreck is given as Mbo, Sembo, Mpondomise, Mpondo, Thembu, Riligwa or Gryghas, Xhosa, with "Batua" beyond. The information from survivors staying with Xhosa suggests that they were west of the Kei.

Contact period – distribution of groups
In the maps at the end of this chapter I have attempted to collate the information given by the early travellers and the traditions on the positions of Cape Nguni groups until 1819. A fugitive group of Xhosa "living in friendship with the Hottentots" is placed west of the Fish in 1702 near the modern Somerset East, which some traditions suggest may have been Gqunukhwebe. Hubner's expedition of 1736 encountered Xhosa under Phalo and the party was killed in his land at a place which Beutler was told was west of the

Kei. At this time the Thembu were beyond the Xhosa, and beyond them "Nomotis" (Beutler). In 1738 a hunter was told that the Keiskamma was the western boundary of the Xhosa territory (Moodie 1835). Beutler in 1756 gave the Keiskamma as the border of the Gonaqua and the Xhosa, the Kei as the eastern boundary of the Xhosa. The Thembu beyond it were under "Tzeba", a name which does not fit any genealogy exactly, but could be Dabe (Ndabe) or Nadibi, of about the correct time. Mbo lay beyond them. The villages were distributed on the Qora and in the Ciskei the Gcaleka lived on the Kwenera, the Buffalo and other rivers.

The distribution at the period of frontier conflict is both better known and more fluid. In 1775 Xhosa villages, but not necessarily their total territory including hunting lands, lay between the Upper Fish and what was two days to the southeast. At the birth of Ngqika in 1775, there were said to be no Xhosa west of the Keiskamma. At this time, the Tsomo marked the boundary of the San and the Thembu, with the Mbo beyond the Thembu.[68] Meanwhile, the eastern boundary of the colony was fixed officially at Bruintjies Hoogte, near what is now Somerset East, in 1770, but was exceeded in 1772. It was extended in 1775 to the Fish in the north and Bushmans River in the south, but the Fish was crossed by colonists by 1777.[69] Xhosa traders visited Bruintjies Hoogte in 1776 to trade. The Xhosa Jeramba was west of the Fish in the same year, and Koba was also to the west in 1778.[70] In 1778 Van Plettenberg gained Xhosa agreement to the Fish as their western boundary and in 1779 Paterson found that he had to journey two days from the Fish mouth to visit Xhosa villages, although they were west of the Keiskamma. In that year fissive groups of the Xhosa cluster crossed west of the Bushmans River and there was conflict on the Upper Fish, marking the first frontier war.[71] In the succeeding years of tension some Xhosa groups were still to cross the Fish.[72] In 1797 there were deserted villages west of the Keiskamma and Ngqika said he had forbidden people to go into this area. Le Vaillant had noted similarly deserted homesteads in 1782.

The Fish remained the official western boundary of the Xhosa during most of the wars until 1819, with a temporary extension to the Kowie. In 1809 the northern border of the Rarabe Ngqika ran from the Amathole east along a tributary of the Kubusi, and along the Kubusi itself. The lower Kei marked the boundary between the Gcaleka and the Rarabe Xhosa. The Mbashe was the eastern Xhosa boundary.[73] The Ngqika huts at the time lay mainly in the Keiskamma basin, with some at the Kat; many other parts were uninhabited or hunting areas.

In 1790 the first Xhosa village Van Reenen encountered on his search for the survivors of the *Grosvenor* lay at the Kat River. There were San between the two Kei Rivers and Thembu at the Tsomo, said to be under "Joobie" as Paramount. Other members of related expeditions reported arriving in the area of "Joobie", the same chief, east of the Kei, and that none of his people were allowed to visit the Thembu. This suggests that this group was separated from the main cluster of Thembu and subject to the Gcaleka, whom Collins met controlling this area in 1809. Muller gives "Love" on the Mtakatyi River as principal over the Mabacqua. The same "Love", spelt Louve, was said by Van Reenen to be a chief under "Joobie", probably Jumba, brother of Ngubencuka over a fissive group. The country from here to the Mthatha by the travellers' northern route had been despoiled by Rarabe, who died about three years before Van Reenen's visit. Many local inhabitants had been reduced to a hunter-gatherer existence inland or on the coast. Villages were encountered of the Mbo (Hambonas), described as yellowish people with longish hair. They may have been one of the clans (Lungu or Tshomane) with origins in inter-marriage between shipwrecked sailors and Nguni.[74] The chief was called "Gamboose", interpreted by Kirby as probably the Gambushe of the Bomvana lineage, but conceivably the Mgabisi of the Mpondomise lineage. This chief's great place was found on the Mgazi, and the "bastaards" described were on the Mgazana.

Survivors of the wreck of the *Grosvenor* similarly reported

▲ 6. San fishing (Matatiele district)

▼ 7. Interaction: cattle (with modern imitations) (Engcobo district)

PLATE 5

▲ 8. *Interaction: horses (Matatiele district)*

▼ 9. *Interaction: European ox-wagon with team and driver (Tsolo district)*

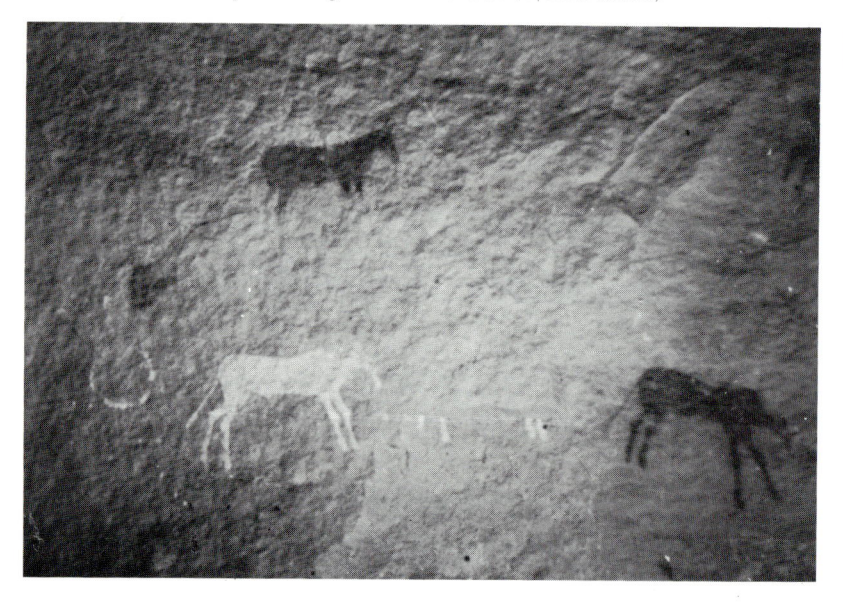

PLATE 6

meeting a succession of groups along the coast, separated by uninhabited areas: "Abonyai" or "Abonzai" east of the Mzimvubu, Mbo, Thembu, Xhosa and "Hottentots". The apparently deserted areas were probably the hunting territories discussed below. From the account of one survivor, Hubberley, there were huts to the east of the wreck, a village on the Mzimvubu and many between there and the Mgazi. There were no villages west of the Mgazi, but towards the Mthatha some deserted huts were noted and a shellfish collector's hut on the coast. Deserted huts were seen east of the Mbashe, but there was little occupation until west of the Qora, then more concentrated on the Kobonqaba and Kei. There was another area with no coastal villages, although scattered individuals were seen in the Ciskei. A final concentration was seen in the suurveld.[75] This accords well with the better-known reports of survivors from the wreck of the *Grosvenor*. The survivors' report presented by Chiron put the Thembu close to the Mzimvubu, but allowed no room for the Mbo, who are reported by others. In another document travellers took five to six days to pass through the land of the Mbo.[76]

The maps on pp. 73–8, based on this documentary material and on oral data, indicate the acceleration of overall settlement change in the period of frontier contact and conflict.

Settlement patterns and change
The written sources on early history, though not the traditions, contain much information which can be used to reconstruct settlement patterns at the level of villages and hut clusters or on a wider scale.[77] My concern here is to advance a settlement model which fits the available information on the pre-1820 period, and to see what changes took place over time. Techniques of locational analysis and the concepts of developing ecological geography which have been expansively adopted in archaeology need to be applied more vigorously to historical contexts of this type. I am concerned here not only with the physically visible aspects of settlement, villages, fields, water resources, but also with the important intangibles of territory, exploitation

The settlement pattern of early Cape Nguni
(a) the village

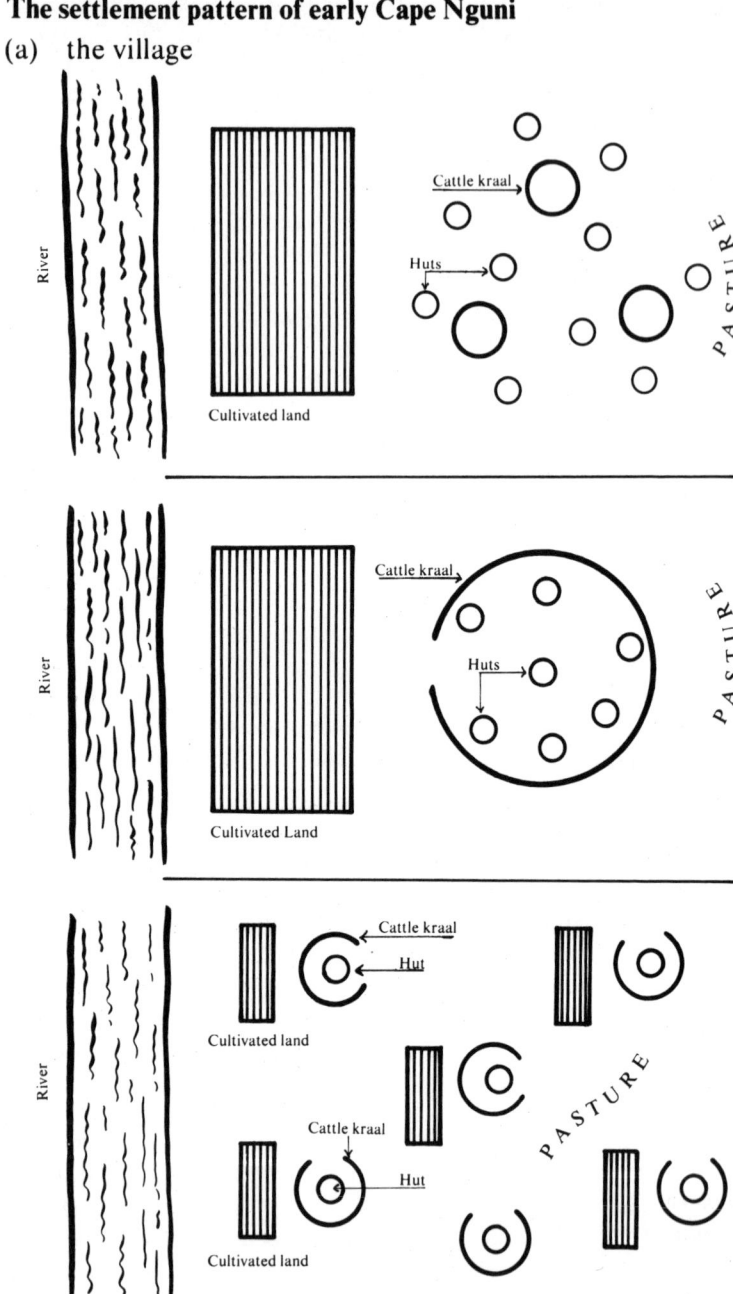

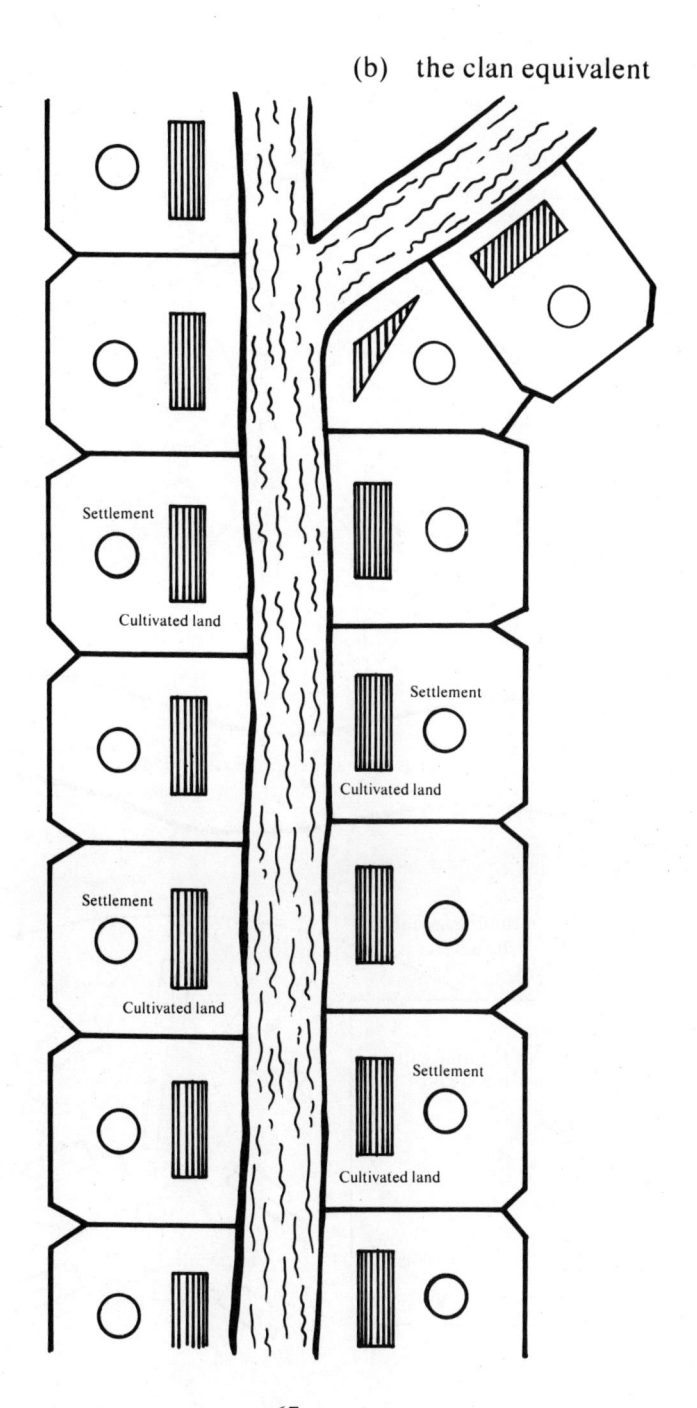

(b) the clan equivalent

(c) the tribal cluster

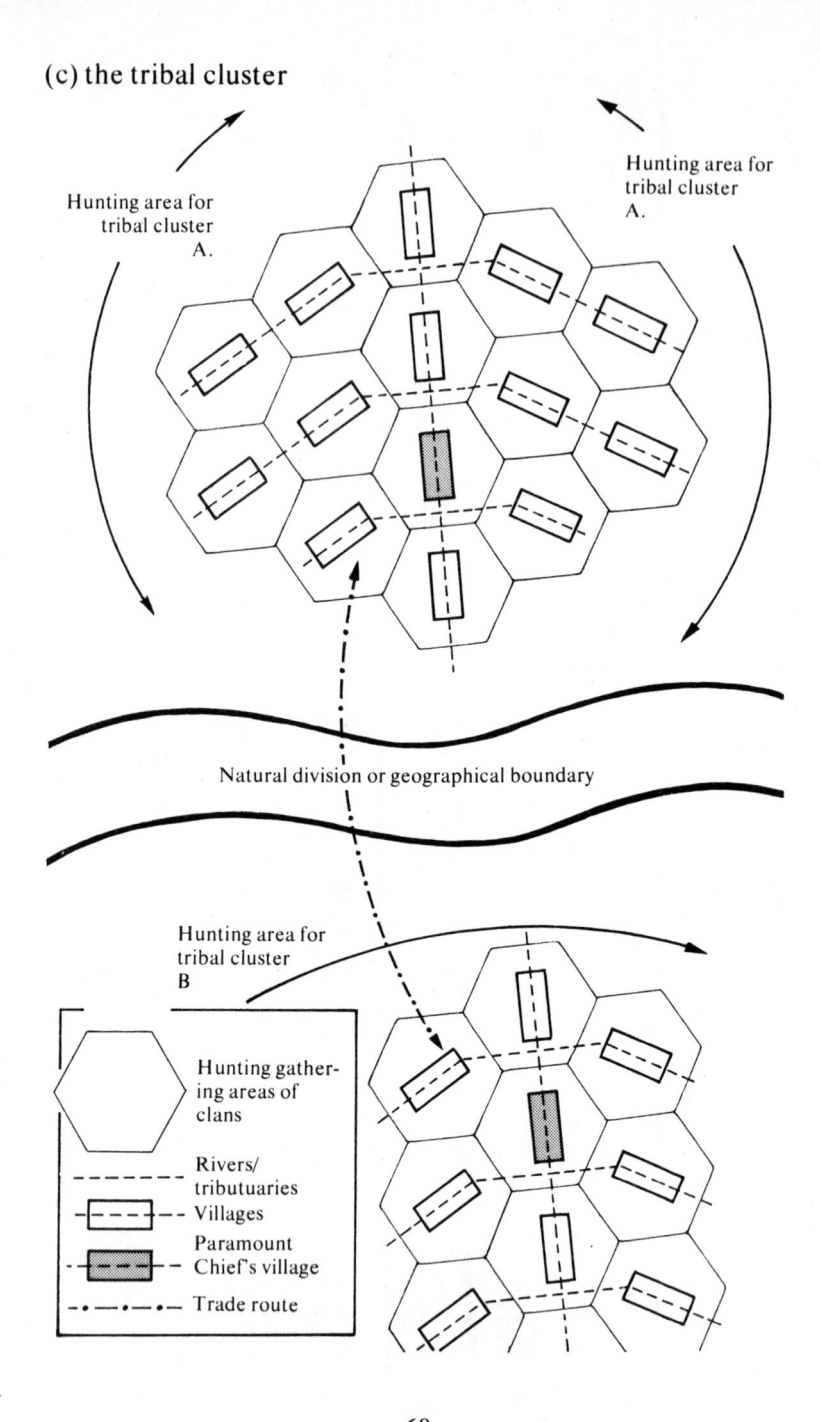

Hunting area for tribal cluster A.

Hunting area for tribal cluster A.

Natural division or geographical boundary

Hunting area for tribal cluster B

⬡	Hunting gathering areas of clans
– – – –	Rivers/tributuaries
▭	Villages
▬	Paramount Chief's village
–·–·–·	Trade route

68

zones, and the social and physical determinants of site location.

The model which I suggest best fits the available data is summarized in the figures on pp. 66–8 as a generalized type; such situations are not claimed to represent actual examples. The model envisages villages, with huts and animal kraals, cultivated land, pasture, water and an area for hunting and gathering. There is territorial distribution of such villages into units of political and environmental solidarity, equivalent for the most part to chiefdoms or clans of recent times. These share a territory for hunting and gathering. A larger tribal cluster of political and territorial unity may be constructed, separated from others by a large area used for hunting expeditions, which authors may describe as "deserted areas".

The 16th and 17th century tribal clusters were clearly so separated, yet individuals were found in the areas between these concentrations. Such areas were, I suggest, hunting and gathering territories of the cluster, areas across which trading routes ran and areas which could contain remnant San. Such areas between tribal clusters remained into the conflict period.

Distances between tribal cluster core areas vary in the records from 14 days and 12 days downwards.[78] The coastal distances were also within this range, but movement between clusters along the coast would seem difficult and unusual. Distances between the core areas of villages and pasture of the "clan equivalent chiefdoms" also vary widely. A regular pattern of fission as groups became too large for the hunting-gathering and pasture territory would be predictable; consequently the number of villages in a clan region and the distance between clan core areas would vary considerably. 16th and 17th century travellers could travel a day's walk between villages; they were, of course, travelling east to west and tending to cut across river valleys rather than up them, hence moving more between hypothetical clan core areas than along them.

The number of villages in a clan cluster seems to have varied with the fissive process. 16th and 17th century travellers speak of plains dotted with villages, a three-league stretch with many kraals, of villages a quarter to half a mile apart in one area[79] or four to five hours apart; of two or three together, or of an isolated situation. Van der Kemp states that villages were about five miles apart and Le Vaillant gives one league square as the territory of one village.

Paths or recognised routes seem to have existed between tribal cluster core areas and between villages and clan core areas. In the *Grosvenor* sources they are spoken of as "well-trod".

Most frequently, hunting and trading expeditions accounted for the main mobility. In 1752 Beutler mentions seasonal movement for pasture in the Ciskei, while the survivors of the *Santo Alberto* observed that the inhabitants seldom went away from the village, except when they pulled it down when a resident died in it. By the conflict period, it is noted, the Xhosa could resettle easily, but would not do so willingly.[80] By this time there was more pressure to leave areas from war. Even from the pre-contact period, though, deserted huts were noted near the coast. Regular seasonal abandonment of huts in movement from one ecozone to another seems unlikely. More probable was the seasonal sending of some animals with herd boys to better pasture. As a chief, Ngqika had a grazing village ten to twelve miles away from his great place.[81] Regular observations of significant travel is common only in the conflict period in the Ciskei and seems a feature of the interaction of paramounts and fissive clans, of colony and Xhosa and Khoi. Thus an image of the Nguni as nomadic is incorrect, except for the movement of a village upon the death of an owner in his homestead.

The design of villages from descriptions shows a range of Nguni settlement corresponding to family needs, population size and economic micro-strategy (see figures pp. 66–68). Village location through all periods seems to have been of the same general pattern, related to rivers and streams, but not upon them. Van der Kemp says huts lay three to four hundred yards away from a river and all authorities agree that settlement was preferred on the slopes above streams. A chief's village could often be central to a clan cluster, although one source observes that it was on top of a range. Coastal settlement, too, seems regular, with fish and shellfish collected by coastal people but despised by others. Village size seems remarkably stable throughout the period under discussion. All huts were of the poles and reed type in the period before 1820, of floor diameter described as 10–12 feet, 14 feet, 18–25 feet and 9 feet.[82] Villages in the pre-contact period are said to have contained 15 huts, 20 huts, 6 huts in a late example, 12–15 huts in the conflict period, 12 in a chief's village, and so on. In 1779 one village contained 50 huts and 300 people altogether.[83]

Population distribution is also difficult. In the pre-contact period a group of 60 with a chief was noted, another group of more than 70 in a 15 hut village, also 100 armed warriors, perhaps the clan equivalent. A trading party of 100 men was met near the Fish. For the conflict period, Van der Kemp estimates 40 males in each village. Lichtenstein puts 40–50 families in one place, clearly an increase. The 300 men exercising with assegais seen by the *Grosvenor* survivors were perhaps the full young male strength of a clan equivalent.

The impression given of the Transkei in the 15th and 16th centuries is not of an area under-exploited, but of a region well utilised by tribal clusters, each with a territory for the important hunting and gathering activities. If these areas were not so exploited, they would certainly still have been used by San, who are not indicated at this period. The inland and coastal regions were used by similar people, with strandloping as a regular aspect of their activities.

Stability was such that fission or movement from population growth or political conflict could be accommodated. Interaction with Khoi (Gonaqua) seems to have been similarly stable in territory and trade, although Gonaqua retreat is attested in the final period.

In the late 18th and early 19th century, in the final contact and conflict period, pressure from the west on the tribal clusters restricted their hunting and gathering areas and hence the area for potential fissive groups, each of which needed its own territory, not just hut space. The frustrations of potential fission led to expansion within existing territory, less buffer room and more conflict, in itself increasing the potential for fission which could no longer be accommodated[84] and contributing to the overall change in Cape Nguni society.

I have argued that events in the period from about 1820 to about 1830 were sufficiently disruptive of traditional society to require us clearly to separate our study of the pre-1820 period from that of the later, better documented period. I suggest that those who use traditions relating to the earlier period should place more emphasis on those collected in the 19th century rather than on Soga and other recent authors.

By employing different disciplines, useful information on settlement areas and settlement patterns can emerge. This information casts doubt on certain popular assumptions, such as a recent arrival in the Transkei of Cape Nguni; an origin in the upper Mzimvubu; abstention from coastal exploitation; and a pattern of mobility or semi-nomadism. Cape Nguni seem to have operated in a stable settlement pattern until increasing disruption occurred in the 18th century.

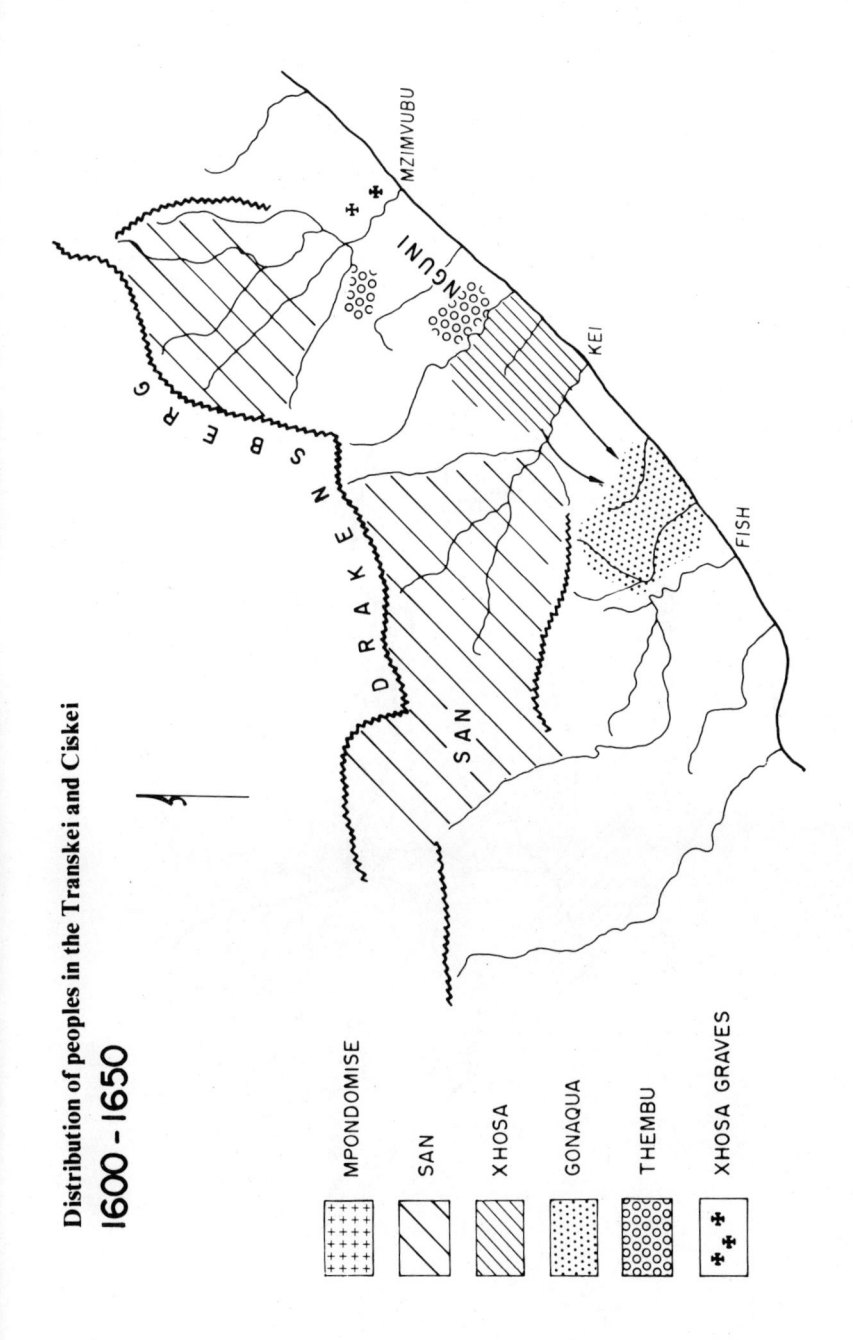

Distribution of peoples in the Transkei and Ciskei
1600 - 1650

1650 - 1700

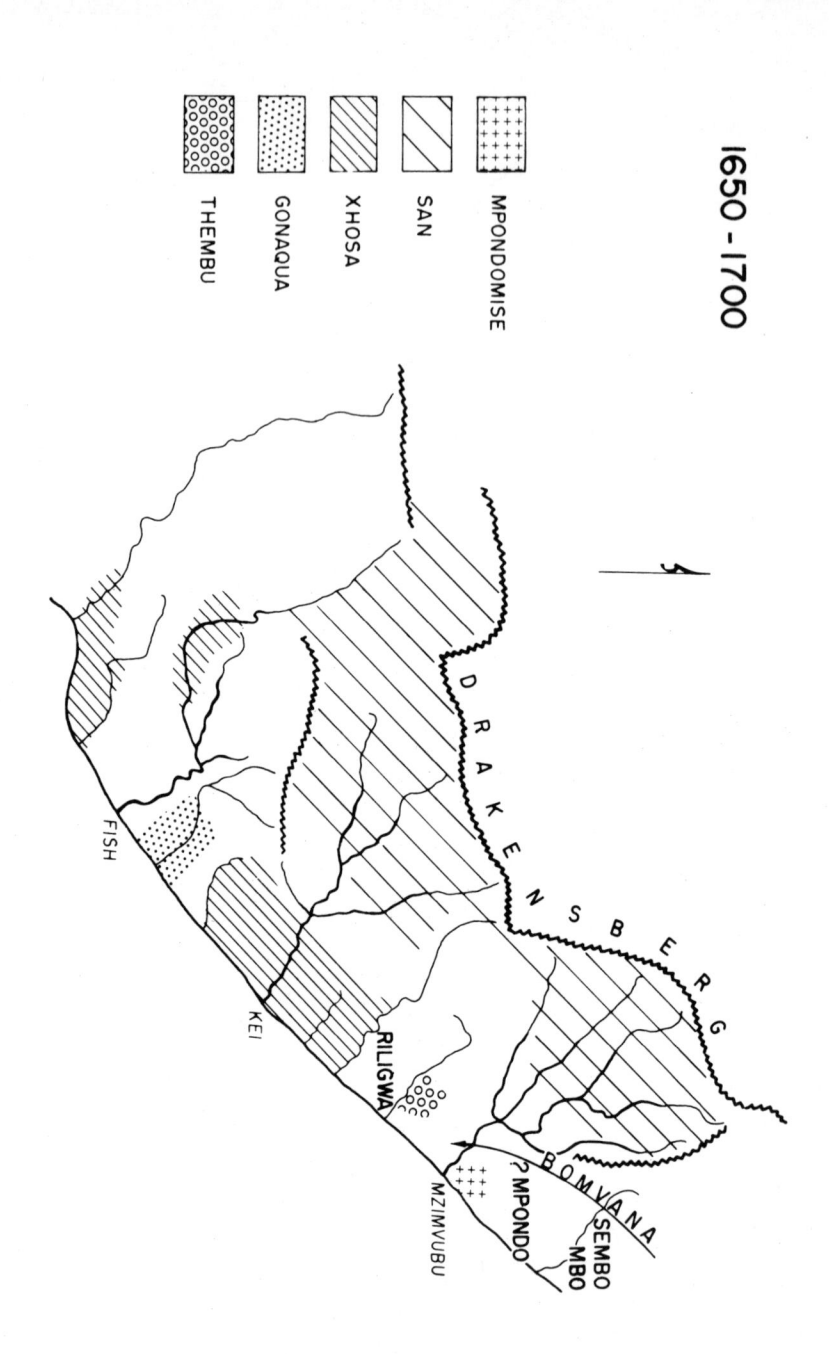

Legend:
- THEMBU
- GONAQUA
- XHOSA
- SAN
- MPONDOMISE

FISH
KEI
RILIGWA
MZIMVUBU
?MPONDO
BOMVANA
SEMBO
MBO
DRAKENSBERG

1700-1750

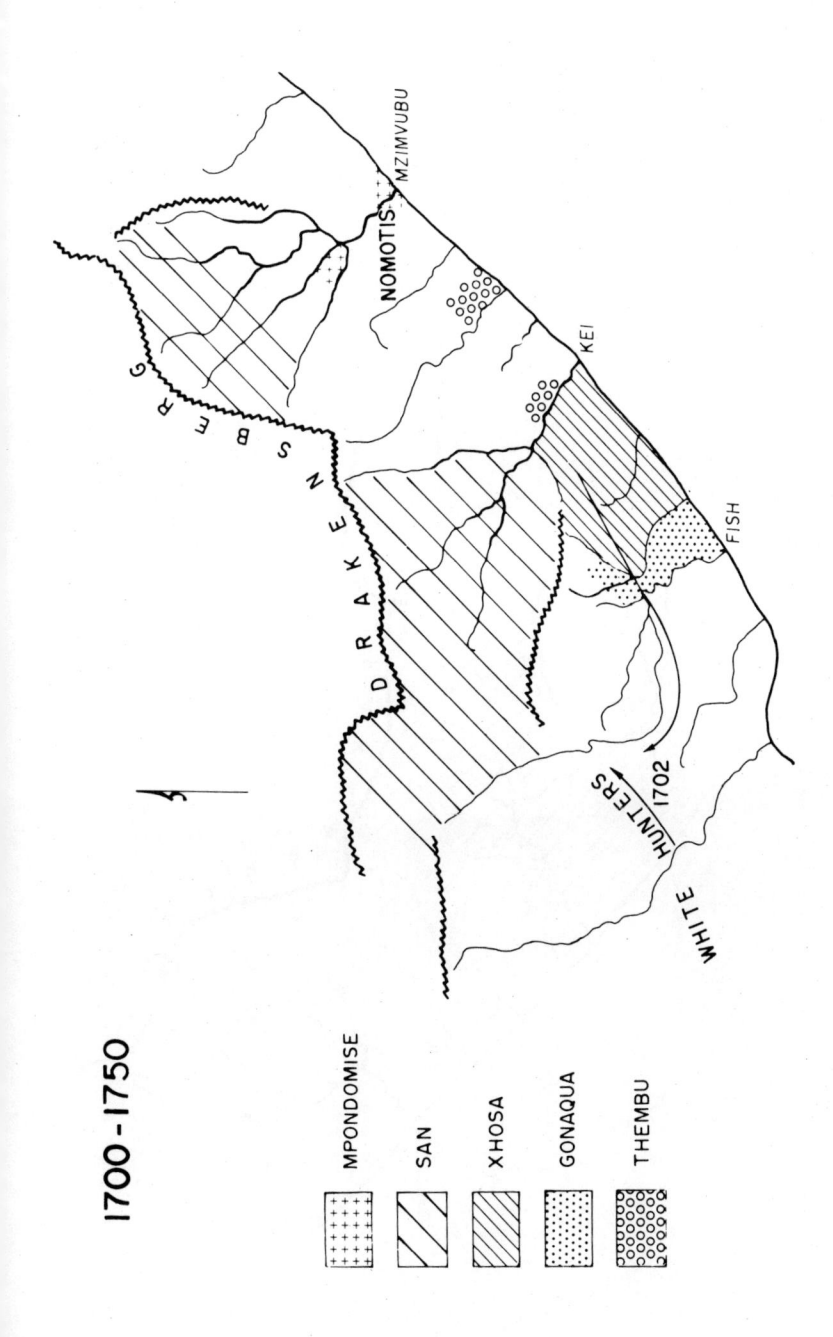

1750-1770

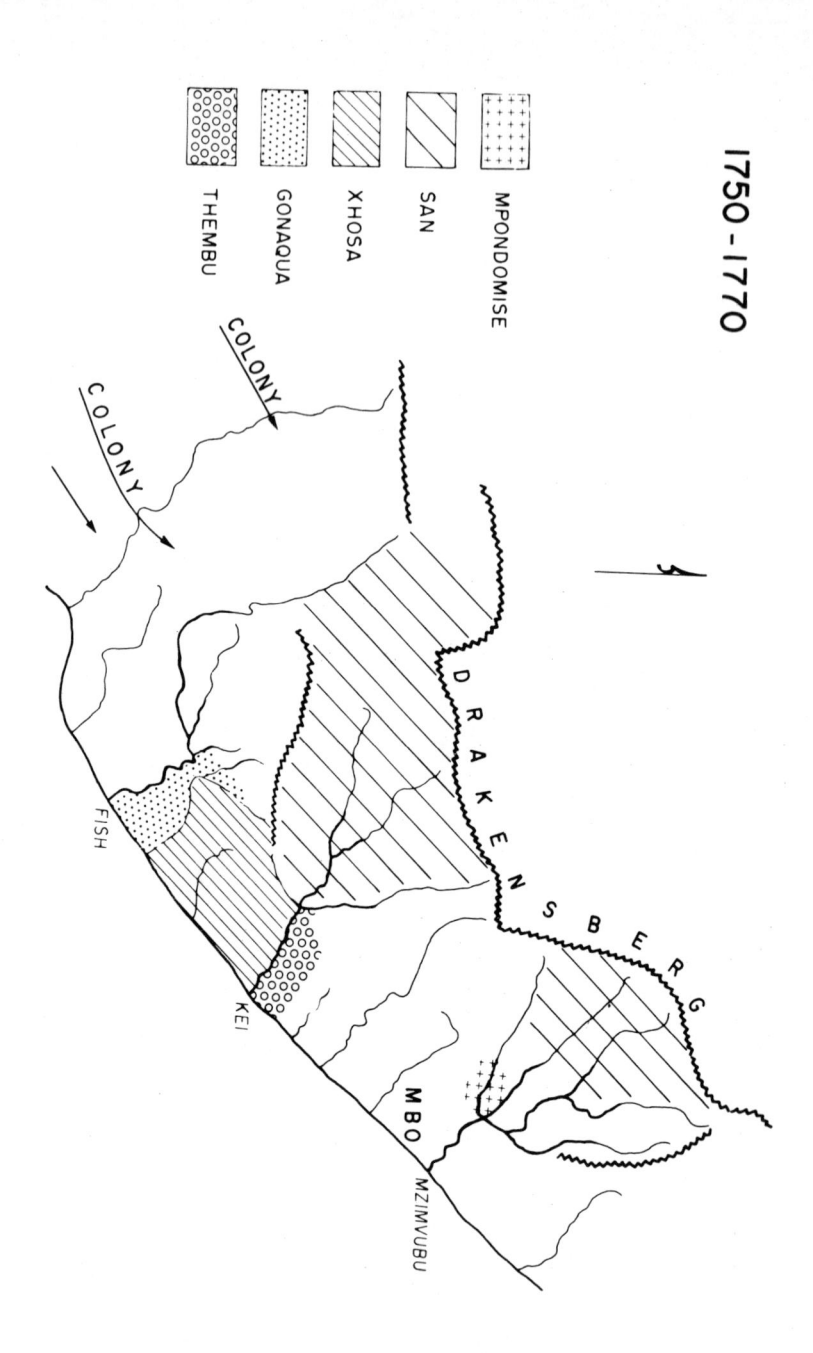

THEMBU
GONAQUA
XHOSA
SAN
MPONDOMISE

1770 - 1779

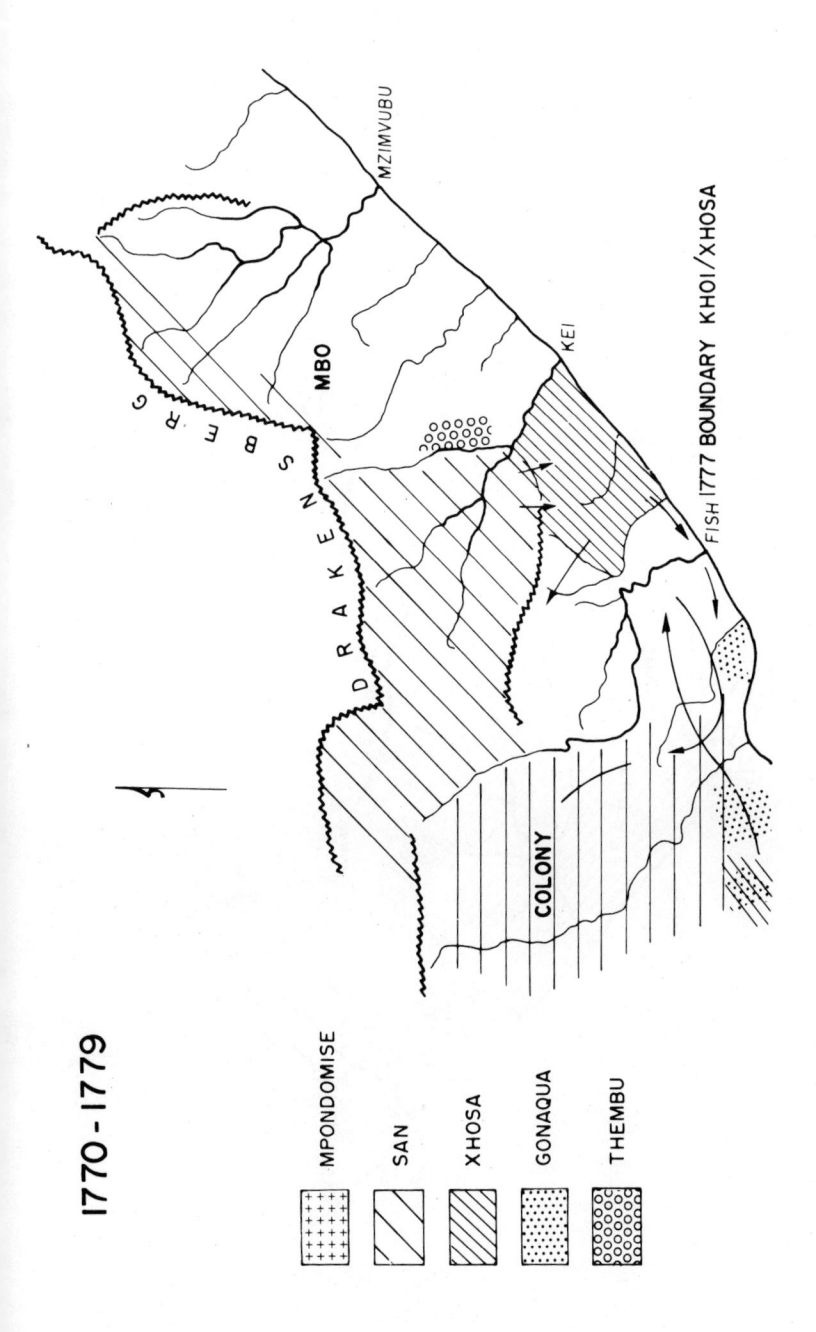

MPONDOMISE
SAN
XHOSA
GONAQUA
THEMBU

MZIMVUBU
MBO
DRAKENSBERG
KEI
FISH 1777 BOUNDARY KHOI/XHOSA
COLONY

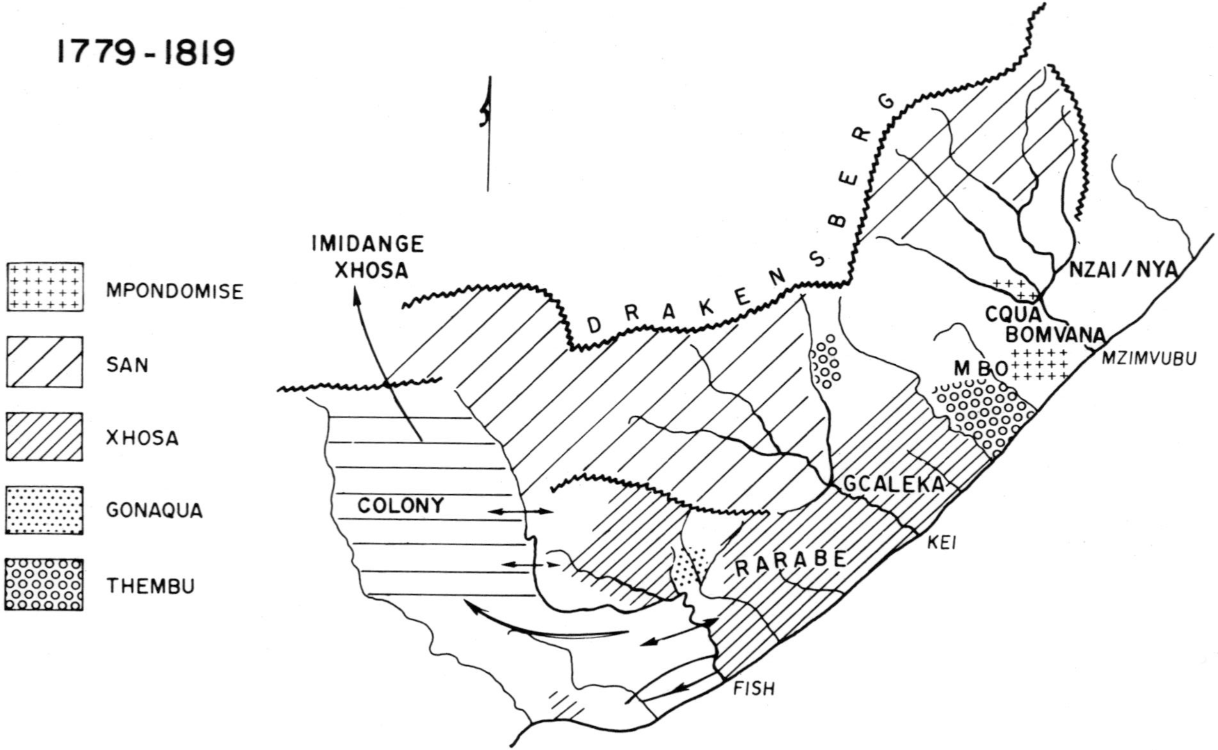
1779-1819
MPONDOMISE
SAN
XHOSA
GONAQUA
THEMBU
IMIDANGE
XHOSA
COLONY
DRAKENSBERG
NZAI / NYA
CQUA
BOMVANA
MZIMVUBU
M BO
GCALEKA
KEI
RARABE
FISH

FOOTNOTES

1. N. J. Van Warmelo, *A Preliminary Survey of the Bantu Tribes of South Africa* (Pretoria 1935); W. D. Hammond-Tooke, Segmentation and Fission in Cape Nguni Political Units, *Africa* 35 (2) 1965, 143–67.
2. Hammond-Tooke, Segmentation; Cape of Good Hope, *Report and Proceedings . . . of the Government Commission on Native Laws and Customs* (Cape Town 1883) pp. 403–9.
3. G. Thompson, *Travels and Adventures in South Africa*, I (Cape Town 1967) 196; M. Wilson and L. Thompson, eds., *Oxford History of South Africa*, I (Oxford 1969) 255.
4. R. C. Germond, *Chronicles of Basutoland* (Morija 1967) pp. 125–9; D. Moodie, *The Record* (Cape Town and Amsterdam 1960) II, 236.
5. M. Wilson, Co-operation and Conflict: The Eastern Cape Frontier, in Wilson and Thompson, *Oxford History*, I.
6. The best bibliography of sources is provided in E. M. Shaw and N. J. Van Warmelo, The Material Culture of the Cape Nguni, part I, Settlement, *Annals of the South African Museum* 58 (1) 1972, 3–14.
7. G. M. Theal, *Records of South-Eastern Africa*, I, II, VIII (London 1898–1902); C. Boxer, *The Tragic History of the Sea* (London 1959); Moodie, *Record* I, 415ff.
8. G. M. Theal, *History of South Africa*, II (London 1888) 64–5, 97, 102–5; Cape Archives C354, p. 313; Moodie, *Record* V, 9ff.; G. Harinck, Interaction between Xhosa and Khoi, in L. Thompson, ed., *African Societies in Southern Africa* (London 1969) p. 165.
9. *Précis of the Archives of the Cape of Good Hope: the Defence of Willem Adriaan Van der Stel* (Cape Town 1897) pp. 133–49.
10. Moodie, *Record* III, 1; V, 22–3, 73–4, 90–9; Wilson and Thompson, *Oxford History* I, 234–5.
11. Beutler in Godée-Molsbergen *Reizen in Zuid-Afrika in de Hollandse tijd* III ('s Gravenhage 1922) 265–336; cf. V. Forbes, Beutler's expedition into the eastern Cape 1752, *AYB* 1953; C. R. Thunberg, *Travels in Europe, Africa and Asia* I (London 1793); A. Sparrman, *A Voyage to the Cape of Good Hope* (Dublin 1785); W. Paterson, *A Narrative of the Hottentots and Caffraria* (London 1789); official sources in Moodie, *Record*.
12. F. le Vaillant, *Travels into the Interior Parts of Africa* (London 1796); H. Lichtenstein, *Travels in Southern Africa* I-II (Cape Town 1928–30); J. Barrow, *Travels into the Interior of Southern Africa* (London 1806); L. Alberti, *Alberti's Account of the Tribal Life and Customs of the Xhosa in 1807* (Cape Town 1968); Janssens in Godée-Molsbergen, *Reizen* IV, 100–209; W. B. E. Paravicini di Capelli, *Reize in de Binnenlanden van Zuid-Afrika* (Cape Town 1965); D. G. van Reenen, *Die Joernaal van Dirk Gysbert van Reenen* (Cape Town 1937); Collins in Moodie, *Record* V, 38–55.

13 J. T. van der Kemp, An Account of . . . Kaffraria, *Trans. London Missionary Society* I (1804) 432–468; *Cape Quarterly Review* I (1882) 331–342.
14 W. Stout, *Interesting particulars of the loss of the American ship Hercules* . . . (London 1810); Theal, *History* III (1891).
15 G. Carter, *The Wreck of the Grosvenor* (Cape Town 1927); P. R. Kirby, *A Source Book on the Wreck of the Grosvenor East Indiaman* (Cape Town 1953); P. R. Kirby, *Jacob van Reenen and the Grosvenor expedition of 1790–1791* (Johannesburg 1958).
16 In G. Thompson, *Travel and Adventures* I, 191–219.
17 R. Godlonton, *Introductory Remarks to a Narrative of the Irruption of the Kafir Hordes* (Grahamstown 1836) p. 209.
18 J. Maclean, *Compendium of Kaffir Laws and Customs* (Mount Cole 1858). This also contains a Xhosa genealogy collected by Dugmore in 1846 which is in general agreement.
19 "Justus", *The Wrongs of the Caffre Nation* (London 1837).
20 A. Kropf, *Das Volk der Xosa-Kaffern* (Berlin 1889); cf. Harinck, Interaction.
21 Cape of Good Hope, *Report and Proceedings with Appendices of the Government Commission on Native Laws and Customs* (Cape Town 1883) pp. 403–9.
22 W. D. Cingo, *Ibali lama Mpondo* (Palmerton 1925); W. D. Cingo, *IBali laba Tembu* (Palmerton 1927); T. B. Soga, *InTlalo ka Xosa* (Lovedale 1937); W. B. Rubusana, *Zemk' inkomo Magwalandini* (London 1906); W. Gqoka, *Isigidimi sama-Xosa;* V. Poto Ndamase, *Ama-Mpondo: Ibali ne-Ntlalo* (Lovedale 1927); A. Z. Ngani, *Ibali lama Gqunukwebe* (Lovedale n.d.).
23 F. Brownlee, *The Transkeian Native Territories: Historical Records* (Lovedale 1923).
24 S. Marks, The Traditions of the Natal "Nguni", in Thompson, *African Societies.*
25 P. A. W. Cook, *Social Organisation and Ceremonial Institutions of the Bomvana* (Cape Town 1931); W. D. Hammond-Tooke, *The Tribes of the Umtata District* (Pretoria 1957); *The Tribes of the Willowvale District* (Pretoria 1957); *The Tribes of the King William's Town District* (Pretoria 1958); P. R. Kirby, Gcuma, Mdepa and the Amatshomane clan, *African Studies* 13 (1954), pp. 1–24.
26 R. M. Derricourt, Archaeological Survey of the Transkei and Ciskei, *Fort Hare Papers* 5 (1972) 213–222; 5 (1973) 449–455.
27 Moodie, *Record* I, 426–7.
28 Moodie, *Record* V, 9f; Le Vaillant, *Travels* II, 273.
29 Lichtenstein, *Travels* I, 338.
30 *Dirk Gysbert van Reenen,* p. 167.
31 J. Campbell, *Travels in South Africa* (London 1815) p. 122.
32 G. Stow, *The Native Races of South Africa* (London 1905) pp. 88, 199–201.
33 B. Holt, *Place-names in the Transkeian Territories* (Johannesburg 1959).

▲ *Khoi soldier in the Cape Corps.* (Cape Archives E 2986)

PLATE 7

▶ *Kat River Coloureds*

Kat River Bastard & his afterrider.
H.B. 1838.

(Cape Archives E 3212, from H. Butler, South African Sketches (London 1841) plate 1 no 3)

PLATE 8

34 E.g. Sparrman, *Voyage*, p. 107.
35 W. Stanford, *The Reminiscences of Sir Walter Stanford* II (Cape Town 1962); W. Stanford, Statement of Silayi, *Trans. Royal Soc. S. Africa* I (1910).
36 Brownlee, *Transkeian Native Territories*, p. 123; Stanford, *Reminiscences;* J. R. L. Kingon, The Place Names of Tsolo, *Report South Afr. Assoc. Advancement of Science* 14 (1916), 603.
37 J. Wright, *Bushman Raiders of the Drakensberg 1840–1870* (Pietermaritzburg 1971) pp. 119, 128–131.
38 Cf. Harinck, Interaction.
39 Collins in Moodie, *Record*, V, 12.
40 J. H. Soga, *The South-Eastern Bantu* (Johannesburg 1930) pp. 116f.
41 Godlonton, *Introductory Remarks*, p. 206.
42 Harinck, Interaction, pp. 151–3.
43 Maclean, *Compendium*.
44 Theal, *History* II, 102.
45 Thunberg, *Travels;* Paterson, *Narrative*.
46 Godlonton, *Introductory Remarks*, p. 206.
47 Van Warmelo, *Preliminary Survey;* cf. also Hammond-Tooke, Segmentation.
48 Wilson & Thompson, *Oxford History* I, 87.
49 Soga, *South-Eastern Bantu*, pp. 92–3.
50 Alberti, *Account of the Tribal Life*, p. 13; J. Ayliff, *A Vocabulary of the Kaffir Language* (1863), introduction.
51 A. Kropf, *Kafir-English dictionary* (1915).
52 I am grateful to Prof. H. W. Pahl and the staff of the Xhosa Dictionary Committee for discussion on these points.
53 C. M. Doke & B. Vilakazi, *Zulu Dictionary* (Johannesburg 1948).
54 A. Steedman, *Wanderings and Adventures in the Interior of Southern Africa* (London 1835), pp. 247–8.
55 Harinck, Interaction, p. 154 note 30.
56 Beutler, in Godée-Molsbergen, *Reizen* III.
57 Brownlee in Thompson, *Travels* I.
58 Beutler in Godée-Molsbergen, *Reizen* III.
59 Soga, *South-Eastern Bantu*, pp. 113, 122.
60 *Ibid.;* F. Brownlee, Burial places of chiefs, *African Affairs* 43 (1944), 23–4.
61 Moodie, *Record* V, 9.
62 Wilson & Thompson, *Oxford History* I, 92.
63 C. Brownlee, *Reminiscences of Kaffir Life and History* (Lovedale 1896) p. 105.
64 Boxer, *Tragic History*.
65 Wilson & Thompson, *Oxford History* I, 79.
66 Boxer, *Tragic History*.
67 Wilson & Thompson, *Oxford History* I, 82.
68 E. Napier, *Excursions in Southern Africa* (London 1850), I, 194; Sparrman, *Voyage*.
69 Moodie, *Record* V, 1, 14, 49, 66–7.

70 Sparrman, *Voyage;* Swellengrebel, Plettenberg and Gordon (illustration) in Godée-Molsbergen, *Reizen* IV.
71 Moodie, *Record* V, 82, 92.
72 Barrow, *Travels;* R. Renshaw, *Voyage to the Cape of Good Hope and up the Red Sea* (Manchester 1804).
73 Collins in Moodie, *Record* V; Lichtenstein, *Travels* I, 348.
74 Cf. Kirby, Gquma.
75 Kirby, *Source book.*
76 Carter, *Wreck of the Grosvenor.*
77 Much of the direct descriptive material is collected in Shaw and van Warmelo, Material culture I.
78 Survivors of the *Santa Alberto* and the *Grosvenor.*
79 Survivors of the *Grosvenor.*
80 Lichtenstein, *Travels.*
81 Barrow, *Travels.*
82 Beutler in Godée-Molsbergen, *Reizen* IV; Collins in Moodie, *Record* V; Van der Kemp, Account; Alberti, *Account.*
83 By Le Vaillant, Barrow, Paterson and the survivors of the *Grosvenor.*
84 Hammond-Tooke, Segmentation.

3

THOUGHTS ON THE STUDY OF THE CAPE EASTERN FRONTIER ZONE

William M. Freund

THE convening of a conference on the history of the Transkei and Ciskei underlines the continued significance for South African historians of the concept of frontier. Despite increasing uncertainty about what defines frontier dynamics and where the ultimate impact of frontier society on modern South Africa lies, the idea of frontier remains as a fundamental category in the study of the South African past. My own research on Cape society in the Batavian period (1803–6) has consisted in part of an investigation into frontier conditions in that era.[1] The results, necessarily posed within the framework of an analysis of colonial policy, appear in a recent article.[2] In this paper I would like to suggest some of the problems both of definition and of social process which emerged in the course of my research, in the hope that this may serve to clarify certain issues for ongoing and future research.

Let us begin by re-examining the use of the term "frontier" in southern African conditions. While we do well to examine the frontier in a comparative context, some foreign frontier models prove problematic for South African historians. The frontier of ancient empires, a concept which continues to haunt our historical imaginations, is handily symbolized by the wall separating "civilization" and "barbarism", whether Hadrian's or the Great Wall of China. Whatever validity this idea holds in Roman or Chinese history, it fails to serve southern African conditions. On the old eastern frontier of the Cape, boundaries (despite the proclamations of Cape Town authorities) were fluid and notoriously unsuccessful at posing barriers to population movement. People of different cultures with formal political loyalties to different (and sometimes distant) centres lived cheek by jowl with one another.

The historiography of the North American frontier, on the other hand, is heavily weighted towards the concept of a "moving frontier", a mounting westward-moving wave of men and women, taking place, given the vastness of the continent, with great speed. Such a frontier only existed in certain times and places in South Africa, notably in the northern and central Cape in the first half of the eighteenth century. On the whole, colonial or settler expansion in South Africa was characterized by great forward leaps (the Great Trek), flanking movements (Natal) and periods of lengthy stalemate and even withdrawal (the eastern Cape, particularly before 1811). It can be argued that only in the 1870s, as one approaches the heyday of British imperialism and following the first great mineral discoveries, a long century after the first colonial settlers reached the far side of the Karroo, did the scale tip on the side of the Europeans in what is today South Africa. The theme of white, or, better, colonial-imperial expansion, is a major one in nineteenth century history but it is only part of the history of the frontier.

Particularly in the eastern Cape, we are concerned with a territory where none of the contesting forces could claim decisive victory for a long period of time. As P. J. van der Merwe has written:

> The conflict with the Bantu on the eastern frontier, the barrenness and [agricultural] precariousness of the northwest and the effective pressure

that the Bushmen exerted after 1770 on the northeastern frontier, obstructed the restless expansion into the interior which had flowed forward rapidly and undisturbed for generations, during the last three decades of the eighteenth century.[3]

This suggests the usefulness of the focus proposed by Dr Martin Legassick for pre-Trek Transorangia upon the frontier zone, rather than the frontier, as the meaningful analytical category in the east as well.[4] What we need to investigate, then, are the social forms that evolved in the era between the initial impact of the colonial Cape in the east (the emergence of new trade patterns with Khoi as effective commercial transmitters between Cape Town and the Xhosa polities) and the final "closing of the frontier" characterized by colonial rule everywhere and the takeover of the economy by white farmers, merchants and industrialists.

Conflict and co-operation

Two themes have dominated the study of this era: those of conflict and co-operation. The South African frontier has for a long time been linked, indeed often in almost mythical form, with clashing of cultures and a hardening of relationships between different ethnic groups into bitter, total opposition. A republican historiography elevated the Great Trek into a Biblical parable whereby white Christian man survived the perils of a harsh environment and heathen savages to mould his own God-given social order. Clearly, some trekkers did see things this way themselves, but, operating from hindsight, we surely need not accept this ideological articulation as social fact. In the eastern Cape, the early Afrikaners lived in a multi-racial society where peace and war, long indecisive, alternated. They formed only one class within a socio-economic unit including slaves, servants and other non-whites, who, taken as a whole, outnumbered the white frontiersmen. The Moses in the wilderness analogy fits particularly badly and must be rejected as a model.

For the same reason, we must seriously question the hostile

but complementary point of view put forward by liberal historians, most notably C. W. de Kiewiet.[5] They too have stressed the overriding importance of conflict, while deploring it and ultimately placing the blame for the contemporary racial situation in the Republic on the "laager mentality". Sheila Patterson's book, *The Last Trek,* yields a good instance:
> If the mentality portrayed in the following song sung at the 1938 centenary persists, it can prove to be the swansong of Nationalist Afrikanerdom: "We look into the future, our symbols stand we by; We shall continue our onward trek, no struggle will we shun; We think of blood-steeped rivers, we see the enemies' stand. O God, knit up our strength, with valour fill our hearts, That we yet may for true freedom offer up our hearts".[6]

There is a contrast, presented implicitly or explicitly, with the "civilizing" influence of British imperialism and its concomitants, industrialism, urbanism and capitalism.

For a different viewpoint, that stressing the theme of frontier co-operation, one turns readily to the contribution of Monica Wilson in the *Oxford History of South Africa.*[7] Professor Wilson develops a strong, convincing case that the frontier situation induced co-operation in various forms between white, Xhosa and Khoi. Indeed, if there is a fundamental assumption to be made about the eastern frontier zone, it is that such a zone was predicated on a power vacuum. It was a disputed area precisely because no one government could enforce its authority over it and in the course of the years co-operative patterns among the resident population were bound to develop.

One might reasonably make a comparison here with the historiography of the American frontier. There are some strong parallels with South Africa. Popular tradition, powerfully re-enforced by the Turner thesis, has idealized the frontier along lines not dissimilar to the Voortrekker legend. The frontier has been seen as a zone of freedom, a liberating experience from the more stratified, tamed societies of the eastern seaboard. The emphasis would be here on social and economic opportunity and on toleration of individual eccentricity and deviance ("rugged individualism").

However, historians such as Roy Harvey Pearce and Arthur K. Moore have denounced in the name of the Enlightenment and industrialism the inadequacies and hypocrisies of the "garden myth" that they believe succoured the frontiersmen.[8] Their critique, although placed along the lines of intellectual rather than political history, has strong affinities to that of South African liberals and, in regard to the American Indians, they also stress the frontier as a source of hardened racial attitudes. It is perhaps a more balanced critique though; they would not claim that Indian wars were more decisive than the introduction of slavery in the development of American racism. Moore faulted the white frontiersmen for their crudeness, lack of cultivation and "distortion of vision", but even he admitted that, so long as the frontier itself prevailed, "considered as a stronghold of democracy and rugged individualism and accordingly a principal formative influence on American society, the West appears in a favourable light." His bias is, moreover, rather anti-egalitarian.

In analysing the social characteristics of the American frontier, historians have also recognized the need to differentiate between times and places in measuring the significance of economic opportunity and the character and extent of interaction between settlers (not always white) and indigenes. Their work overall is highly suggestive for the historian of South Africa suspicious both of the idealized and stigmatized frontier traditions. Certain American frontier situations, where the staying power of the Indians was strong and the norms of American society were only imposed slowly (perhaps the far Southwest in the nineteenth century) might point to sharp and particular parallels to the contact/conflict frontier zone of the eastern Cape as pictured by Wilson.

Presenting a more complex picture of a jumbled bag of "conflict" and "co-operation" elements is not good enough for us, though, if we wish to develop a full understanding of frontier zone society. Professor Wilson's work presents us with a suggestive and interesting point of departure, but we need to continue our analysis beyond hers. If conflict and co-operation were both part of the frontier scene, how can one meaningfully distinguish between the frontier and other sections of contemporary (and later) South Africa? We must pose for ourselves the question of the real autonomy of the social conditions of the frontier zone. Is the frontier merely a hazy no man's land between the distinct centres (such as the Xhosa heartland in the Ciskei-Transkei and the established colonial society of the Boland) or does it have its own social composition?[9]

Frontier society
Examing the pattern of frontier "race relations" is one way of getting at this problem. Clearly, on the basis of Professor Wilson's evidence and my own research, the conflict model of harsh, discrete opposed units segregated by race on a level incomparable with the rest of the colony, is unrealistic. Until imperial Britain came to fill the power vacuum, whites had no choice but to deal with Africans as something other than servants or foreigners or beaten foes.

The policy of the Batavian commander, Lodewijk Alberti, the first *landdrost* of Uitenhage, exemplified this necessity. He adhered to formal government policy aimed at subjugating the Khoi who had rebelled against their white masters in 1799 and in ultimately driving Ndlambe and other Xhosa chiefs east of the Fish River. In practice, he was unable to carry out such a policy. He had neither the ammunition nor the soldiers to impose the wishes of the Castle on his unruly dominion. He wrote in 1803 to Gerotz, the interim *landdrost* of Graaff Reinet:

> For a short time yet, one must tolerate the Kaffirs' presence within the borders of this Colony; the

use of force, even though one has it at hand, is not always the most suitable for attaining a goal.[10] Alberti's colleague in Graaff Reinet, the elder Andries Stockenström, shared his attitude: "Insofar as the Kaffirs are concerned, in the present circumstances and as long as they use no force, it is best to practise patience."[11]

Consequently, Alberti's actual policy consisted of amicable consultation with Xhosa chiefs, some conciliatory measures towards the most important Khoi bands and, generally speaking, an attempt to retain in peace the *status post bellum*. The frontier made Alberti and others into diplomats. White frontiersmen travelled into Xhosaland and traded with Khoi and Xhosa associates. The Graaff Reinet rebels of 1793 were quite willing to entertain the notion of alliance with Xhosa chiefs against the government, just as Xhosa chiefs attempted to use colonial authorities and local white farmers for assistance in their internecine feuds.

The power vacuum obliged individuals and small groups to conduct their lives autonomously and in potential violation of the master-servant pattern of social organization. If persistent accusations that white frontiersmen used this freedom to abuse their servants arbitrarily have any basis in fact, one should at least consider another piece of evidence: that non-whites emigrated east from the Cape (and, in much larger numbers, northwards) because they knew frontier conditions offered them a freer and better life.[12] The traveller Lichtenstein described the ex-colonial Khoi of the Orange river valley as follows:

> They were interbred with Christians and slaves, had learned from the European ancestors the better way of rearing cattle, had taken up not only the names (Pienaar, Cloete, Kok) but even customs and certain Christian religious practices, which they always, even in the wanderings of an irregular nomadic life, made sure of keeping as purely as possible... The daily bible reading had always remained in use among them and

very many of them could read, a few even write,
before there ever was a missionary among them.[13]

In the same report, Lichtenstein noted that the half-white, half-Khoi missionary, Jan Matthys Kok, with whom he was very favourably impressed, had left the settled colony specifically to get away from the prejudices of colonial society against the half-caste.

If white frontiersmen were no more tolerant, they were not therefore more rigid in their thinking on race than other colonial whites. One should perhaps rather stress the ideological similarities that were inescapable given the political and economic links that intimately connected the eastern and western settlers. Even before the development of wool, the cattle and sheep trade, based on eastern and northern production, was the mainstay of the whole colonial economy.[14] Annual trips to the capital by many eastern frontiersmen and women, based on this trade nexus, powerfully enforced contact, at least into the early nineteenth century. So did the bonds of religion and the intimate ties of kinship.

The pattern of "race relations" in the western Cape is itself not very well-known in the eighteenth and nineteenth centuries. About 1800, the prevalent atmosphere in Cape Town was one of intense racial prejudice and snobbery not yet given legal expression. Racial lines probably followed class lines roughly. Yet there was a sizeable and not entirely impoverished "free black" population whose status was ambivalent. The *opgaafrolle* suggest a certain amount of intermarriage between white males and non-white females. There was no doubt a good deal of what would later be called "passing for white." We know little of the life and ideas of the poorer classes in town whose racial mores may have been rather flexible. There is so little assurance about what the norm was, that it would be foolhardy at this stage to assert that the frontier in 1800 fitted or deviated from a colonial norm. Evidence suggests that the most rigid social colour code was prevalent in the rural Boland with more flexibility both on the frontier and in town. One must stress though that this is far from proved.

On the colonial farm in the frontier areas servitude prevailed rather than, as elsewhere, slavery. Slavery was relatively weak as an institution on the frontier; there is rather a predominant and distinctive pattern of master-servant relations between white farmers and Khoi clients cum labourers. Khoi could not be enslaved legally. They were a 'free' people according to VOC law which initially paid at least nominal due to their status as original occupants of the land. Certainly in early times it would have been difficult to keep indigenous people from escaping to the hinterland to join their free kinsmen. The relation of Khoi herders to white farmers owed much in practice to ancient clientage relationships, preceding the arrival of whites, although a closer examination of the institution from this point of view remains to be made.

The status of the servant changed over time. Before the mineral discoveries, the history of labour relations in colonial or settler-controlled South Africa is in part that of master-servant relations and analysis is needed of changes and patterns in the development of this bond. The 1828 ordinance and subsequent laws form only one part of this history. We need a chronological schema placing the formal regulations on labour in order but we need as well to question the effective enforcement of the various ordinances.

The Batavians have often been credited for their liberal and original labour contract regulations. Yet in practice they established contracts which were certainly no more beneficial and probably less beneficial to the servant than their British predecessors.[15] The specific working conditions for non-white clients and servants are an important gauge of their position in frontier areas.

At the beginning of the 19th century the rights of the Khoi labourer were extremely circumscribed, although he was technically free. He was often virtually bound to the land, unless unsettled conditions facilitated an escape. He had the right to complain against ill-treatment to magistrates under VOC rule and thereafter. Yet in practice, he could not easily obtain redress. Magistrates were often distant and not always impartial. Generally, he had to rely on the good will of the master to pay him regularly and treat him decently. Worst of all, the right of the labourer to leave his employer was restricted by the threat that the employer would hold on to his stock, or even his family.[16] As the elder Andries Stockenström wrote to Governor J. W. Janssens, the labourer would put up with the worst treatment if seeking redress meant leaving wife, children and cattle to the farmer's mercy for the time being.[17]

Should we in fact distinguish fundamentally between the status of slaves and servants? Would Eugene Genovese's methodological umbrella of seigneurialism in Brazil, covering both slavery and other forms of dependent labour, which he argues are there fundamentally similar, be applicable to the South African situation?[18] How essential to the work system is the clientage relationship, that social form so deeply rooted in African soil to which clearly white farmers made some adaption? How vitally does the situation change with the emancipation of the slaves, the 1828 Ordinance and the new developments in Natal and on the Highveld from the 1830s? These are questions which, when answered, will enable us to get a clearer picture of the special rôle of the frontier, and the eastern frontier zone specifically, in South African history. It underlines too the absolute necessity for discussing race relations within the wider social and economic context for it to have any specific conceptual historical meaning.

The "other side" of the frontier
As the title of Professor Hammond-Tooke's article in the collection *African Societies in Southern Africa* aptly brings out, there is also "another side" of eastern frontier history.[19] The African context of the frontier zone has been much less explored than the colonial context. Much of our knowledge of Xhosa politics is based on what are, in effect, the

constitutional norms, the "rules of the game" sometimes honoured only in the breach. Xhosa society allowed for the fission of political units every generation but in practice some generations knew no fission while others experienced more than the "legal" share. Fissiparous tendencies were strikingly powerful in the late eighteenth and early nineteenth centuries. The chart on Xhosa genealogy in the *Oxford History* indicates this.[20] One can contrast the relatively orderly chiefly succession of the descendants of Gcaleka who dominated the central and eastern Xhosa with the complex splits in the house of Rarabe in the west. Rarabe himself was a contemporary of the first permanent European settlers on the colonial eastern frontier. This difference cannot entirely be explained by the normal course of the laws of inheritance.

Much of Xhosa politics in the last decade of the eighteenth century and the first quarter of the nineteenth revolved around the rivalry of Ndlambe and Ngqika, son and grandson of Rarabe. Ndlambe was not a legitimate heir to the chiefdom according to Xhosa tradition; he headed neither the Great nor the Right-Hand House. He was a successful and energetic leader, though, who came to the fore as regent for his nephew when Ngqika was a minor. In making his bid for power, he moved west across the Fish into colonially-claimed land before 1800.[21] Here he joined a number of other Xhosa segments whose precise degree of independence is unclear (most prominently, the Gqunukhwebe and the Ntinde). For those seeking autonomy and an effective power base, the cis-Fish frontier zone exerted a special attraction in this era.

Traditionally, southern African societies focussed upon a thickly settled centre with power and population thinning out as one proceeded outwards. Frontiers between African political units were characteristically virtually uninhabited no-man's lands. By contrast, the Xhosa western flank by the late eighteenth century would seem to have drawn to it considerable groupings of people interested in trade. Writing on Xhosa-Khoi relations, Gerrit Harinck would apparently push this westward attraction back into the seventeenth century. This does not necessarily vitiate the factor of a colonial "pull" however, given his own evidence of the growing importance of Xhosa-colonial trade in the seventeenth century, at first through the medium of the Khoi as middlemen but increasingly direct as the colonial frontier moved eastwards.[22]

Soon after the establishment of white-owned farms in the east, Xhosa labourers began to work on them. By the time of De Mist and Janssens, government disapproval was already proving insufficient to stop the employment of Xhosa on farms. Indeed the Batavian government recognized the right of farmers to continue to employ Xhosa who had worked for them for more than a year.[23] We do not know to what extent these first Xhosa labourers were refugees from the effects of war and to what extent they were voluntarily entering white service in order to build up their herds and buy needed or wanted articles of trade. The degree to which they approached white farmers with their own resources, especially in cattle, would be a key factor in determining this. Probably given the overall power alignment, their options were far more open than in later days. Exploring the frontier factor in Xhosa history along such lines and comparing conditions in different places and times seems a useful approach for coming to grips with these phenomena.

There is also a third factor in the history of the eastern frontier: the Khoi factor. This factor is of crucial importance in the eighteenth century and well into the nineteenth. One of the most startling and dramatic events in eastern frontier history was the great Khoi rising of 1799 in conjunction with Ndlambe and some other Xhosa chiefs. By paralyzing the eastern economy and by their command of European weaponry and military skills, the rebels posed the greatest challenge ever raised to colonial hegemony in the eastern Cape. Khoi aims, at least as revealed by the testimony of one leader, David Stuurman, were a not very clearly articulated blend of improvement in labour conditions and real independence from white political and economic control through land restitution. The collapse of the movement in 1803 is something of a puzzle, unless we can take it as an instance of bold but "primitive rebels" in Hobsbawm's sense, lacking an ideology that could develop a successful political movement. Most of the tunes played in 1799–1803 are closely repeated half a century later in the Kat River rising.[24] We are bound to develop a stronger sense of the frontier's historical role when we take up more fully the story of Khoi disintegration and integration and the very neglected one of the social formation of the Coloured people in the nineteenth century.

The importance of the eastern Cape frontier
In conclusion, I should like to stress that continued special study of the South African frontier zones, especially the eastern frontier, seems still of great importance. A number of remarkable events occurred there. One was the rise of a missionary tradition hostile to the colonial border which began with J. T. van der Kemp and was carried through by John Philip. Van der Kemp arrived in South Africa in 1799 under the auspices of the London Missionary Society and soon afterward made his way to the eastern frontier to preach first among the Xhosa and then the Khoi. Particularly after he settled in Bethelsdorp in 1803, he developed a radical critique of the existing social order. The problems of the disorderly frontier he blamed on the white settlers. He began to act as a spokesman for Khoi demands and to function as a respected and successful arbiter among non-white forces in the east. His role quickly led him into conflict with the Batavian, and then the British administration, which ultimately put its power behind the interest of the white farmers. Clearly this development has something to do with the missionary being placed in a power vacuum where it was unclear on whose shoulders political authority lay. This not only forced upon him a more searching evaluation of the political and social scene than in areas where the colonial order was well-established; it also enabled him to exert real influence and power.

The missionary factor emerged with greater force in the person of John Philip who was influenced by van der Kemp and continued and expanded his ideas.[25]

The evolution of the Great Trek, to take a second instance and an event in South African history of utmost importance, also must be studied in the perspective of an understanding of the social and economic conditions in the eastern Cape. The trekkers were in good part men and women of the eastern Cape, brought up amid the special political and social conditions of the frontier zone. To what extent was the trek a real departure for them ideologically as well as spatially? How much of their ideas on politics and race was a carry-over from ideas formed in the eastern Cape? More research into the history of the Cape in the first third of the nineteenth century should lead to better perspectives on this problem.

Thirdly, the eastern frontier would seem to be the cauldron out of which emerged new currents of ideas among Africans, ultimately leading to the special political rôle played in the twentieth century by eastern Cape Africans. On the eastern frontier, Africans enjoyed special opportunities through contact with the colony and colonial society although they also bore special burdens as a consequence. Professor Wilson, C. C. Saunders and Donovan Williams have gone over some of this ground already. It needs to be yet more firmly and precisely related to social and economic factors.

Fourthly, the pressures of the frontier zone played a major role in determining imperial and colonial policy generally. For one thing, disorder, potential and actual, posed the problem for administrators as to whether, when and how they should expand full colonial control. The Batavians made the decision to hold on to the cis-Fish lands, apparently because of their economic value. Given this decision, only in the short term could the power balance of the beginning of the nineteenth century between white settlers, the administration, Xhosa chiefs and Khoi groups hold.

The British after 1806 retained the Batavian commitment to this territory and moved in 1811 to exert a total authority by expelling the Xhosa across the Fish. Then followed the gradual extension of colonial rule eastward over the next sixty years. Both the inherent conflict and the inherent links between different groups engendered by the conditions of the frontier zone ultimately played a major role in stimulating imperial expansion. Here the comparison may be drawn with the physical extension of European empire in other parts of Africa and Asia during the nineteenth century. The specific conditions of frontier life affected the general character and intentions of the imperial power.

As one follows the social and economic transformation of the eastern frontier zone through the middle and later nineteenth century, one becomes aware of the particularities of the frontier becoming altered into the particularities of a specific region. The stress on regional dynamics logically replaces one on frontier dynamics. At this point especially, it would seem worthwhile to think through the similarities and differences of the different South African frontiers. Apart from general forces which affect the entire sub-continent, does a close understanding of the eastern Cape at the beginning of the nineteenth century help especially in understanding other frontier zones, say the mid-nineteenth century Caledon valley or the Marico of the H. C. Bosman stories? It may be that the special factors, political and economic of a particular frontier region are those which are analytically decisive, and that the frontier zone has only a limited conceptual use as general typology. This is the conclusion to which some historians of the American frontier have come, observing the vast differences between, say, the Connecticut Valley in the late seventeenth century and the Dakotas two centuries later. Further research on South African frontier history may mean that we shall have to discard or refine earlier models, conceptual and ideological. Such research will, however, continue to shed valuable light on social process and historical development in South Africa.

FOOTNOTES

1. W. Freund, Society and Government in Dutch South Africa: The Cape and the Batavians 1803–06 (Ph.D. Yale 1971).
2. W. Freund, The Eastern Frontier of the Cape Colony during the Batavian Period, *JAH* XIII (4) 1972.
3. P. J. van der Merwe, *Die Noordwaartse Beweging van die Boere voor die Groot Trek 1770–1842* (The Hague 1939) pp. 104–5. (Author's translation.)
4. M. Legassick, The Griqua, the Sotho-Tswana and the Missionaries 1780–1840: The Politics of a Frontier Zone (Ph.D. UCLA 1969).
5. A strong critique of this point of view is made in M. Legassick, The Frontier Tradition in South African Historiography, *Collected Seminar Papers on the Societies of Southern Africa in the Nineteenth and Twentieth Centuries,* II (Institute of Commonwealth Studies London 1971). Much of the thinking in these pages has been stimulated by this paper, especially in making this argument and in discussing frontier race relations.
6. S. Patterson, *The Last Trek* (London 1957) p. 305.
7. M. Wilson, Co-operation and Conflict: The Eastern Cape Frontier, in M. Wilson and L. Thompson, eds., *Oxford History of South Africa* I (Oxford 1969).
8. R. H. Pearce, *The Savages of America: A Study of the Indian and the Idea of Civilisation* (Baltimore 1965); A. K. Moore, *The Frontier Mind* (Kentucky 1957). I am grateful to my colleague, Dr David Locke, for these references and discussion of American parallels.
9. P. J. van der Merwe's studies of the northern frontier suggest a striking social continuity into the twentieth century of 'frontier' socio-economic patterns in the northwestern Cape. Is this unique to that desolate area or could analogies be made to other parts of rural South Africa?
10. Alberti to Gerotz, 31 Nov. 1803, Inventory Batavian Republic 43 p. 185 (Cape Archives). (Author's translation.)
11. Stockenström to Governor Janssens, 2 Jan. 1805, Inventory Magistrates' Office, 2/4 Graaff Reinet 16/13 (Cape Archives). (Author's translation.)
12. The *opgaafrolle* of the Batavian period reveal the presence of prosperous "Baster" eastern frontiersmen. For the northern frontier see Legassick, The Griqua.
13. H. Lichtenstein, Over het Instituut . . ., Sept. 1805, Verzameling J. W. Janssens, VII (Algemeen Rijksarchief The Hague). (Author's translation.)
14. See S. Daniel Neumark, *Economic Influences on the South African Frontier 1652–1836* (Stanford 1957) and Freund, Society and Government.
15. Freund, Society and Government, pp. 257–59.
16. Some of this still appears to have relevance over a century later in J. B. Loudon's account of life in rural Natal in the mid-twentieth

century, *White Farmers, Black Labourers* (African Social Research Documents, I, Leiden Afrika Studiecentrum and Cambridge African Studies Centre 1970).
17. See Freund, The Eastern Frontier . . ., p. 640.
18. Eugene Genovese, *The World the Slaveholders Made: Two Essays in Interpretation* (New York 1969) pp. 71–95.
19. D. Hammond-Tooke, The 'other side' of frontier history: a model of Cape Nguni Political Process, in L. Thompson, ed., *African Societies in Southern Africa* (London 1969).
20. M. Wilson, The Nguni People, in Wilson and Thompson, eds., *Oxford History*, I, 88.
21. Hammond-Tooke, The 'other side', p. 238.
22. G. Harinck, Interaction between Xhosa and Khoi: emphasis on the period 1620–1750, in L. Thompson, ed., *African Societies in Southern Africa*.
23. W. Paravicini di Capelli, *Reizen in de Binnen-Landen van Zuid-Afrika* (trans. and ed. Cape Town 1965) pp. 76–77; D. G. van Reenen, *Die Joernaal van* . . . (trans. and ed. Cape Town 1937) pp. 86, 131.
24. T. Kirk, Some Notes on the Financial State of the eastern Cape 1840–50 (Institute of Commonwealth Studies London seminar paper 1971).
25. W. Freund, The Career of J. T. van der Kemp, *Tijdschrift voor Geschiedenis* (Leiden) forthcoming.

4

THE MFENGU, SELF-DEFENCE AND THE CAPE FRONTIER WARS

Richard A. Moyer

MANY volumes have been written about the wars which occurred in the eastern Cape between 1779 and 1879. Invariably they have concentrated upon the activities of the white participants and their adversaries. This emphasis obscures the fact that the whites relied heavily upon non-white auxiliaries in all nine wars.[1] From the 1835 war onwards the Mfengu progressively became the greatest military collaborators with the whites. In no single study have their contributions to the British and colonial efforts in subjugating the Xhosa been assessed.[2] Though several Cape Governors favourably compared the Mfengu with the Sepoys of India, even so distinguished a historian as John Galbraith has accepted the British Colonial Office view that no people assumed such a role in South Africa.[3] The evidence suggests that the Colonial Office was wrong.

The reasons for this neglect are multiple and, given the exigencies of economic and social life in the eastern Cape during the mid nineteenth century, understandable. Through ethnocentrism contemporary white commentators naturally concentrated upon the activities of the British army and colonists. They also assumed European technology and military know-how was decisive in securing victory. Non-white auxiliaries were mentioned only when unavoidable or when they acted in co-operation with white troops. Some commentators appear to have either deliberately or subconsciously ignored or perverted the activities of the Mfengu.

The colonists resented their dependence upon the Mfengu in confronting and suppressing the Xhosa. To have fully acknowledged their dependence upon non-whites would have been an open admission of their own weakness. Some believed that acknowledgement could encourage the Mfengu to overestimate their strength and turn upon the colony. Whites and Mfengu were engaged in a keen competition for land. To give full acknowledgement to Mfengu contributions would justify their requests for more and better land. Having witnessed the Mfengu in battle, however, several Cape Governors were convinced that they were more efficient and effective than either whites or Khoi/coloureds in preventing Xhosa penetration into the colony.[4]

Lack of familiarity with English prevented the Mfengu from publicising their military contributions and their particular attitude to warfare. They frequently had to rely for recognition upon the efforts of white spokesmen who were easily stereotyped as Mfengu apologists.[5] As British army officers appear to have made only minimal efforts to communicate with Mfengu soldiers, frequent misinterpretations of their activities in the field resulted. Consequently, many of their field activities were reported in a highly unflattering manner, and whites became obsessed with their alleged "barbarousness".[6] This helped them to overlook the very startling military accomplishments of the Mfengu.

The 1846–47 war was well in progress before the British reconciled their approach to war with that of the Mfengu. Until then, British officers frequently submitted reports criticising the Mfengu for failure to adhere to rigid discipline and for being insubordinate.[7] In turn, the Mfengu considered British discipline and strategy a liability when practised in the terrain of the eastern Cape and against the tactics of the Xhosa when the latter refused to meet them in open combat.

Some army observers expressed surprise at Mfengu "bloodthirstiness", their unwillingness to take Xhosa captives or show mercy to the injured, and at the readiness of both Mfengu and Xhosa to fight to the death or commit suicide rather than be taken captive. Their primary explanation for this dogged determination to take life was the supposed hatred of the Mfengu for the Xhosa.[8] But the Nguni always fought to take life. Modification of the assegai to facilitate close quarter fighting and the adoption of firearms increased their capacity to cause death. Moreover, the harsh experiences of the Mfengu during the Mfecane must have removed from them any capacity to demonstrate mercy. Not to have fought to the death would have labelled them cowards and that was a stigma neither Mfengu nor Xhosa wanted to bear.

The zealousness of the Mfengu may be attributed to other factors as well. They may have believed it important to impress their white officers and prove themselves equal to or better than the British. They must have been aware that many colonists distrusted them, believing they had sympathy with the Xhosa. A doggedness in battle could possibly allay white fears. They may also have misinterpreted British tactics. The British were relentless in pursuing the Xhosa and creating situations in which it was easier to attack and kill them. It may be that the Mfengu could not rationalise this with a subsequent concern for the saving of life and the taking of captives. A man shown mercy could fight again on another occasion.

The unwillingness of the whites to trust the loyalty of non-whites or have complete confidence in their fighting capacity compelled both the Mfengu and the Khoi/coloureds to confront the Xhosa at a distinct disadvantage. At the outset of the 1846–47 war, for example, few Mfengu possessed firearms and those that did possess them appear not to have known how to use them effectively.[9] Once armed, the Mfengu, like the Khoi/coloureds, had ammunition rationed to them in very small quantities.[10]

In battle the British preferred to meet the Xhosa on open ground as this conformed to their previous experience in combat.[11] The Xhosa were well aware of this and preferred to meet the British under conditions where they could exploit the terrain and their skill with assegais, in the dense bush and rocky mountain passes, where firearms were not very effective. Rather than adapt to Xhosa tactics, the British either attempted to provoke them into fighting in the open or sought to adhere to disciplined tactics even in the bush. The Mfengu quickly realised that discipline was effective in the open but suicidal in the bush and so when in the bush they repeatedly disobeyed orders, broke rank and confronted the Xhosa on their own terms. Their frequent successes did not mollify the consternation of the rigid British.[12]

The first tactic employed by the British to draw the Xhosa into the open was a scorched earth policy.[13] When Mfengu joined British ranks in the last months of the 1834–35 war, British officers soon discovered that their presence was sufficient provocation to the Xhosa to make them abandon their strategy. Mfengu were then deployed to draw the Xhosa into ambushes or were tactically located in specific sections of marching columns. It was observed that the Xhosa would invariably first attack the section with the Mfengu, usually the rear.[14] This knowledge enabled white troops to march through the bush with virtual impunity. They knew that they would always have adequate time to respond to an attack. The only occasion when this device backfired was in the war of 1850–53. Following an attack, the Mfengu panicked and rushed down upon the whites, causing such havoc that the lives of several whites were lost.[15]

In addition to actually fighting, the Mfengu performed

numerous activities which were of great military significance but which drew little public attention. They did picket duties, intelligence gathering, guide work, message carrying, and quartermastering. They also acted as decoys. Xhosa and Mfengu sources both maintain that the fighting of the Mfengu and their successful performance of these other duties were together instrumental in causing Xhosa defeat.[16]

Ambiguities in colonial legislation were often exploited by whites in an attempt to define the Mfengu out of their just rewards. The Mfengu responded immediately to entreaties to enlist in colonial levies but were never referred to as British subjects or colonials. Instead they were called "the loyal Mfengu" or "faithful allies", terms preferred because they suggested that the Mfengu were of another nation or community and subject to a supreme Mfengu authority. There has never been such an authority and from the day Governor D'Urban proclaimed them British subjects few Mfengu appear to have considered themselves anything else.[17] They were probably unaware that colonial regulations had re-classified them as "native foreigners".[18] "Foreigners" suggested they were mercenaries, and for mercenaries rewards of cash and cattle rather than land could be considered adequate compensation.

Some colonists begrudged the Mfengu any compensation for participating in the frontier wars. Others conceded that they were entitled to a share of captured cattle and goods, but only a fraction of that allocated to whites. Many were of the opinion that the opportunity to help defeat the Xhosa should be reward enough. They argued that it was only the presence of the British army and white colonists which prevented the Xhosa from "re-enslaving" the Mfengu.[19] Good sense dictated that they fight to prevent a Xhosa victory.

Some whites, speaking from the sanctuary of hindsight, maintained that in the 1846–47 and 1850–53 wars the Mfengu troops had been more trouble than they were worth.

Some could refer to specific instances to justify this claim, but few knowledgeable people denied that the Mfengu had been assigned many of the most dangerous tasks and that without them the successful conclusion of the wars would have been more difficult.[20] There was no question of the British not committing the resources required to win the wars, but Mfengu assistance shortened their length, minimized their cost and reduced the number of injuries and deaths among white combatants.

By 1850 many Mfengu appear to have been confident of their military potential and the dependence of the whites upon them. Some capitalised upon this condition of dependence as a lever to attempt to extract concessions of land from the British. When rumours of dissatisfaction and potential disaffection circulated on the frontier, the British either tried to appease the Mfengu through grants of additional land or sought to undermine their military potential and "take them down a notch".[21] In 1854 Governor George Grey told London that the rumours of Mfengu disaffection indicated they were a potential threat to the colony. He formulated a sophisticated plan to undermine their position as the principle guarantee of peace on the frontier.[22] Before Grey left office in 1861 some Mfengu had become so annoyed by his policies that they contemplated rebellion.[23] It is unlikely that many contemplated rebellion seriously; they were too pragmatic and realistic. White officials nevertheless had to acknowledge that should the Mfengu revolt they would provide the most dangerous and competent opposition the whites would have faced to that date in South Africa.[24]

In an abstract sense, then, the Mfengu claims had some merit. Had the Xhosa remained neutral or assisted the Mfengu in a fight against the whites, an overseas commitment far in excess of any previously made would have been required. During the period before aid arrived there would have been great losses of colonial property and life. The one sobering thought which the recalcitrant Mfengu probably never lost sight of was their enmity with the Xhosa.

If they were to fight the whites, it was almost certain that the Xhosa would have temporarily forgotten their grievances against the colonists and joined in the fight against them. This would have allowed the Xhosa to exact a measure of revenge without fear of antagonising the British. It might also have meant that they could recover some of their territory and perhaps effect a beneficial rapprochement with the whites.

Why the Mfengu fought
The Mfengu had been well received by the Xhosa when they arrived in the Transkei and Ciskei.[25] Initially Xhosa-Mfengu relations were cordial and assimilation appeared inevitable. By 1835 cordiality had given way to hostility and many Mfengu were searching for more favourable circumstances. The 1834–35 war provided 17 000 Mfengu with an excellent opportunity to abandon the Xhosa and enrich themselves in the process. Their actions naturally offended the Gcaleka Xhosa: they provided the British army with warriors, took 20 000 head of Gcaleka cattle and settled on lands which had belonged to the Ciskei Xhosa. The Xhosa came to perceive the Mfengu as a treacherous and ungrateful people. They believed that the Gcaleka had been used and then spurned when an opportunity for gain presented itself. The Mfengu were transformed from incipient Xhosa into bitter enemies who merited all the injury and harassment the Xhosa could marshal. To the Xhosa the Mfengu became collaborators in that word's most perjorative sense.[26] Even today there are many Xhosa who consider the Mfengu to be a treacherous segment of the Xhosa chiefdom and still subject to the Xhosa paramount chief.[27]

Naturally, the Mfengu perceived their activities in an entirely different light. Initially collaboration with the British was justified because of the prejudicial treatment they had been receiving. After the war they did not distinguish themselves from other British subjects. Their continued collaboration with the British was like that of two partners co-operating in a positive act. They did not fight the

Xhosa because of an irrational hatred, as many whites believed.[28] As British subjects they fought the Xhosa for the same reasons the whites did. They fought for more land and cattle, to protect their families, homes and wealth, and to create an environment in which they could have greater security and prosperity.

For a considerable time after 1835 many whites believed that the Mfengu were a militarily weak, even helpless, people.[29] Certainly, they believed that they were no match for the Xhosa. The principal reason for this notion was the myth propagated by Governor D'Urban that the Mfengu had been shattered as a military force during the Mfecane and then cruelly enslaved by the Xhosa. The Mfengu did undoubtedly suffer many hardships during the Mfecane and receive unpleasant treatment from the Xhosa, but there is no proof that they were disarmed or incapable of fighting others or protecting themselves. In fact, many of the people who have been labelled Mfengu had considerable reputations as fighters, most notably the Ngwane and Hlubi. Even those most shattered by the Mfecane were never without assegais and they frequently had to resort to their use for protection and the acquisition of food. Some oral informants claim that the word *siyamfenguza,* which gave rise to the name Mfengu, was meant to convey a peaceful intent even though the people saying it were bearing arms.

This view is substantiated by the subsequent relationship of the Mfengu to the Gcaleka. The Gcaleka allowed the Mfengu to settle in their country because they believed them to be a military and economic asset. Hintsa, believing them trustworthy and acknowledging their military potential, located some of them along the Mbashe River to protect his territory from northern invaders.[30] Some informants even claim that Hintsa kept large numbers of Mfengu at his great place because he considered them more trustworthy than his own Gcaleka.

John Ayliff, probably the source of the slavery myth, was

well aware of Mfengu military potential. His writings testify to the willingness of the Mfengu to defend Butterworth mission station and the Transkei whites following the outbreak of the 1834-35 war.[31] He comments on their intelligence-gathering activities and the messages they carried to the British army. The first reports by the British army on entering Gcalekaland describe how the Mfengu offered them 970 fighting men and how well trained and impressive the Mfengu soldiers were.[32]

From late April 1835 until the termination of the war in September of that year, Mfengu played an active role in defeating the Xhosa. They aided Harry Smith in his campaign in Gcalekaland and fought effectively when the scene of battle shifted back to the Ciskei.[33] It was the Mfengu who enticed the Xhosa from the bush so that British firepower could assert itself.

The Mfengu rôle 1835-46
Governor D'Urban claimed that the removal of the Mfengu from Gcalekaland was a humanitarian act. In reality he intended them to perform a highly hazardous role in the future defence of the colony.[34] Having extended the colony past the Keiskamma River, D'Urban envisioned the Mfengu serving as a human barrier between white and Xhosa. In Gcalekaland the Mfengu were told that the British would provide them with protection, but on crossing the Keiskamma they learned that they must contribute to their own defence and the defence of the colony.[35] This frightened them and many fled into the "old colony" or returned to the Xhosa. Those who settled on the frontier lived under an almost constant state of siege.

The white troops stationed at Peddie to help defend the Mfengu evinced little willingness to do so, particularly after Queen Adelaide Province was abandoned. Moreover, Lt. Governor A. Stockenström had little sympathy for the Mfengu and believed them to be a constant source of irritation to the Xhosa.[36] Compounding their unhappy situation, in early 1837 the British officer in command of

Fort Peddie proscribed the Mfengu from bearing arms within two miles of the fort.[37]

In August 1837 Mfengu vulnerability became painfully clear. Several Xhosa chiefs led by the Ndlambe Seyolo provoked an incident at Peddie to demonstrate their newly acquired authority over Queen Adelaide Province. Six hundred Xhosa met the Diplomatic Agent J. M. Bowker to protest about a theft of some cattle by the Mfengu. Bowker requested Mhlambiso, the most senior Mfengu chief, to join the parley. When he did so, he was immediately assegaied, eleven other Mfengu and one white were killed and an estimated 1 500 head of cattle taken.[38] Rather than retaliate, Stockenström accepted a token return of 79 cattle, laid the blame for the incident upon the Mfengu and then removed 2 000 Mfengu into the colony to lessen tension on the border.[39] The Mfengu who remained at Peddie then knew that they could expect little assistance from the British in protecting themselves.

Aside from the occasional petty raid or minor armed skirmish, no major incident occurred in the Peddie district until the outbreak of war in 1846. During this period the Mfengu protected both themselves and the colony as D'Urban had envisioned them doing.[40] They minimised the thefts of colonial cattle by dilligently guarding their own cattle and the colonial border. They also apprehended many Xhosa attempting to enter the colony without valid passes.

Between 1835 and 1846 the Mfengu did not capitalise upon their favoured position with respect to the British to acquire firearms for themselves. Several newspaper accounts mention Mfengu bearing arms for their own use, but two reliable accounts in 1845 and 1846 attest to their general lack of firearms. Anticipating a war in 1845, Theophilus Shepstone, the Diplomatic Agent at Peddie, requested permission to give the Mfengu arms and train them in their use. He said few Mfengu owned guns and even those who did were incapable of using them effectively.[41] When war did erupt in 1846, James Thackwray, on being appointed Captain of the Grahamstown Mfengu Levy, requested guns for his troops.[42] This was refused and the Mfengu had to fight for several months armed solely with assegais before the Governor felt confident enough of their loyalty to issue them with guns.

The 1846–47 war

Had animosity between white and Xhosa not provoked the 1846–47 war, it is likely that antagonism between Mfengu and Xhosa would have done so. Since 1837 Mfengu had been allowed by Gqunukhwebe chiefs to plant gardens in their territory. They explicitly told the Mfengu that the gardens were temporary and that no permanent homes should be constructed. By 1845 Mfengu belonging to the clans of Njokweni and Matomela had violated these conditions.[43] Chief Phato appealed to Theophilus Shepstone to remove them, but he ignored the request. Phato then petitioned the Governor but still received no satisfaction.[44] In desperation he threatened Shepstone's life, compelling him to keep a bodyguard and, ultimately, to abandon Peddie. When war erupted, Phato, long an ally of the British, immediately ordered his followers to attack Peddie and kill every Mfengu in that and their own district.[45] Indeed, Phato had become so recalcitrant that he was the last Xhosa chief to surrender in the war.[46] Naïvely, Shepstone believed the Gqunukhwebe animosity towards the Mfengu and himself was solely a result of their successful efforts to patrol the colonial border and prevent cattle thefts.[47]

For the Mfengu the 1846–47 war had four phases: the attack upon the Peddie Mfengu, the attack by the Xhosa on the "old colony", the pursuit and confrontation of the Xhosa in Xhosa territory and the "mopping up". The initial attack at Peddie was made upon Njokweni, who was driven from his kraal at Newtondale.[48] Most Mfengu were compelled to move from their kraals to Fort Peddie. When a settlement was attacked, a detachment of troops was sent from the fort. The most notable aspect of this phase of the war was the lack of white enthusiasm in assisting the Mfengu. On one occasion news of an attack reached the fort but it was several hours before the white troops responded. On arriving at the scene of conflict, they made one half-hearted charge and then immediately withdrew, leaving the Mfengu to their fate. The unsatisfactory explanation was that the land was unsuitable for horses and that the men and horses were tired from a long march on the previous day.[49] In another incident a Xhosa army estimated by the British at 10 000 attacked Fort Peddie. Before the battle the commander of the fort ordered all whites inside and closed the gates. The Mfengu were left to seek shelter against the outside walls of the fort. When the attack commenced the only assistance the Mfengu received was several half-hearted rifle volleys and a few shots from the fort's cannon. The Mfengu, nevertheless, repelled the attack, pursued the Xhosa and recaptured most of their cattle.[50] The failure of this attack appears to have broken the offensive spirit of the Ndlambe and Gqunukhwebe. Within days, 450 Mfengu were released from the fort to join Colonel Henry Somerset in pursuit of other Xhosa.

Concurrent with the attack on the Peddie district, other Xhosa invaded the "old colony". Though both white and Mfengu came under attack, Mfengu were denied access to fortified positions in colonial towns. Nevertheless they did not seek an accommodation with the Xhosa, but fought them and acquitted themselves well.

Some Mfengu remained at their homes in order to defend them. Others, encouraged by missionaries and British officials, enlisted in the newly-created Mfengu levies. The levies were officered by white captains and subalterns, most of whom had previous affiliations with the Mfengu.[51] Mfengu were assigned positions of lesser rank, as sergeants and corporals. Those selected to be officers were a varied lot. One was colourfully described by the *Grahamstown Journal* as a veteran of the war with the Ngwane and the proud possessor of thirteen battle scars.[52] Others held the rank of chief or headman. The British believed the Mfengu levies would fight more effectively when they followed traditional leaders. In later years efforts were made to recruit sons of chiefs as army officers as well.[53] Commoners appointed officers were initially selected, it would appear, because of previous experience amongst whites and an ability to speak a colonial language. The most famous Mfengu commoner officer, Veldman Bikitsha, first served in this war.[54]

At least 1 200 Mfengu were formally enrolled in levies during the 1846–47 war and it is likely that the actual number serving was much higher. At least one levy was organised in each of the following places: Grahamstown, Uitenhage, Port Elizabeth, Tsitsikamma, Cradock, Salem, Farmerfield, Shiloh, Kat River, Fort Beaufort, Fort Thompson, Fort Brown and Fort Peddie. James Thackwray, who provides the most detailed information about the Mfengu levies, describes their heroic efforts in the defence of Grahamstown, though denied the use of firearms. Several Mfengu prevented great destruction in lower Albany when they discovered a large Xhosa encampment with at least 100 fires and convinced Colonel Somerset of the danger. Somerset followed them to the encampment and the Xhosa were routed.

With the colony apparently secure, the scene of fighting shifted into Xhosa country. Many Mfengu accompanied the army, while others were stationed at strategic posts along the border to protect the colony. Of these Thackwray writes that no plunder was allowed to pass them without being intercepted or retaken. "Had the Mfengu been placed at an earlier period in the war at the posts ... an immense amount of property would have been saved."[55]

The Mfengu were involved in all levels of pursuit and confrontation with the Xhosa. They transported supplies, including cattle, from the colony and coastal ports to the army. Thackwray maintains that they never lost a head of cattle, a surprising statement as others claimed they never lost an opportunity to plunder cattle, whether it belonged to Xhosa or an ally.⁵⁶ In previous wars Khoi/coloureds performed most of the intelligence and guide work. In this and succeeding wars these activities were increasingly performed by the Mfengu.

As those attacked first, they unavoidably received the full impact of the Xhosa. When it was necessary to scale a mountain or penetrate the dense bush to reach the Xhosa, the Mfengu were the first to be sent into battle. Though they usually obeyed instructions without question, they several times flatly refused, claiming that to comply would be to act like sheep being sent to slaughter. In this and later wars the Mfengu protested about the tendency of the white troops to fire at them when engaged in battle.⁵⁷ The white reply was often that Mfengu and Xhosa were physically indistinguishable and that they could not believe that the Mfengu had moved through the bush and engaged the enemy so quickly.

The 1846–47 war was a transitional one for both Mfengu and British. The Mfengu began the war relying upon the stabbing assegai. By the end of the war many had acquired guns and learned how to use them effectively. The British, in turn, learned how to use the Mfengu. At the outset of the war they were determined to make the Mfengu fight as they did. When the Xhosa were confronted in the open, the Mfengu maintained discipline and drew praise from their officers. When in the bush, however, they broke rank and fought like the Xhosa, which appalled the British. Eventually the British realised their mistake and began devising strategems to capitalise upon the demonstrated skills of their allies.⁵⁸

Though the Mfengu performed well, many whites still lacked complete faith in them. On the pretext that they mishandled their guns in camp and squandered ammunition while in the bush, the British kept a strict inventory on arms and carefully rationed out ammunition in small quantities.⁵⁹ It is probable that many whites feared the Mfengu might trade their guns to the Xhosa, as some had done before the war, or that the weapons would be captured if Mfengu were killed.

The "irregular" activities of the Mfengu, when they were authorised to break ranks and scour the bush for Xhosa and cattle, elicited numerous comments from observers. Some were amazed at their ability to find Xhosa and cattle.[60] Others became aware of just how seriously the Mfengu took war to be. They often watched in horror when the Mfengu killed an individual Xhosa or tortured and then killed individuals who had been taken captive.

As war drew to a close the Mfengu attitude towards warfare might well have cost them the land which they had been promised at the outset of hostilities by Governor Maitland. They practised total war when the issue of victory was in doubt, but when they determined that victory was inevitable many immediately lost interest in fighting and wanted to resume their civilian lives.[61] They saw no need to imprison all the Xhosa chiefs or secure an unconditional surrender. They knew the Xhosa would never adhere to forced promises. When their terms of enlistment were up, most refused to re-enlist and returned to their homes. Those who still had time left rebelled at the strict regimentation and were reluctant to participate in "meaningless" manoeuvres. Co-operation was often secured only through increased allocation of captured booty, even if that booty was obviously colonial in origin.[62]

When Lt. Governor H. Young wanted to enlist a permanent Mfengu force to patrol the dense Fish River bush, the Grahamstown Mfengu informed him that they had done long and arduous duty and were tired. If there was a new danger they would serve, but Mfengu should now be asked who had not as yet served. William Shaw, the superintendent of the Wesleyan Mission Society, who was assisting Young, told him that even if he offered the Mfengu rations for themselves and their families, they could still earn more than he was prepared to pay by working in the colony. Young had to content himself with using the more costly and less effective Khoi/coloureds and whites.[63]

The failure of the British to give the Mfengu the land promised them caused considerable disenchantment. Resentment increased following the expulsion of Mfengu squatters from land they had occupied, merely to suit the whim of government agents and the appetite for land of white colonists. A considerable furore developed when the Hlubi Chief Luzipo, an officer in a Mfengu levy, was expelled several times from unoccupied land during the two years following the end of the war.[64] Officially, the Mfengu were only allowed to occupy large tracts of Xhosa land in late 1848, but by then the Xhosa had recovered their strength and were once again on the "brink" of war.

It was claimed that this callous treatment led some Mfengu to contemplate either neutrality or a change of allegiance should a new war erupt.[65] It is unlikely that many Mfengu would have abandoned the British, for they recognised that the Xhosa could never hope to win a war and drive the whites from South Africa. They probably doubted that the Xhosa would treat them kindly had they offered them their assistance. The Xhosa did not take the rumours of Mfengu disaffection seriously and many of the initial attacks of the war were against Mfengu. These attacks must have convinced even the most anti-British Mfengu that they could not effect a rapprochement with the Xhosa and could only hope for better treatment from the British.

A further inducement to participate in the 1850–53 war alongside the British was the overcrowding which existed on the Mfengu locations. Their numbers increased owing to natural growth, the settlement on the locations of Mfengu who had previously resided within the "old colony", and the settlement in the Ciskei of several thousand Mfengu who had been evacuated from Gcalekaland during the previous war. Thus it was self-preservation and self-interest which pragmatically determined their allegiance. Many colonists duly noted, however, that if the British wanted to keep the allegiance of the Mfengu during the ensuing decades, they would have to keep the promises made to the Mfengu this time.[66]

The 1850-53 war
In early 1851 a large number of Khoi/coloured people, including members of the Cape Mounted Rifles, rebelled against the British and joined the Xhosa. The reasons usually given were animosity towards the white colonists and British, as well as a desire for greater autonomy.[67] A cause which is generally overlooked is their antagonism towards the Mfengu. Prior to the war, Khoi/coloured had allowed Mfengu to squat on their lands, but by 1851 many believed the Mfengu were trying to force them off their land permanently. Others resented having been pushed out of the labour market by the Mfengu, because the latter were prepared to work harder and for less money than the Khoi/coloureds. Some were said to be jealous of the Mfengu because they had usurped their position as the favourite "coloured" people of the colonists.[68]

The activities of the rebels confirm this. The initial act of the Theopolis rebels was to kill as many of the Mfengu in that district as they could find.[69] At the Kat River, James Read, Jr., himself a coloured, told John Green "that Englishmen need have no worries as the Hottentots were only after cattle and arms belonging to the Fingoes".[70] During the rebellion contests between Mfengu and Khoi/coloureds were particularly fierce and captured rebels were treated as harshly as Xhosa. When Khoi/coloured women were discovered bringing supplies to their men, the British had great difficulty in restraining the Mfengu from beating or killing them. When Shiloh mission station was attacked, the Khoi/coloureds living there refused to aid the Mfengu who were defending the station.[71]

Because of the rebellion even greater reliance was placed upon the Mfengu than in previous wars, and the successful defence of several colonial towns can be attributed to them. To ensure Mfengu enlistment in the levies British officers again requested the aid of missionaries. James Read Jr., as in the previous war, organised a company from his congregation and served for a time as its officer.[72] John Ayliff encouraged the Fort Beaufort Mfengu to enlist and they did so enthusiastically.[73] When that town was attacked by the rebels of Hermanus Matroos, both enrolled and unenrolled Mfengu helped to rout the enemy. They are even credited with causing Matroos' death. This inspired John Ayliff to write another series of articles praising the Mfengu and gave Governor Harry Smith an opportunity to congratulate himself for having been involved in their removal from Gcalekaland in 1835.[74]

Though Mfengu soldiers had used firearms in the previous war, most of the new enlistees appear to have had no knowledge of their use and came into camps armed only with assegais. It is possible that veterans with guns remained in their locations with chiefs and fought independently. When the war ended most Mfengu soldiers returned home with guns. Many were captured as booty from fallen opposition, especially Khoi/coloureds.[75] In one unusual incident Captain Cobb demanded a captured rifle from William Dema, a Christian Mfengu, and a fight broke out. In the struggle the gun went off and Cobb was killed. To maintain Mfengu loyalty and morale, the committee investigating the incident dismissed it as an accident and no action was taken against Dema.[76] Though the Mfengu were issued with firearms, they were still only rationed ammunition in small quantities. The result was sometimes disastrous. On one occasion, a mixed force of Mfengu and Khoi/coloureds encountered the Xhosa, were surrounded and fought admirably until they exhausted their limited supply of ammunition, when they were all slaughtered.[77]

Though colonial whites had deep-seated fears about Mfengu loyalty, relations between Mfengu and most British soldiers appear to have been amicable. The two groups camped apart because the Mfengu sung and danced every night, but intercourse between the two camps was regular. The British enjoyed observing the Mfengu at their "pleasures", particularly their dancing and smoking of dagga, which one British officer admitted trying himself.[78] Only one account of hostility between Mfengu and British in a bivouac has been discovered. This incident occurred on a cold evening after a Xhosa village had been captured. Both Mfengu and British occupied huts, but the British wanted to destroy those occupied by the Mfengu for firewood. The Mfengu rebelled and a fight broke out, but the British prevailed because while some were fighting others were dismantling the Mfengu huts.[79]

During this war the British formalised far-ranging "irregular" activities by the Mfengu. In conjunction with unenrolled Mfengu, Mfengu from various levies were released from duty to make raids upon Xhosa villages in the Ciskei and Transkei.[80] They were directed to disrupt the villages and capture as many cattle as they could find. The Mfengu volunteered for these raids with enthusiasm as they were allowed to keep all of the captured cattle. As the Xhosa relied upon cattle for food during wartime, any losses they suffered greatly curtailed their capacity to prolong the war. No records were kept of these raids so it is not known who was attacked or the extent of the damage they did. One can only assume that as they were continued, they must have been effective.

As in the two previous wars, the Transkei was invaded. When war appeared imminent in Gcalekaland, Mfengu resident there attempted to remove their cattle to safety in Mpondo country, but were attacked by the Thembu chief Joyi, whom they assumed had been encouraged to attack them by Sarili. They retaliated against Joyi but became convinced that they had no future in Gcalekaland. When the British army crossed the Kei, Mfengu rallied to its aid. After hostilities ended, upwards of 7 000 Mfengu had to be withdrawn into the colony for their own safety.[81]

Some Mfengu from the Ciskei quite naturally accompanied the troops into Gcalekaland. Others, like a force of men from Peddie, had enlisted in the army solely on the understanding that they would be allowed to fight in Gcalekaland. They may have been motivated by smouldering resentment for ill-treatment prior to 1835, a desire to assist relatives and friends still resident in Gcalekaland who were in danger, and a belief that the Gcaleka still had large herds of cattle which could be taken as spoils. On leaving Gcalekaland, the Mfengu took over 20 000 head of cattle and 14 000 goats, far in excess of what they had removed in 1835.[82]

As the war drew to a close, some whites again criticised the Mfengu. Their "unruliness and lack of discipline" were publicised and notice was taken of the great quantities of booty they had ostensibly acquired.[83] This was done in an effort to minimise the quantity of land that was to be parcelled out to them. Fortunately for the Mfengu, Governors Smith and Cathcart had been eyewitnesses to their efforts and respected their achievements. Cathcart perceived them as the key to maintaining peace on the frontier once overt hostilities had ceased. He was also aware that several hundred Mfengu were still helping British forces in their efforts against Moshweshwe. In a despatch to London he wrote that the Mfengu were "in respect to the military exigencies of South Africa, what the Sepoys are to those of the East India Company in Asia . . ."[84]

The Mfengu rôle 1853–79
At the close of the 1850–53 war, Cathcart created a permanent force of 240 Mfengu to patrol the border. In spite of low pay (fourpence a day and rations only when on manoeuvres), he had little difficulty in finding men to enlist.[85] As a concession to white fears, this force was reviewed and re-enlisted every six months. Soon after it first met, the white-dominated Cape Assembly appointed an enquiry into the state of defence in the eastern Cape. A rumour was circulating that Mfengu and Xhosa were negotiating a rapprochement[86] and attempts were made to have Cathcart's patrol disbanded and the Mfengu disarmed, but these proved unsuccessful.

Cathcart's successor, Sir George Grey, having suppressed the Maoris in New Zealand, was intent upon a similar success with the Xhosa. Whites welcomed him with pleas that he disarm both the Xhosa and the Mfengu, many of whom served with the regular army and the Frontier Armed and Mounted Police. Grey respected the military potential of the Mfengu, but realised the danger were 7 000 men capable of bearing arms to turn on the colony.[87] They were loyal at the moment, but he did not believe it wise to entrust the defence of the colony to anyone but the politically dominant community. He therefore sought ways of undermining the military potential of the Mfengu and weaning them from their chiefs.[88] During the cattle-killing small-scale fights erupted with considerable frequency between Xhosa who had been killing their cattle and Mfengu who had not. James Ayliff, Superintendent of the Crown Reserve, suggested that Grey hoped that one of these fights might become something larger which might debilitate both Mfengu and Xhosa.[89] When the upheaval had been brought under control, however, Grey decided that Sarili and the Gcaleka should be driven across the Mbashe River and that Mfengu should be used to help do this. They also served in the units which policed Gcalekaland and kept it depopulated for the next seven years.

In 1865 Governor Wodehouse decided to reduce the population pressures which were building up in the eastern Cape. Denied permission to settle whites in Gcalekaland, he resolved to move Mfengu there from the Ciskei. He believed that Mfengu could serve as an effective lightening rod for Xhosa hostility in the Transkei. Mfengu were therefore settled in the three districts which became Fingoland and a portion of the Idutywa Reserve. By 1877 resentment among the Gcaleka towards the Mfengu reached uncontrollable proportions and following a fight between Mfengu and Gcaleka at a Mfengu beer drink the war of Ngcayecibi erupted.

In the first months of the war, before colonial troops could be mobilised effectively, most of the fighting was done by

Mfengu. Inspired and led by Captain Veldman Bikitsha, the Mfengu prevailed in several large-scale battles. Just before the Gcaleka appeared ready to capitulate, Sandile's Rarabe Xhosa broke into revolt. When fighting shifted southwards, the Mfengu continued to fight in large numbers, and it was they who caused Sandile's death.[90]

When this, the last frontier war, drew to a close, it was obvious that the Xhosa were no longer a threat to the colony or to the white settlers who had been filtering into the Transkei. Legislation was then enacted to disarm all Cape Africans. As Mfengu military assistance was thought to be no longer required, they were included within the order. They protested that they had done nothing to justify such "betrayal" and that it would leave them vulnerable to attacks by the Xhosa and other enemies, but their protests were to no avail. Like all Xhosa-speakers, they were disarmed. Their fears proved justified: in 1880–81 rebellion broke out and when the Mfengu refused to join they too were attacked. As always they remained loyal and came to the aid of the whites.

The hundred year struggle for domination in the eastern Cape was now at an end. The African population was effectively subdued and subjugated and would never again pose a real military threat to white hegemony. The Xhosa were, of course, the greatest losers. Owing to their recalcitrance they had lost most of their land and fallen well behind the Mfengu in acquiring western education and cash wealth. By 1879, however, all Africans, including the Mfengu, had lost something. On being disarmed the Mfengu realised they had been used and were, after all, no different than the Xhosa. Their only consolation was the price they had exacted from the British for their assistance during the previous forty-five years. Though the whites were next to seek to undermine their control of their land and their economic and social achievements, their collaboration with the British had enabled them to acquire sufficient political power to delay this process and at least retain a position of "pre-eminence", however tainted, amongst Africans until well into the twentieth century.

FOOTNOTES

1. The frontier wars began in the following years: 1779, 1792, 1799, 1812, 1818, 1834, 1846, 1850 and 1877. Khoi and coloureds aided the whites in all the wars. In the 1799 and 1850 wars a great many joined the opposition. Some Xhosa, for various reasons, aided the whites against other Xhosa in most of the wars. The Mfengu aided the whites in the last four wars.
2. J. Ayliff and J. Whiteside, *History of the Abambo* (Transkei 1912) and R. T. Kawa, *Ibali lama Mfengu* (Lovedale 1929) devote sections to the Mfengu in the frontier wars, but they are brief and contain no original material.
3. J. Galbraith, *Reluctant Empire* (Berkeley 1963) p. 272.
4. E.g. Governor Cathcart, 9 July 1853, L.G. 651 (Cape Archives).
5. The Rev. John Ayliff was their best known spokesman and apologist.
6. E.g. S. Loxton, 11 August 1854, Committee on Frontier Defence, C.O. 48/353, pp. 403-6 (P.R.O.); *Graaff-Reinet Herald,* 27 June 1855.
7. 1847-8 *Accounts and Proceedings,* 43, 77; T. Baines, *Journal of Residence in Africa,* ed. R. Kennedy, II (Cape Town 1964) 204.
8. E. Napier, *Excursions in Southern Africa* (London 1840) p. 267.
9. J. Maclean to Lt. Gov., Fort Peddie, 23 March 1846, L.G. 403, p. 30 (Cape Archives); J. Thackwray to J. Ayliff, 3 Dec. 1849, MS. 15, 545 (Cory Library).
10. 1847–48 *Accounts* 43, 77.
11. G. M. Theal, *The Story of a Nation – South Africa* (London 1899) p. 189; *Br. Parl. Papers, Select Committee on Aborigines* 1836–37, p. 316.
12. Baines, *Journal,* II, 219.
13. W. M. Macmillan, *Bantu, Boer and Briton* (Oxford 1963) p. 131.
14. D'Urban Papers (Cape Archives) II, 15; *Grahamstown Journal,* 17 August 1835.
15. Lt. Col. J. Fordyce, 15 Sept. 1851, C.O. 48/316, p. 155 (P.R.O.).
16. Cape Committee on Frontier Defence, 1854, p. 21, W. Stanton Jr.
17. H. Calderwood, *Caffres and Caffre Missions* (London 1858) p. 195. The Mfengu were not a united people; they accepted the name to distinguish themselves from the Xhosa.
18. W. Porter, memo. on status of Mfengu, 1853, L.G. 676, p. 252 (Cape Archives).
19. *Grahamstown Journal,* 31 Jan. 1851.
20. Baines, *Journal,* II, 205; R. Godlonton and E. Irving, *Narrative of the Kaffir War* (London 1851) p. 197.
21. *Further Papers Relative to the State of the Kaffir Tribes in the Cape of Good Hope,* 1855, p. 34: Darling to Gov. Grey, 4 Nov. 1854.

22. *Ibid*, p. 35: Gov. Grey to Sir G. Grey, 12 Dec. 1854.
23. E.g. C.O. 48/377 (P.R.O.), p. 31: Statement of Umjaxa, 18 March 1859.
24. *Further Papers,* 1855, p. 35.
25. Diary of W. Shrewsbury (Cory library MS. 12, 252), p. 13: 10 Dec. 1826.
26. "To co-operate with or assist (usually traitorously) an enemy, especially conquerors occupying one's country" *(Websters New International Dictionary,* 1945, p. 524).
27. See, e.g. "The Fingo Manifesto", petition submitted by the Ciskei Fingo Day Committee to the Dept. of Bantu Administration and Development, 1967.
28. Napier, *Excursions,* p. 267; C.O. 48/358 (P.R.O.), p. 16.
29. Theal, *Story of a Nation,* p. 211.
30. Most Ngwane do not consider themselves Mfengu but some were classified Mfengu in the mid-19th century and are so classified today.
30. *Cape Parl. Papers,* G 4, 1883, Appendix p. 16, evidence G. Woods.
31. Cf. Ayliff to his sons, 27 August 1861, MS. 15, 289 no. 8 (Cory library).
32. *Grahamstown Journal,* 23 April 1835; D'urban Papers, 21, 190: T. Shepstone, camp on the Dabakazi, 22 April 1835.
33. D'Urban Papers, II, 15; *Grahamstown Journal,* 17 August 1835.
34. C.O. 48/360 (P.R.O.): General Order, 3 May 1835.
35. G. M. Theal, *Documents Relating to the Kaffir War of 1835,* p. 255: Instructions for the guidance of commissioners, 13 July 1835.
36. D'Urban Letters, collected by Theal (South African Library) II, 33: Stockenström to Somerset, 11 August 1837.
37. *Grahamstown Journal,* 26 Jan. 1837.
38. *Grahamstown Journal,* 10 August 1837.
39. R. Godlonton, *The Case of the Colonists of the Eastern Frontier of the Cape of Good Hope, in reference to the Kaffir Wars of 1835–36 and 1846* (Grahamstown 1879) pp. 52, 77.
40. T. Shepstone, 12 July 1845, L.G. 451, p. 45 (Cape Archives).
41. ibid.
42. J. Thackwray to Ayliff, 3 Dec. 1849, MS. 15, 545 (Cory Library).
43. T. Shepstone, 12 July and 29 August 1845, L.G. 451, pp. 45–9, 188 (Cape Archives).
44. Statements by Phato and Cobus Cungwa to Gov. recorded by G. Cyrus, 5 June 1845 L.G. 451, p. 204 (Cape Archives).
45. 1847 *Accounts,* vol. 38, p. 89: Lt. Gov. Hare to Maitland.
46. Macmillan, *Bantu, Boer and Briton,* p. 298.
47. T. Shepstone, 12 July 1845, L.G. 451, p. 45 (Cape Archives).
48. J. Appleyard, *The Xhosa Bible and the War of the Axe* (Cape Town 1971) p. 46; *Grahamstown Journal,* 6 May 1846.
49. Appleyard, *Xhosa Bible,* p. 46; G. Cory, *The Rise of South Africa,* IV (London 1926) 437.
50. *The Cape Frontier Times,* 6 June 1848; *Grahamstown Journal,* 30 May 1848; Appleyard, *Xhosa Bible,* p. 83; Harriet Ward, *The Cape and the Kaffirs* (London 1851) p. 280.
51. *South African Commercial Advertiser,* 6 May 1851. Four of John

Ayliff's sons served in the Mfengu levies, two of William Shepstone's sons and so too did a number of men who had worked at mission stations largely peopled by Mfengu.
52. *Grahamstown Journal,* 16 May 1851.
53. *South African Commercial Advertiser,* 6 August 1851; MS. 1851 (Cory Library).
54. E. Hurlcombe in *Daily Dispatch,* 22 Oct. 1922; Ayliff and Whiteside, *Abambo,* pp. 73–75.
55. MS. 15, 545 (Cory Library).
56. Napier, *Excursions,* p. 352.
57. W. King, *Campaigning in Kaffirland* (London 1853) p. 203; Baines, *Journal,* II, 211, 219.
58. *South African Commerical Advertiser,* 27 May 1846.
59. *1847 Accounts,* 38, 77.
60. Napier, *Excursions,* pp. 266–69.
61. Lt. Gov. H. Young to Pottinger, 26 May 1847, L.G. 619, p. 814 (Cape Archives).
62. Cape Committee on Frontier Defence, 1854, p. 21, W. Stanton Jr.
63. L.G. 619, p. 814 (Cape Archives).
64. MS. 1851 (Cory Library).
65. G. Brown, *Personal Adventure in South Africa* (London 1855) p. 49.
66. C.O. 48/358, p. 429. Committee on Frontier Defence, testimony A. Stockenström (P.R.O.).
67. E.g. E. Walker, *A History of Southern Africa* (London 1957) p. 251.
68. J. S. Marais, *The Cape Coloured People 1652–1937* (London 1939) p. 235.
69. Baines, *Journal,* II, 194.
70. J. Green, *The Kat River Settlement in 1853* (Grahamstown 1853) p. 68.
71. Baines, *Journal,* II, 225 and 236; *South African Commerical Advertiser,* 6 August 1851; B. Kruger, *The Pear Tree Blossoms* (Genadendal 1969) p. 236.
72. London Missionary Society Papers 24/1/a, 1846, James Read Jr.
73. MS. 15, 380, 7 Jan. 1851 (Cory Library).
74. Smith to Earl Grey, 7 June 1851, C.O. 48/316, p. 198 (P.R.O.).
75. *Grahamstown Journal,* 18 August 1851; Clerk of Peace, Grahamstown to W. F. Liddie, 11 June 1853, L.G. 663 (Cape Archives).
76. *South African Commercial Advertiser,* 1, 8 and 15 March 1851.
77. *Grahamstown Journal,* 25 March 1851.
78. Baines, *Journal,* II, 212; King, *Campaigning,* pp. 25, 162.
79. Baines, *Journal,* II, 271.
80. *Grahamstown Journal,* 27 Nov. 1851.
81. *Grahamstown Journal,* 4 Nov. 1851, 24 Jan. 1852.
82. L.G. 659, p. 123 (Cape Archives); *Eastern Province News,* 14 Feb. 1852.
83. *Grahamstown Journal,* 13 March 1853; Cape Committee on Frontier Defence, 1854, p. 21.
84. G. Cathcart, *Correspondence* (London 1857) p. 209. Cf. King, *Campaigning,* p. 317.

85. *Cape Frontier Times,* 30 March 1853; C.O. 48/338, p. 109 (P.R.O.).
86. *Further Papers* 1855, pp. 430-44. Report on Fingo Locations by H. Calderwood.
87. *ibid.*
88. *Further Papers* 1855, p. 37: Gov. Grey.
89. J. Ayliff, Recollections Written for Members of His Family (found at home of Mrs. Ayliff Goss in Grahamstown, 1971; copy in Cory Library).
90. Ayliff and Whiteside, *Abambo,* p. 64.

5

THE GRIQUA IN THE POLITICS OF THE EASTERN TRANSKEI

Robert Ross

IN this chapter an attempt is made to analyse the way in which the Griqua contrived to establish their hegemony over the African peoples of the eastern Transkei in the decade between their arrival there in 1863 and the British take-over in 1874. Situations of alien domination are common enough in Africa, and are well nigh universal in cases of colonial rule, but any understanding of the dynamics of political life in such circumstances depends on isolating the important variables on both sides of the line, among the dominators as well as among the dominated.[1] This paper does not attempt to build any kind of model of the possible interrelationships, for this is beyond its scope, but rather to present a detailed account of a particular instance of this process, and so to point to fruitful comparisons that may illumine not only Griqua-African relations, but equally the problems that faced both whites and Africans in establishing their domination in southern Africa, and, specifically, in the Transkei.

The arrival of the Griqua in Nomansland

The Griqua people had emerged during the eighteenth century in the Cape Colony. They were drawn from the marginal "Bastaards" who could not find acceptance in the increasingly racially stratified, white-dominated society, but yet felt themselves to be of that society as independent farmers and stock keepers, rather than as labourers. They had set themselves up along the Orange River, where their political organisation developed a considerable sophistication. They saw themselves as superior to the Sotho-Tswana with whom they came into contact, and in the years around 1840 they made a concerted effort to assert their hegemony over much of Transorangia, attempting to gain control particularly over the Thlaping, by using as intermediaries and collaborators those of the Tswana who had come under mission influence.[2] This attempt failed, and the Griqua in Transorangia became steadily less powerful, in competition with the Boer population that was moving north.

By the late 1850s the Griqua of Philippolis were in an intolerable position. Although sheep farming had raised a substantial number of them to a position of considerable wealth, the political pressures to which they were subjected by the Orange Free State, in whose territory they lived and with whose burghers they were interspersed, grew to such an extent that they considered that the only way in which to survive as an entity, and thus preserve any semblance of their wealth, was to trek. They could do this because they knew the land in Nomansland, across the Drakensberg, to be empty, and they visited it in 1859 and were well satisfied. The immediate spur for their decision to move was the failure of Sir George Grey's confederation scheme, which would have brought the Griqua into the Cape's orbit as British subjects, and the consequent election of Marthinus Wessel Pretorius as President of the Orange Free State. They left Philippolis from the end of 1861 onwards, spent the winter of 1862 disastrously in the Witteberg, losing many of their cattle and sheep to the combined efforts of drought and Sotho raiders, and debouched into Nomansland during the summer of 1862–3, after an epic crossing which entailed building a wagon road over the High Drakensberg at Ongeluks Nek.

The legal status both of the area into which they moved,

▲ *Charles Brownlee,*
African administrator and the Cape's first Secretary for Native Affairs (1872-8).

PLATE 9

▶ *Dr James Stewart and Lovedale students.*

(Lovedale collection, Cory Library)

PLATE 10

roughly the modern districts of Matatiele, Mount Currie and Umzimkulu, and of the Griqua themselves, during and after the trek, is highly complicated. Although it may be possible to sort out the various conceptions that the actors held of the situation, from a historical point of view its ambiguity is most important. Essentially the area had been claimed by Faku of the Mpondo in his treaty with the British of 1844, but as a pre-emptive measure, for he could not establish effective control over the Bhaca, the Mpondomise and the Xesibe, who lived north of the Mpondo settlements. In 1850, in consequence of his inability to cope with cattle raids into Natal, conducted primarily by San, in alliance with the Bhaca under Ncaphayi,[3] he ceded the area to Natal on the condition of its effective occupation.[4] This was never forthcoming, primarily because the schemes of Theophilus Shepstone to remove large numbers of Natal's Africans into the area were quashed by Sir George Grey. Grey it was who consented to the Griqua being allowed to move into Nomansland, despite protests from the government of Natal, but they were to move as British subjects and a British Resident was to be placed among them.[5] As it was, no such resident was appointed, and so the Griqua enjoyed the prestige of the British connection without the constraints of supervision.

The area into which they moved was in large measure thinly populated. Although it would appear to have been the region from which many of the Cape Nguni had dispersed,[6] the highland sourveld along the southern slopes of the Drakensberg can never have been thickly inhabited with Africans, primarily because it only provided grazing for half the year.[7] Rather it remained, in conjunction with the Highlands of Lesotho, the haunt of San hunter-gatherers until the mid-nineteenth century, only being evacuated by them in the decade and a half before the Griqua trek.[8] This does not, however, mean that the Griqua entered a political vacuum. On the contrary, they came into contact with numerous African peoples, over whom they attempted to establish hegemony. It is this ultimately unsuccessful process that the discussion that follows attempts to describe.

Rivalries in the eastern Transkei
The various groups of Nguni-speakers in the eastern Transkei had, effectively, a short history, for events before the Mfecane no longer affected the political relations extant in the early 1860s. Nevertheless, in the intervening forty years much had happened to determine the reactions of individuals to the Griqua trek. The Mfecane had seen the establishment of two major powers in the area, each with their own designs and enemies, namely the Mpondo and the Bhaca. Initially moderately amicable, they fell out as the threat from the "Fetcani hordes", notably the Qwabe, diminished, and the regent of the Bhaca, their notable leader Ncaphayi, was killed by the Mpondo. This led to the splitting of the Bhaca into two sections, one under Ncaphayi's son, Makaula,[9] which remained in Mount Frere, and the other under Mdutyana, which congregated on the right bank of the Mzimkulu River.[10] This struggle formed part of an attempt by Faku to gain paramountcy over the whole of the eastern Transkei, which was helped by the treaty with the colonial government in 1844, but which ultimately failed. In pursuance of this policy, Faku came into conflict with a variety of African groups, but as they were all primarily concerned to maintain their own independence, they did not ally with the Griqua to obtain safety from the Mpondo, for Adam Kok was generally, and correctly, seen as a greater threat than Faku. Moreover, the internal fission that divided the Mpondomise and Bhaca into sections created cross-cutting enmities of great complexity.

One major rivalry, however, did persist from the Mfecane until the Le Fleur revolt of 1896, namely that between the Bhaca and the Hlangweni.[11] Originating in the aftermath of Shaka's devastation in southern Natal, it was maintained despite the fission of both groups, for the Hlangweni adhering to both Fodo and Sidoi appear to have retained memories of scores to be settled, as did all Bhaca. It was, moreover, exacerbated by the depositions of Fodo and

Sidoi by the British Government in Natal, on the earlier occasion in consequence of attacks made on Bhaca who were moving into the province. Fodo, who had played a considerable and important role as henchman of the Voortrekkers during their raid on Ncaphayi, was removed in 1846, and then migrated to Nomansland, where many of his followers gathered around him. Sidoi's did likewise after he fled from the colonial forces in 1857.[12] Across the Mzimkulu, the two groups continued a bickering warfare of raid and counter-raid, into which the Griqua were drawn for two main reasons. First, a group of "Hottentots", who had been rebels on the Kat River and who were led by Smith Pommer, fell foul of the Bhaca under Mdutyana because of their random cattle raiding from their base near Mount Currie. These men naturally assimilated to the Griqua on their arrival, for Pommer had been in contact with Kok before the trek. As Pommer gained a position of eminence within Griqua society, in consequence of his following and force of personality, the Griqua naturally became party to his quarrels.[13] Furthermore, a party of Griqua, who appear to have been on a hunting trip over the Berg in advance of the main trek, were massacred by Bhaca who stormed a laager that included Griqua as well as the Hlangweni who had been raiding Bhaca cattle.[14]

Rival Claimants to Nomansland
The Griqua were by no means the only people who coveted and moved into Nomansland around 1860. As one of the few areas of empty country in South Africa, it was widely desired at a time when the increase of population made land much scarcer than heretofore. The various "coloureds" either in Pommer's following or among the more peaceable inhabitants of Pearcetown, on the Ibesi River, or in the Gatberg were not, however, the greatest threat to Griqua hegemony, for this came from Nehemiah Moshweshwe, who from 1859 onwards had been attempting to set up a principality around Matatiele. He had moved down from Lesotho in part in an attempt to forestall the establishment of a rival Sotho state under Letele, the senior Kwena chief, and Lehana, successor to

Sekonyella as head of the Tlokwa.[15] The frustrations of being a highly able junior son, who had no chance of power within the Sotho state, must also have weighed with him. Nehemiah could not by himself command much force – according to Sir Walter Currie, he had but 50 fighting men with him in 1861[16] – but he could call on the numbers and experience of Lesotho, and above all of the mountain bandits of the south, notably Poshuli, whose power had already been exercised over the Drakensberg against the Mpondomise.[17] Moreover he was attempting to fill the same niche as the Griqua themselves, as educated overlord of the Bantu-speaking tribes, and was, so it was rumoured, in cahoots with the Mpondo to drive out the Griqua, for the better division of Nomansland.[18] It is thus not surprising that a "regular system of stealing developed between Nehemiah's followers and those of Adam Kok". With the outbreak of the war between the Sotho and the Orange Free State at the beginning of 1865, Nehemiah's position became untenable, for it had always rested on the power across the mountains that was now fully engaged, and the smallest show of Griqua force, not even directly aimed at him, was sufficient to drive him away.[19] Thus the Griqua position was secured, and further enhanced at Sotho expense when a highly successful raid was launched on the Sotho flocks and herds that had been moved to the highlands, away from the Free State armies. The economic resurgence of the Griqua, such as it was, dates from this raid.[20]

With the threat of competition from Nehemiah removed, and their own level of subsistence, which had been very greatly reduced by the rigours of the trek and the difficulties of accustoming themselves and their stock to the new environment, increasing, the Griqua were able to cope effectively with those amongst whom they lived. They could not, evidently, treat all their neighbours in like fashion. Although they had managed to baulk Natal's efforts to gain control over Nomansland and had thus incurred a long-lasting enmity, the Griqua had to maintain a façade of politeness towards the Natal government, and to refrain from open conflict. Their own position depended in part on the prestige that they gained from the British connection, for in an ill-defined and informal way the British were, even before annexation, the arbiters of inter-tribal rivalries throughout the Transkei. The intense dislike the Griqua felt for Natal was well known by the Cape Government and in London, and so, aided by the possibility of playing Cape Town off against Pietermaritzburg, Adam Kok was able to keep the Natalians out of his territory. On one occasion he even sought to increase the extent that was recognised as his by granting some, which was refused as too paltry, to Natal.[21] Border incidents were not infrequent, especially after Natal annexed Alfred county in 1866, for this area formed the route by which Griqua raided Mpondo and were raided by them.[22] The fulminations of successive governors of Natal against the iniquities of Griqua rule in Nomansland perhaps increased the odium in which the community was held, and so lessened their chances of continued independence.

A similar relationship of hostile neutrality existed between the Griqua and the Mpondo. Both of these powers, as also Natal, had as their ultimate aim suzerainty over the eastern Transkei, and Faku had protested as vigorously and as unavailingly as Shepstone or Scott against the Griqua trek.[23] Nevertheless, although the Griqua did not scruple to aid Jojo of the Xesibe or the Nci in their attempts to gain their independence from Faku – because of the cattle forthcoming from the various raids, if for no other reason – neither Adam Kok and his councillors, nor Faku, Mqikela, his successor, and theirs, dared commit significant resources to a challenge of the other party. In part this arose from a mutual acknowledgement of military parity. The Griqua were always conscious of their own lack of numbers, and had not succeeded in building a large enough following among the subject African populations to cope with the strength of the Mpondo who, in their turn, realised that the cannon and mounted riflemen of the Griqua constituted the single most effective force in the Transkei.[24] In addition, of course, the eyes of the British, both in the

Cape and in Natal, were on the relationship, and would not permit an open struggle for paramountcy between them, for the British had settled the border lines between the two powers and, in the interests both of prestige and border security, wished these to be maintained. The Natal government was thus instrumental in settling one particular bout of cattle raiding through the Ingeli mountains.[25] It can thus be seen that both Griqua and Mpondo leaders realised that they did not operate in a political vacuum, and could not afford to base their calculations on such an assumption. Forces external to the pure problems of diplomatic mechanics were too great to be disregarded, if any desired solution was to be achieved. North of the Ingeli mountains, such constraints operated much more loosely. It was over the modern districts of Umzimkulu, Mount Currie, Mount Frere, Matatiele, Mount Fletcher and perhaps Mount Ayliff, that the Griqua attempted to establish their hegemony, while trying to build up a following among the "coloureds", many of them of Griqua origin, in the Gatberg, modern Maclear. Rather over 2 000 Griqua were thus to be an aristocracy over more than 40 000 Africans.[26] The task of control was immense, although the fact that many of the African tribes only arrived in the area after the Griqua themselves eased the problem somewhat. Only Umzimkulu and Mount Frere were at all thickly populated in 1860, for Mount Fletcher was settled in 1869 as a deliberate move on the part of the British Government to reduce the pressure on land in the Witteberg reserve while Matatiele, which contained a few Sotho at the time of the Griqua trek, received many more as the 1860s progressed, particularly in the aftermath of the Orange Free State-Sotho war.

The Nature of Griqua rule
It is important to note that Griqualand remained, even as late as the 1870s, an open society, in that it received individuals of whatever background. It is thus rather difficult to write of the "Griqua", as distinct from the "Bantu" or the "Africans", for there were many people whom it would be difficult to assign to any category. Jan July, for

instance, was born a Sotho, and may well have died one, for he was prominent in the Basotho rebellion of 1880, unlike almost all other Griqua, but, having gained the confidence of Adam Kok, he was a leading figure in the Griqua government from the trek to annexation, and became a *Veld Kornet*.[27] It would appear that his case was not unique, but rather that a steady trickle of persons of Sotho or Nguni origin, who had for some reason or other become detached from their original society, was accepted into the Griqua community. Although there was a clear distinction made between those who lived a "tribal" life and were thus liable for hut-tax, and those who were "Griqua" and eligible for a "plaas", the line could be crossed by individuals in both directions.

Donald Strachan was an example of this ambiguity. Ethnically he was undoubtedly white, being a first generation immigrant from Europe, and he was always accepted as such by the white community of Natal and the Cape, for he served for a time as magistrate under the Cape Government, was a member of a major parliamentary commission and was for one session M.L.A. for East Griqualand. As against this, he was a Griqua burgher throughout the 1860s and 1870s, having preceded the Griqua into Nomansland, setting up a successful trading business for himself and his brother Thomas. He was so far accepted that they made him both *Veld Kornet* and Magistrate over Umzimkulu, where he lived.[28] Moreover, he was highly fluent in all the Bantu dialects with which he came into contact, and was trusted enough to be able to build up a regiment of Africans under his personal command.[29] The precise composition of this body is unfortunately unknown, but no doubt many of its members were men without affiliation or power in the tribal system, who looked to Strachan and through him to the Griqua captaincy for status and for law.

This was one of the ways in which the African population of Umzimkulu was brought under the Griqua system of control. Some members of small kraals accepted the control of whoever was able to impose it. The great proportion of the inhabitants of Umzimkulu were, however, either Bhaca or Hlangweni. Sidoi, as we have seen, was always a firm ally of the Griqua, especially as the fortunes of Smith Pommer, his closest acquaintance and partner, waxed within the captaincy. For all that Sidoi had married a daughter of the Bhaca chief Ncaphayi,[30] the Hlangweni alliance between him and Fodo appears to have held, and Fodo maintained a close relationship to the Griqua, perhaps in part because they gave him support against his brother Nondabula. In this case, however, it is difficult to see who was using whom, for Fodo and his son, Nkisiwana, were able to exploit the divisions between Pommer and Donald Strachan, so that they gave Pommer the chance to move into Strachan's ward and "eat up" Nondabula. Strachan, in fact, appears to have been able to prevent the relevant Griqua government commission coming to a decision, for, in the relationship of power then current at Mount Currie, any definite outcome would have gone against him.[31]

The Bhaca of Umzimkulu present an even more complicated picture. Essentially, the Griqua attempted to divide and rule, but although their divisive techniques were highly successful, this did not increase their ability to rule, as both the occasions on which they attempted to impose their authority led merely to the emigration of the chief whom they were disciplining, along with his followers. On the first occasion, on the death of Mdutyana, the Bhaca under him showed all the classic symptoms of impending fission. The chief of the great house, Cijisiwe, was a minor, as was the chief of the right hand house, Nomtsheketshe, who had been favoured by his father. Thiba, the uncle and regent, was thus in a strong position, until Nomtsheketshe came of age, when he returned from living with another section of the Bhaca people and demanded an inheritance to which he was not strictly entitled. After a certain amount of fighting between the two factions, the Griqua imposed a solution, dividing the Bhaca people between Nomtsheketshe and Thiba, while the two protagonists were fined one and four hundred cattle respectively.[32] The Griqua government were no doubt highly gratified at establishing a puppet, for Thiba had previously displayed reluctance in the vital matter of paying taxes.[33] This rebounded against them, however, for in the next year, an attempt to collect a small fine from Thiba was prosecuted with considerable vigour, Thiba himself showed signs of resistance, and on the appearance of a large Griqua force he fled across the river into Natal, with most of his followers and stock.[34] Although a fair number of these Bhaca later returned to their old lands, where, chiefless, they were more easily governable, many others, including Thiba and Cijisiwe, remained in Natal, or began engaging in such activities as transport riding, which later enabled them to buy up Griqua farms.[35] Nomtsheketshe, in his turn, fell foul of the Griqua authorities some two years later, apparently for condoning the smelling out of witches, which resulted in the burning of two. He was forced to move to Pondoland, although, again, the evidence suggests that many of his followers remained in Umzimkulu.[36]

West of the main Griqua settlements, the Sotho who filled the country did so on the understanding that they came under Griqua authority, even though they later claimed that such authority was bestowed by the British government. As has been noted, the greatest influx came during and after the Free State War, as was the case with the most important of these, Magwai, whose "mountain fortress" was stormed in December 1867,[37] while other headmen, such as Mosi Lipheana and Letuka Morosi, had been in the area since the expulsion of Nehemiah.[38] By 1875, Matatiele district contained, according to the census, 5 728 Sotho and 2 529 Mfengu, who had drifted up from the west, seeking land, or, in at least one notable case, refuge.[39]

These groups were all small, unlike the three units that migrated from Herschel district into Mount Fletcher at the instance of Sir Philip Wodehouse in 1868. There they remained and the Griqua never seem to have made any attempt to impose their control over any of them, although the squabbles between Lehana, the Tlokwa chief, and the

Mpondomise, and between him, Lebenya, a Sotho leader, and Zibi, the Hlubi chief, may well have been sufficient to allow effective intervention, had the area remained independent much longer. In that case events may well have taken the course exemplified by Griqua dealings with Makaula, the Bhaca chief who lived in Mount Frere. Although initially he and the Griqua had been moderately amicable, as the Griqua became more securely settled in Nomansland relations deteriorated, and, almost inevitably, a series of cattle raids and counter-raids developed. On the Griqua side, these were conducted primarily, so it would seem, by Mfengu and Sotho from Matatiele, rather than by Griqua themselves. A certain Ncukana, a Hlubi, was the most prominent of these raiders. This does not mean, however, that the Griqua did not realise what was going on, or were not responsible for the border warfare, for, as occurred when similar expeditions went into Pondoland, it was possible for the Griqua to restrain their subjects if necessary.[40] No doubt Makaula could have imposed similar restrictions on his border kraals should he so have desired. Both sides believed that they were right, and were able to convince their missionaries that they were. Thus William Dower at Mount Currie wrote:

> A Kaffir tribe lying on our northern border has been making frequent raids into Griqua territory, killing, burning and stealing and, as it turns out now, all with a view to provoke hostilities. Capt. Kok sent once and again a deputation or commission of peace, but without effect. I had hoped that an outbreak might be prevented but all efforts in that direction failed. Capt. Kok did not call out his commando before several of his subjects had been killed and several huts burnt down and a quantity of stock stolen, chiefly belonging to the Basuto residing under Adam Kok's rule.[41]

In contrast Charles White, the Wesleyan missionary with Makaula, related that "Makaula says it is because he stopped the stealing of cattle from Natal and sent them back that Adam Kok has sent his army laying his country waste."[42] At all events, the Griqua commando, which, as it only comprised burghers of two *Veld Kornetcies* and the Africans from across the Mzimvubu, was far from the largest force the Griqua could field,[43] rampaged through Makaula's country, burnt a large number of huts and captured in all 1 400 cattle, 500 horses and 1 700 sheep,[44] with the consequence that Makaula soon sued for peace, as he and his followers had been driven over the Tina River into Mpondomise country.

The war with the Bhaca was the last time that the Griqua had to assert their authority. In general, in fact, they were able to rule Nomansland with remarkably little difficulty. This was for four main reasons. In the first place, they were obviously more formidable than any African tribe on its own, and the Transkei was sufficiently split between various factions and sub-tribes to make large scale alliance against the Griqua impossible. Secondly, the Griqua were moderately astute in their handling of these factional differences, so that some, at least, of the African tribes held to the Griqua in order to use them against other Africans. Thirdly, the Griqua controlled what was by the 1860s the only land in the area that was still unoccupied, and thus had a valuable asset with which the loyalties of landless men could be secured. Fourthly, the duties that the Griqua imposed on those who came under their rule were far from heavy, although they were vital to the survival of the Griqua in Nomansland. The military service was scarcely onerous, especially as it was frequently directed against those who were the old or recent enemies of the militia itself. It was perhaps a greater strain on the loyalties of the Africans when they were forbidden to indulge in what were potentially highly lucrative cattle raids.[45] Thus the Griqua had little difficulty in compensating for their own lack of numbers, for all that African troops do not ever seem to have been as effective in the field as the Griqua themselves.

The Griqua also felt a duty to impose a code of laws more in accord with the ways of the Cape Colony – of Christian civilisation as they saw it – than with the traditional systems of the peoples they ruled. In part this was to avoid the taunt of savagery that was being hurled at them by Natalians who coveted their farms, but the Griqua had a long history of imitating white ways of government. Adam Kok did, however, realise that the imposition of new laws might strain the legal competence of his state beyond the limit, and thus initially virtually all the judicial functions remained with the chiefs, and were only gradually transferred to the courts run by the Griqua at the centre of the captaincy. Thus it was announced that murder would be made a capital offence well in advance of the actual implementation of the promulgation, while the major crime that the Griqua were concerned to stamp out was the practice of "smelling out" for witchcraft, which, as it had been an integral part of the system of social control, was of considerable moment.[46] Although, increasingly, large-scale theft was brought under the jurisdiction of the Griqua, who had, of course, always been prepared to bring chiefs to their own justice when they considered it expedient, the routine running of affairs in the locations remained in the hands of Africans. Thus local customs as to marriage, land tenure and so forth (of which the Griqua were ignorant) might be maintained, while the expensive use of interpreters, who were necessary in the Griqua courts, was obviated. Disputes between Griqua and African were, however, always dealt with by the Griqua judiciary. Despite this they by no means invariably resulted in the verdict going to the Griqua party, as even the most prominent officials on government business might be arraigned for misuse of their powers.[47] There was even an African chief, Mosi Lipheana, who was dignified by the title of *Veld Kornet,* primarily because he had among his entourage an Irishman by the name of Paddy O'Reilly, who could conduct the business of that office,[48] but in general the local officials were Griqua who attempted to use their prestige to maintain order in difficult border areas, for they were normally of high rank.[49]

Lastly and most importantly, the Africans under Griqua rule were required to pay a hut-tax, variously reported as 5/- or 7/6 per hut. By 1874, approximately 43% of Griqua government income came from this source.[50] Indeed, the escape of the Griqua from debt, which had been nearly accomplished by the time of the British take-over, was largely a consequence of the hut-tax, which might be paid in kind if no cash was available. For non-payment individuals might be driven out, but, in fact, the amount of resistance to the Griqua authorities was remarkably small. Only Thiba ever raised major objections and even they were not so much against the principle of paying taxes as against the government he was paying. Probably the fact that most of the Africans in Nomansland were immigrants is important. Many must have paid such taxes before, whether in the Cape Colony or in Natal, and so become accustomed to such practices.

The settlements upon which these taxes were levied were almost invariably designated locations, upon which there was a certain amount of pressure from land-hungry Griqua, who may well have hoped to raise income from rents to the same Africans. More than anyone it was the Kaptyn himself who contained this pressure,[51] probably because he was more aware of the need for the Griqua nation to placate those among whom they lived than were many of his subjects. Africans who lived on Griqua farms might be expelled by the owner, but interlopers into locations other than their own suffered similarly.[52] The pattern of aristocratic rule was thus complete, even if the Griqua were far too poor ever to be aristocrats, and took much less care about restricting the movements of those under their rule than those across the border in Natal, for the Griqua government only issued passes to those who required such documents for travel in Natal or the Cape Colony.[53]

Obviously, in the short time that they had at their disposal – barely ten years – the Griqua were unable to develop unquestioning acceptance of their rule among their subjects. Their rule was still very definitely backed by the threat and the need for force. In this of course, they were no different from the British who succeeded them. The Griqua were poorer than the British, they did not have the might of the British empire behind them, and they could not use missionaries or traders to establish their power. But they had less to distract them, for their responsibilities were far narrower, they had more officials in the area, officials, moreover, who had a tighter grasp of the African reality than many colonial dignitaries, and they were not bedevilled to the same extent by inconvenient racial attitudes. But, as intruding powers, aided by the rifle and the chancery, in their attempts to establish dominance the Griqua and the British had much in common. The possible permutations of colonial rule were not that large, for the population that was being ruled remained unchanged, except through the passage of time, and the ruling groups emanated from the same cultural, if not political, tradition.

FOOTNOTES

1. D. A. Low, *Lion Rampant* (London 1973) ch. 1.
2. For elaboration of this theme see M. C. Legassick, The Griqua, the Sotho-Tswana and the Missionaries (Ph.D. UCLA 1969) chs. VII, VIII.
3. See J. B. Wright, *Bushman Raiders of the Drakensberg* (Pietermaritzburg 1972) pp. 114–138.
4. *Cape Parl. Papers,* A 118, 1861, p. 7: Pine to Governor-General, 25 Nov. 1850.
5. *Ibid,* pp. 19–21: Sir George Grey to Newcastle, 19 Feb. 1861.
6. M. Wilson, The Early History of the Transkei and Ciskei, *African Studies* 18 (4) 1959, pp. 175–8.
7. P. L. Carter, Late Stone Age Exploitation Patterns in Southern Natal, *S. Afr. Arch. Bull.* 1971.
8. Wright, *Bushman Raiders,* ch. 6.
9. He was also known as Silonyana. As he was a minor, his half-brother Diko ruled initially. See W. D. Hammond-Tooke, *The Tribes of Mount Frere District* (Pretoria 1955) pp. 42–3.
10. See D. G. L. Cragg, The Relations of the Amampondo and the Colonial Authorities (D.Phil. Oxford 1959) pp. 94–6.
11. This section may perhaps go some way towards answering the questions about the involvement of the two groups in the revolt of 1896 raised by C. van Onselen in his article Reactions to Rinderpest in Southern Africa in *J.A.H.* XIII (3) 1972, p. 479.
12. See *South African Archival Records, Natal No. II* (Cape Town 1960) pp. 110–21. Also D. Welsh, *The Roots of Segregation* (Cape Town 1972) pp. 112, 120–1; A. T. Bryant, *Olden Times in Zululand and Natal* (London 1929) pp. 351–2.

13. R. Richards, Pommer and Sidoi, *Natal Magazine* 1879, pp. 317–24.
14. Hulley Papers (Killie Campbell Library, Durban), sec. 3.
15. J. van der Poel, Basutoland as a Factor in South African Politics, *AYB,* 1941, I, 184–5.
16. Currie to Grey, 29 June 1861, encl. in Grey to Newcastle, 12 July 1861, G.H. 28/76 (Cape Archives).
17. G. Theal, ed., *Basutoland Records,* II (Cape Town 1883) 588–93: Memo of J. M. Orpen, 26 June 1861.
18. *Cape Parl. Papers,* G 16, 1876, pp. 96–7: Special commissioners to the Col. Sec. 25 Oct. 1875.
19. *Ibid.*
20. Thomas Jenkins, the Wesleyan Missionary with the Mpondo, heard that the Griqua took 1 700 cattle, 1 300 sheep and 300 horses (Wesleyan Methodist Missionary Society Archives, S.A. Box XX: Jenkins to Secs. 27 Dec. 1865); Donald Strachan, who knew the Griqua better, gives the same figures, except that he claims they took 6 000 sheep (*Cape Parl. Papers,* G 58, 1879, p. 51).
21. *Cape Parl. Papers,* G 58, 1879 (Report of a Commission into the Recent Outbreak in Griqualand East), pp. 58–9: Wodehouse, Memo. of Agreement, 10 March 1869.
22. See, e.g., Shepstone to Harding, 18 Jan. 1871, encl. in Keate to Barkly, 10 August 1871, G.H. 9/9 (Cape Archives).
23. Jenkins, for Mqikela, to Grey, n.d., G.H. 8/48 (Cape Archives).
24. The success of Mhlontlo in defeating Mditshwa in the Mpondomise feud demonstrated the success of such troops (see W. D. Hammond-Tooke, The "other side" of frontier history, in L. Thompson, ed., *African Societies in Southern Africa* (London 1969) p. 241).
25. On this see the voluminous correspondence in the Natal Archives (S.N.A. files 1/1/24, 1/1/25).
26. Figures from census returns after annexation and are highly approximate (see *Cape Parl. Papers,* G 27, 1874, p. 55; G 17, 1878, pp. 72–3).
27. *Cape Parl. Papers,* G 37, 1876 (Report of a Commission into the Affairs of Griqualand East), pp. 63–4; G.O.3, 10 May 1872 (Cape Archives).
28. Perhaps Adam Kok was influenced in this by the fact that this particular area contained many white settlers and Africans and few Griqua.
29. *Cape Parl. Papers,* G 58, 1879, p. 28.
30. Hammond-Tooke, *Tribes of Mount Frere,* p. 44.
31. E. Stafford to Henrique Shepstone (magistrate of Alfred County), n.d. (7 March 1871) and H. Shepstone to S.N.A. Natal, 9 March 1871, encl. in Keate to Barkly, 10 August 1871, G.H. 9/9 (Cape Archives).
32. Meeting of 22 Jan. 1868 in G.O.1 (Cape Archives) and *Natal Witness,* 14 Jan. 1868.
33. He "did not feel like paying Hottentots" (statement of Duta and Mehlwana, 14 March 1865, encl. in Maclean to Wodehouse, 28 March 1865, G.H. 9/6 (Cape Archives)).

34. There is a voluminous correspondence on this episode in G.H. 9/8 (Cape Archives).
35. See R. Hulley to Resident Magistrate, Umzimkulu, 28 March 1956 (courtesy of Prof. W. D. Hammond-Tooke).
36. Hulley Papers.
37. A. Atmore, The Passing of Sotho Independence, in Thompson, ed., *African Societies,* p. 65.
38. G.O.1, 30 Jan. 1866 (Cape Archives).
39. *Cape Parl. Papers,* G 21, 1875, p. 119.
40. The Griqua in fact declared the injuries done to Ncukana the chief cause of the war (Gedye to Shepstone, 23 Sept. 1871, encl. in Keate to Barkly, 7 Oct. 1871, G.H. 9/9 (Cape Archives)).
41. Dower to Mullen, 12 Oct. 1871, S.A. Box 35/5/B (L.M.S. Archives).
42. White to Shepstone, 29 Sept. 1871, in Keate to Barkly, 7 Oct. 1871, G.H. 9/9 (Cape Archives).
43. G.O.1, 5 Sept. 1871 (Cape Archives).
44. G.O.9 (Cape Archives).
45. Kok to Letuka Morosi, Stephanus Lepheane, Lebu Lepheane and Mosi Lepheane, 30 Jan. 1867, G.O.1 (Cape Archives).
46. This section follows the evidence of G. C. Brisley to the Commission on Native Laws and Customs *(Cape Parl. Papers,* G 4, 1883, pp. 510–2); it is confirmed by the records of the case of Monjonjo's murder (G.O.4, 15 July 1871 (Cape Archives)).
47. G.O.1, 8 Sept. 1866, Dioi vs "Rooi" Jan Pienaar (Cape Archives).
48. G.O.9, hut tax record for 1867 (Cape Archives). O'Reilly's "real" name was Murphy (see *Kokstad Advertiser,* 19 Dec. 1902).
49. *Cape Parl. Papers,* G 58, 1879, p. 50.
50. *Cape Parl. Papers,* G 21, 1875: Memo. of Brisley, 15 Oct. 1874.
51. *Cape Parl. Papers,* G 16, 1876, p. 9: Special commissioners to Col. Sec. 25 Oct. 1875.
52. G.O.3, 5 Sept. 1872: complaints of J. de Vreis and Sakopula (Cape Archives).
53. See book of passes in G.O.9 (Cape Archives).

Adam Kok III (1811–75), Griqua kaptyn.

▲ *Tiyo Soga (1829-71), African missionary.*

PLATE 12

6

THE RÔLE OF THE WESLEYAN MISSIONARIES IN RELATIONS BETWEEN THE MPONDO AND THE COLONIAL AUTHORITIES

D. G. L. Cragg

THE third decade of the nineteenth century was a period of transition for the Mpondo.[1] On two occasions the impis of Shaka swept the area: in the early twenties they chased the Mpondo to the western bank of the Mzimvubu; and in June 1828 drove them from their kraals and plundered their cattle. Mpondo ambassadors were sent to offer submission to Shaka and were present when he was murdered by Dingane and his associates on 22 September 1828. Even more disruptive than these Zulu attacks was the incursion of refugees from the northeast. Some passed through Pondoland to the regions beyond; others settled among the Mpondo and eventually became part of the chiefdom; yet others, notably the Bhaca, maintained their independence against strong opposition. These migrations led to continual conflict and a considerable disorganisation of tribal life even after the Zulu threat had ceased to matter.

The Mfecane destroyed an old order. At the same time there were hints of a new age. White men settled at Port Natal in 1824, and one of their number, Henry Francis Fynn, became a regular visitor to Pondoland.[2] Other traders came from the direction of Cape Colony. In 1828 the Mpondo chief, Faku[3], received an official visit from a British officer who was hoping to meet Zulu messengers.[4] With a white trading outpost at Port Natal and a growing British community in the Eastern Cape, such contacts were likely to multiply and to bring further changes in the Mpondo way of life.

It was at this juncture that the Wesleyan mission arrived in Pondoland. Its leader was the Rev. William Shaw who had come to South Africa in 1820 as chaplain to the Sephton party of British settlers.[5] He had made all Albany his parish and organised a lively Wesleyan Church among the settlers. From the outset he planned to establish a chain of mission stations from the Cape to Natal. Towards the end of 1823 he settled at Wesleyville among the Gqunukhwebe. Further links in the chain were forged in 1825, 1827 and 1829; and in May 1829 Shaw visited Faku and received permission for a mission to the Mpondo. Faku's eagerness for a missionary is reflected in the Mpondo tradition that he fetched the missionaries from Grahamstown with an elephant tusk. This enthusiasm had little to do with religion. Shaka had boasted white friends and the possession of a missionary was becoming a status-symbol in the Transkei. He was likely to be an asset in the struggle for supremacy among the chiefdoms and in dealings with the white man.

Shaw returned to Pondoland a year later with the Rev. W. B. Boyce[6] who established Buntingville, near the Great Place. There were four changes of missionary in the first eight years and little was achieved. However, in 1838 the Rev. Thomas Jenkins,[7] an Albany settler, began a ministry among the Mpondo which ended only with his death in 1868. Jenkins became a close friend of Faku and won enormous respect among the Mpondo. In the late thirties Faku moved his Great Place to the Quakeni, which was east of the Mzimvubu River. Jenkins followed him in 1845 and established Palmerton. In 1862 he also began the Mfundisweni Mission at the chief's request.[8]

After Jenkins' death the London headquarters of the Wesleyan Methodist Missionary Society refused to appoint an adequate successor, and the mission in Eastern Pondoland became a neglected backwater, staffed by well-meaning but ineffective young men.[9] There was a change for the better in 1882 when the Rev. Peter Hargreaves moved to Mfundisweni. Hargreaves had spent twenty years at Clarkebury in Thembuland where he had gained considerable influence with the local chiefs. His experience and reputation were a great advantage in the confused years which culminated in the annexation of Pondoland in 1894.[10]

The missionary rôle
The purpose of this chapter is to examine the rôle of the Wesleyan missionaries in the relationships between the Mpondo and the colonial authorities at the Cape and Natal in the period outlined above. The average Wesleyan was not a politician by inclination. His aim was evangelistic; his concern was the souls of his people. Moreover, his political activities were inhibited by very definite instructions from his society:

> We cannot omit, without neglecting our duty, to warn you against meddling with political matters or secular disputes. You are teachers of religion and that alone should be kept in view.[11]

These instructions were re-affirmed after the unpleasant interlude of the frontier war in 1834–5,[12] but were interpreted very broadly. It was, in fact, impossible for a missionary beyond the colonial frontier to dissociate himself completely from secular affairs. In the early days he was usually the only white man resident with the chiefdom and was certainly the best educated and most trustworthy. He thus became a means of communication between Government and chiefdom, writing letters for the chief and transmitting messages from colonial officials. A respected missionary would not long remain a mere amanuensis. The chief would ask his advice in dealing with the whites, and the Government would welcome information and consider his opinions. Moreover, secular affairs affected the welfare of the mission and the missionary was usually ready to advocate policies which advanced his cause and to criticise those which retarded it.

Shaw and Jenkins

This was the case in the first twenty-six years of the mission to the Mpondo. William Shaw superintended the Wesleyan Mission in South-east Africa until 1856. He had won universal respect as pastor of the Albany Settlement, and his missionary activities had given him considerable knowledge of affairs beyond the frontier. He had the ear of most Governors of the Cape, corresponding with them on frontier affairs and approaching them directly when they came to Grahamstown. On the other hand, he was trusted by Faku, who also relied increasingly upon Thomas Jenkins as the years went by. The conditions for missionary influence upon relationships between the Mpondo and the colonial authorities were well-nigh ideal.

The attitudes and actions of Shaw and Jenkins were shaped by four inter-related factors. They wanted to defend the land of the Mpondo and their neighbours from white encroachment; to ensure that they were treated justly; to establish peace between peoples constantly quarrelling with each other; and to promote the work of the Wesleyan Mission. Such humanitarian considerations carried weight in the age of Buxton and had some attraction for governors like Sir George Napier and Sir Peregrine Maitland. But it would be wrong to overestimate their importance. Even in the heyday of humanitarianism they only shaped government policy if they were supported by other factors which appealed more strongly to the colonial authorities. One such factor was the security of the Eastern Frontier, and the missionaries were at pains to show that this would be enhanced by the security and friendship of the Mpondo.

This analysis of the missionary rôle may be illustrated by three incidents. Shaw had been disturbed by the attitude of the Voortrekkers to the land-rights of the blacks. When they arrived in Natal he was afraid that they would encroach upon the Mpondo. He therefore informed the Cape Governor, Sir George Napier, that Faku claimed the Mzimkulu River as his boundary and suggested that any encroachment upon his territory would push the Mpondo down upon the frontier and cause trouble for the Colony. Napier noted the possibility but gave a non-committal reply, for there was no immediate danger. It was different in December 1840 when a Voortrekker commando attacked the Bhaca chief, Ncaphayi,[13] in reprisal for alleged cattle-thieving, and carried off a number of captives and a considerable amount of livestock. The missionaries on the spot reported the incident to Shaw in great detail and with reasonable objectivity. They also forwarded an appeal for protection from Faku, who feared that his turn would be next. Shaw passed on the correspondence to Napier whose humanitarian instincts were shocked by what he read. More important, however, was Faku's appeal for protection. Ncaphayi had the reputation of a freebooter and might have deserved his fate; Faku was a friend of the Colony who deserved protection. Moreover, should the Mpondo be attacked and driven in upon the Xhosa, the Eastern Frontier would be endangered. Napier was therefore quite ready to adopt Shaw's proposal that a British force be stationed near the Mzimvubu River to maintain order. It would warn the Voortrekkers without infringing the boundaries they claimed; and it would enhance frontier security by placing a garrison in the rear of the Xhosa.

This affair was a turning point in Napier's dealings with the Voortrekkers at Natal. There had been a remote hope of negotiations before the incident, but this was now banished beyond recall. Furthermore, Napier became very sensitive to any threat to the integrity of Pondoland. When the Natal Volksraad proposed in August 1841 to remove "surplus" Africans from Natal to the area between the Mzimvubu and Mthamvuna Rivers, Napier detected a threat to the Eastern Frontier. This influenced his decision in December 1841 to occupy Port Natal. By linking the claims of humanitarianism and of frontier security, the missionaries had focussed official attention on the Mpondo and significantly affected the fortunes of the Republic of Natal.[14]

Another illustration of the convergence of missionary

motives and political considerations was the Treaty of Amity with the Mpondo which was signed by Governor Sir Peregrine Maitland at Fort Beaufort in October 1844 and approved by Faku in December of that year.[15] This document was a masterpiece of paternalism: it was drawn up apparently without any discussion with the Mpondo, to whom it was simply presented and explained; and the real parties to the negotiations were the Government and the Wesleyan missionaries. It is possible that William Shaw suggested the treaty and even prepared a draft. He was certainly in close touch with Governor Maitland at the time, and was responsible for a number of features in the treaty. The Mpondo Treaty State, which was guaranteed "against all claims or pretensions ... of British subjects", was defined as the area between the Mthatha and Mzimkulu Rivers, and the Khahlamba (Drakensberg) Mountains and the sea. When the Governor left Cape Town for the Eastern Province in September 1844, the south-western boundary of Natal had not yet been decided, and the choice of the Mzimkulu River probably owed much to Shaw, who had repeatedly urged Faku's claim upon the Government. The state included large areas which were either empty or occupied by virtually independent groups, but the missionaries' aim was to protect African rather than narrowly Mpondo interests, and to allow for an expanding population. This explains a further provision which protected the existing rights of petty chiefs within the Treaty State. Shaw later claimed responsibility for this article and there is no reason to doubt him. We may also detect missionary influence in an article which bound Faku to settle inter-tribal disputes by peaceful means and to call for British mediation should his just rights be violated. The suppression of tribal warfare mattered much to the Wesleyans but hardly affected a distant Colonial Government. Finally, it is hardly conceivable that the article protecting both missionaries and their converts had any other than a missionary origin.

These humanitarian provisions were laudable, but they would hardly have persuaded the Governor to conclude a treaty. In fact he believed that there were good political reasons for doing so. The Mpondo would occupy a similar position on the southwestern boundary of Natal to the Xhosa on the Cape Eastern Frontier. It was therefore sensible to make similar arrangements for the return of stolen stock and the apprehension of criminals. Even more important in Napier's eyes was the need for an ally against the frontier tribes whose restlessness had brought him to the Eastern Cape. He was led to believe that the Mpondo were more powerful than the Xhosa, and that an alliance with the former would discourage the latter from attacking the Colony. Experience was to prove this an empty hope, but it seemed reasonable enough at the time, and Maitland naïvely remarked to the Secretary of State for the Colonies that "the good effects of [the knowledge of the alliance] were speedily seen in the submissive spirit of the more refractory part of the kaffirs."[16]

A third illustration of the missionaries' rôle is their struggle to maintain the integrity of the Treaty State.[17] There was a distinct possibility in 1848–50 that all or some of it would be swallowed by the whites. In February 1848 the High Commissioner, Sir Harry Smith, visited Natal in an attempt to check the departure of Voortrekkers who were disgruntled with British rule. In a fit of shortsighted generosity he promised large farms to all who would stay and declared that the blacks should be segregated from the whites. The land commissioners who had to find the necessary land soon revived the old scheme of a native settlement between the Mzimkulu and Mzimvubu Rivers. The threat to Pondoland was intensified by the pressure of immigration, for Sir Harry himself encouraged the idea that it was available for white settlement. In 1849 he was actually considering its acquisition for a Roman Catholic settlement sponsored by the Earl of Arundel.

Shaw was aware of these developments. He knew that he would be powerless to defeat a scheme which was approved by Sir Harry Smith, although he was prepared to appeal to public opinion in the Cape should the Arundel scheme involve convicts. However, Shaw was determined that any alteration to the boundary should be done openly and fairly.

In April 1850 Walter Harding visited Pondoland as a representative of the Natal Government. Among other things he asked Faku to cede to Natal the area between the Mthamvuna and Mzimkulu Rivers, and seems to have suggested that this would relieve him of responsibility for alleged stock thefts from Natal. Jenkins wanted Faku to delay until Shaw's advice could be obtained, but the chief was more anxious to shed responsibility than to retain sovereignty over an area which was not occupied by his own people. He therefore signed the cession, with Jenkins as a witness. The missionaries swallowed their disappointment and commended the country to divine providence. There was no attempt to dispute what had been done freely, openly and in writing.

They reacted differently to developments later in the year. In the interim Benjamin Pine had become Lieutenant-Governor of Natal. He quickly realised that the April cession had solved no problems: thefts were continuing; the newly-acquired land seemed useless for white settlement; and the Imperial Government had ruled out a native location west of the Mzimkulu. His solution was to insist that the Treaty should be strictly observed and, by showing Faku what this involved, to persuade the chief to hand over the entire area to Natal. Harding was therefore sent back to Pondoland with instructions to demand the restoration of all stolen cattle and compensation for any that were not found. This would amount to 1 024 head. Should Faku plead inability to meet his obligations, Harding was to offer the assistance of his party in dealing with recalcitrant chiefs. On paper it seemed straightforward enough. In practice it was bungled. Harding insisted that the cattle should be handed over *before* he would assist Faku; and Henry Fynn, who was now the British Resident, cajoled Faku into surrendering a portion of the fine and himself collected the balance from surrounding tribes. Faku was very annoyed, and said so.

He did not see why he should be responsible for the conduct of independent peoples simply because the Treaty made him "paramount chief" of a theoretical state. (The concept was ridiculous, anyhow, for a chief is paramount over people, not land). Fynn reproduced these sentiments in a letter which also begged the Government to "take the country under their management."[18] Faku apparently affixed his mark and it was sent after Harding.

Pine was elated with the success of his scheme. He assumed that Faku was offering all Pondoland to Natal, and asked Sir Harry Smith for immediate annexation. Meanwhile he returned 600 cattle to Faku and appointed a commission to examine the country for the purposes of immigration. He had reckoned without the missionaries! When Shaw heard of the affair he went straight to Sir Harry, who was in Grahamstown. The High Commissioner was annoyed that Pine should have acted without consulting him and asked the latter for a full report, "as the good faith of Faku for so many years deserves every consideration."[19] Significantly, he understood Faku's letter to Natal as a justifiable remonstrance and not as an offer of cession! There was further trouble in store. Jenkins had been in Pietermaritzburg at the time of the incident. When he returned to Palmerton he discussed it with Faku who categorically denied that he had agreed to the contents of the letter and protested against Fynn's behaviour. Jenkins thereupon wrote another letter for Faku which repudiated the alleged cession, stated his grievances and requested a copy of the earlier missive.

These blows from Grahamstown and Palmerton were enough to destroy Pine's scheme. The offer of land was forgotten, the cattle were returned, and the Treaty State remained intact. Clearly the missionaries had triumphed, but only because the political situation had favoured them. Smith was facing a dangerous situation on the Eastern Frontier where war broke out in December 1850, and he did not want to alienate an ally in the rear of the Xhosa. Furthermore, Pine had offended Smith's dignity. Had the

Lieutenant-Governor not acted unilaterally, it is doubtful whether the missionaries could have saved their Mpondo protege.

The period before 1856, therefore, saw missionary influence at its height. Shaw had the ear of the Cape Governors, and both he and Jenkins were trusted by Faku. Even so, their humanitarian plans were accepted only if they were commended by other considerations, and especially by the security of the Cape Eastern Frontier.

New tensions
A second stage in missionary influence extended from Shaw's return to England in 1856 to the deaths of Faku in 1867 and Jenkins in 1868. The situation differed in several respects from that which had prevailed in the earlier period. Shaw's successors in Grahamstown did not inherit his influence with the Government, and the Wesleyans and Faku therefore lost that immediate access to the Cape Governors which had been so important. The authorities respected Jenkins but it was easy to ignore his written representations. In Pondoland itself times were changing. Faku's great son, Mqikela,[20] was becoming more powerful, and his young men were less disposed to heed the missionary and less eager to please the Government. Moreover, Jenkins himself had been careful not to interfere in political matters except at the express request of Faku or the Government and had apparently relied greatly upon Shaw's advice. He now proved unwilling or unable to act decisively when events demanded it. Finally, the Cattle Killing of 1857 temporarily destroyed the military power of the Xhosa and so reduced the supposed value of the Mpondo as allies of the Cape Colony against the frontier chiefdoms. This removed a political consideration which had served the Mpondo well in the past.

In these circumstances it is not surprising that two points of tension arose which were to poison relationships between the Mpondo and the Cape for over twenty years. The first concerned the inland boundary of the Treaty

State.[21] Governor Sir George Grey proposed to settle Adam Kok and his Griqua on the unpeopled plateau south-east of the Drakensberg. At a fairly late stage the Governor was reminded that Faku was an interested party and sent Sir Walter Currie to settle matters with him. Currie met Faku in April 1861 and was elated with what transpired, for the latter suggested a revised inland boundary which would exclude from his control almost all the land between the Mzimkulu and Mthatha Rivers which was unoccupied or occupied by other chiefdoms. The chief clearly intended this as a basis for discussion, for he would not have settled the boundary between the Mzimvubu and Mthatha in the absence of his son, Ndamase, who controlled the area and was virtually independent. Moreover, on previous occasions such proposals had been confirmed by a written treaty. But Currie was a policeman, not a diplomat. He took Faku's proposal as a firm offer and did not bother to confirm it in writing. When the chief protested to Grey, Currie was sent back to settle matters. His second visit was a fiasco: he would not wait for Ndamase to arrive for the meeting; he maintained that a chief's word was as good as his writing; and he insisted that the time for discussion was past. This was all so unnecessary, for the Mpondo were only questioning details of the boundary in Ndamase's territory and were not going back on their proposal. They would have been satisfied by a full discussion, a few adjustments and a written document. They were not impressed by bullying. Jenkins advised the chief to ask for further discussions and himself wrote to the High Commissioner in these terms, but his representations were ignored. Unfortunately Jenkins did not persevere in his efforts. Even he could not have foreseen the ultimate effects of the dispute.

The other issue was the control of Port St Johns which came to the fore after 1860.[22] The port was valued not so much for what it was as for what it might become. It seemed likely to become the main outlet for the trade of the Transkei and was nearer to the Orange Free State, as the crow flies, than either Durban or Cape Town. Natal feared that its growing trade would adversely affect her own commerce and customs revenue, and was anxious about rumours of gun-running from the Cape. However, in the sixties the most important argument for British control was a fear that the Orange Free State would attempt to seize the port. This fear was insubstantial, but it underlay a tentative enquiry in 1861 and a definite approach to the Mpondo in 1866. Jenkins himself was not averse to British control which would have checked undesirable trade, but he realised that the Mpondo were suspicious and were afraid that it would lead to further encroachment on their land. In 1861 he advised Grey to drop the matter and the Governor complied. In 1866 Governor Wodehouse approached Faku through Jenkins' brother-in-law. Jenkins refused to advise the Mpondo one way or the other, for he did not want to drive a wedge between the mission and the people by giving unpopular advice. Whether he was wise to take this attitude is open to debate. It is clear, however, that his silence virtually assured a Mpondo refusal, and that this refusal further complicated relationships with the Cape.

It would be wrong to suppose that Jenkins was without influence in these latter years. His relationship with Faku was as close as ever, and the young men were not without respect for him. Nevertheless, he could not act effectively in two major crises, partly because of his own temperament and partly because he lacked Shaw's standing with the colonial authorities.

Influence lost

Wesleyan missionaries hardly figured in the political history of Pondoland in the third period which extended from 1868 to 1882.[23] We have already noted that mission headquarters refused to appoint an adequate successor to Jenkins, and that the work was carried on by well-meaning but ineffective young men. This meant that the political influence of the missionaries almost disappeared. Some of them acted as amanuenses for the new chief, Mqikela, and his advisers, but they were regarded as "children" by the Mpondo and discounted as ignorant by colonial officials.

This was particularly unfortunate because the decade after Jenkins' death was one of increasing contact and growing alienation between the Mpondo and the colonial authorities. The issues of the inland boundary and Port St Johns remained unsettled and became more explosive as the Cape advanced into the Transkei. When Griqualand East eventually came under the Cape Government in 1875, the Mpondo were brought into day-to-day contact with white authority along an artificial boundary. By 1878 relationships had broken down completely and the High Commissioner, Sir Bartle Frere, issued a proclamation which withdrew recognition of Mqikela as "paramount chief", declared British sovereignty over Port St Johns, and imposed a Resident who would transmit the orders of the Government to the Mpondo.[24] The Mpondo east of the Mzimvubu remained loyal to Mqikela and adopted an attitude of sullen non-co-operation, which was matched by unnecessary inflexibility on the part of the Cape which had badly misjudged the depth of tribal feeling.

The most distressing feature of these developments was the almost total lack of understanding between the parties concerned. From the early seventies the Mpondo were often unduly suspicious of colonial intentions, while Frere's attitude revealed an understanding of the past and of recent events that was extremely unfair to the Mpondo. Tragically there was nobody who had the confidence of both parties and could appreciate and explain the divergent points of view. Mrs Jenkins remained in Pondoland until her death in 1880, but she was dismissed as a passionate partisan of the Mpondo; whereas J. Oxley Oxland, the Anglican missionary in Pondoland, adopted the British point of view and counted for little with the tribe. A senior and respected Wesleyan missionary at Palmerton or Mfundisweni would probably have been a moderating influence, and the pennypinching policy of the Mission House was most unfortunate. It is ironical that the General Secretary responsible for this policy was none other than the Rev.

W. B. Boyce who had established Buntingville and had played an active part in frontier politics during his years in South Africa.

Hargreaves and a revival of influence
The political influence of the Wesleyan Mission revived somewhat during the ministry of the Rev. Peter Hargreaves at Mfundisweni after 1882.[25] His reputation as a friend of the Thembu helped him to gain the confidence of the Mpondo but did not guarantee that they would listen to him. By this time the chiefs had come under the influence of white adventurers and concession-hunters who did their best to undermine Hargreaves' position. When affairs were relatively quiet, brandy spoke louder than sound advice; but Hargreaves was consulted and trusted in times of crisis. If his relationship with the tribe was less easy than Jenkins', so also was his relationship with the colonial authorities. Now that the Cape had responsible government, Mpondo affairs were in the hands of colonists who generally had little time for missionaries and their views. Hargreaves therefore had little chance of influencing policy at its source. He was fortunate, however, in his relationship with Walter Stanford, who became Chief Magistrate of Griqualand East in 1885 and was involved in Mpondo affairs for the next ten years. The two men became close friends and reached a large measure of agreement on political matters. In this way Hargreaves had some influence upon day-to-day developments and indirectly, through Stanford, upon the thinking of the Cape Government.

Hargreaves was very sensitive to the injustices suffered by the Mpondo but was also aware of their faults. He believed that a settlement with the Cape Government was imperative and his influence with the chiefs helped to bring about the Agreement of 1886 which overcame the difficulties of the past twenty years.[26] Unfortunately the Agreement did not ensure a peaceful future. Mqikela died in 1887 and was succeeded by Sigcawu, who sincerely tried to govern his people well and to live at peace with the

Colony. But the odds were against him. White speculators plied him with brandy. His cousin Mdlangaso, who had virtually ruled the Mpondo in Mqikela's declining years, went into rebellion when Sigcawu clipped his wings and made it clear he would rule in person. The governments of the Cape and Natal bemoaned Sigcawu's inability to keep order, but promoted disorder by allowing Mdlangaso's supporters to cross the colonial boundaries with impunity. Finally, from 1888 the Cape tried to impose a resident in the person of J. H. Scott. The Mpondo were quite satisfied to work through Stanford at Kokstad and feared that a resident was the first step to annexation. Hargreaves looked on with mingled irritation and sympathy. He did what he could to help the young chief who, for all his faults, was being treated unfairly by the colonial authorities. Matters came to a head when the Cape Government offered Sigcawu the alternatives of voluntary submission or conquest. In Hargreaves' opinion this was unjust. However, he realised that resistance would involve bloodshed and the loss of land, and persuaded Sigcawu and his councillors to negotiate. With Stanford as the government representative, the terms were reasonable and the submission took place on 17 March 1894.[27]

Hargreaves' last major involvement in Mpondo politics came in 1895. Sigcawu found it difficult to accept subjection and proved unco-operative on several occasions. During 1895 he was accused – unjustly, as it proved – of interfering with hut registration, and Stanford ordered his arrest. Once again Hargreaves felt the action was unjust, and for a time his relations with Stanford were strained. But Hargreaves knew that the Government was stronger than the Mpondo and that resistance would only bring greater suffering in its train. He therefore persuaded Sigcawu to give himself up and accompanied him to the Kokstad gaol. It was a dangerous gamble on Hargreaves' part: had the Cape Premier, Cecil Rhodes, had his way, Sigcawu would have been banished and Hargreaves would probably have been blamed; as it was, Sigcawu's attorney appealed to the Cape Supreme Court where Sir H. de

Villiers ruled the proclamation of banishment *ultra vires* and ordered the chief's immediate release.[28] The case went on appeal to the Privy Council, which upheld de Villiers' judgement.[29]

The events of 1894 and 1895 illustrate the frustrating nature of Hargreaves' political rôle. He sympathised with the Mpondo but was powerless to overcome the injustice with which they were treated. He knew the realities of power and had to advise courses of action that were unpopular and could have destroyed his usefulness as a missionary. Yet to have dodged the issue and refused to advise would have been tantamount to condemning the Mpondo to defeat and destruction. Hargreaves' Christian responsibility and courage were best seen in those actions which least commend him to the African nationalist of to-day.

Times had changed since the days of William Shaw, when a missionary had direct access to the Governor and significantly influenced his policy. The position of Peter Hargreaves was far closer to that of the modern missionary who is often the powerless adviser of those without power.

FOOTNOTES

1. A. T. Bryant, *Olden Times in Zululand and Natal* (London 1934) *passim;* J. Stuart and D. Malcolm, eds., *The Diary of H. F. Fynn* (Pietermaritzburg 1950) *passim;* D. G. L. Cragg, The Relations of the Amampondo and the Colonial Authorities, 1830–1886, with special reference to the rôle of the Wesleyan Missionaries (D.Phil. Oxford 1959) ch. 1.
2. Stuart and Malcolm, eds., *H. F. Fynn,* pp. 96–110, 130, 207, 222–5 et al.
3. *D.S.A.B.* I (Cape Town 1968) 283: Faku.
4. C.O. 48/125: Bourke to Huskisson 26.8.1828 (P.R.O.).
5. *D.S.A.B.* I, 711: W. Shaw. D. G. L. Cragg, Godfearing men and women they were, *Lantern* 20 (1), 1970.
6. *D.S.A.B.* I, 109: W. B. Boyce.

7. *Ibid*, 408: T. Jenkins.
8. For the Mpondo Mission under Jenkins see Cragg, Amampondo and Colonial Authorities, ch. 2.
9. Cragg, *ibid*, ch. 11.
10. Cragg, *ibid*, ch. 14; *D.S.A.B.* I, 350.
11. Instructions to Wesleyan Missionaries: extracts were printed at the commencement of the *Annual Report of the Wesleyan Methodist Missionary Society* after 1821.
12. B. E. Seton, Wesleyan Missions and the Sixth Frontier War (Ph.D. University of Cape Town 1962).
13. *D.S.A.B.* I, 585: Ncaphayi.
14. D. G. L. Cragg, ed., Copies of Correspondence betwixt Wm. Shaw, Wesleyan Missionary, and the Colonial Government of the Cape of Good Hope : – Relative to the Attack made by the Emigrant Dutch Farmers on the Tribe of the Chief Ncapaye, *Journal of the Methodist Historical Society of South Africa*, 3 (5 and 6), 1960 and 1961; Cragg, Amampondo and Colonial Authorities, ch. 3.
15. *Treaties entered into by Governors of the Colony of the Cape of Good Hope . . . with native chieftains . . . between the years 1803 and 1854*, (Cape Town 1857) p. 135; Cragg, Amampondo and Colonial Authorities, ch. 4.
16. Maitland to Stanley, 7.12.1844, *Br. Parl. Papers 1851, xxxviii (424)*.
17. Cragg, Amampondo and Colonial Authorities, ch. 6. The major manuscript source, other than the official archives, is the Jenkins Private Papers of which typescript copies are preserved in the Cory Library for Historical Research, Rhodes University and in the archives of the Methodist Missionary Society, London. Relevant developments in Natal are discussed in A. F. Hattersley, *The British Settlement of Natal* (Cambridge 1950) and L. Young, The Native Policy of Benjamin Pine in Natal, 1850–55 (*AYB* xiv, 2, Cape Town 1951).
18. C.O. 48/407: Faku to Colonial Government, 7.10.1850, encl. in Grey to Newcastle, 26, 6.3.1861 (P.R.O.).
19. C.O. 48/407: Montagu to Moodie, 11.11.1850, encl. in Grey to Newcastle, 26, 6.3.1861 (P.R.O.).
20. *D.S.A.B.* II, 498: Mqikela.
21. Cragg, Amampondo and Colonial Authorities, ch. 9.
22. *Ibid*, ch. 10. The Jenkins Private Papers are an important source.
23. This period is discussed in Cragg, Amampondo and Colonial Authorities, chs. 11 to 13; *D.S.A.B.* II, 460: Mdlangaso; 489: Mqikela.
24. Encl. in Frere to Hicks Beach, 26.12.1878, *Br. Parl. Papers* 1878–9 LII (C 2252).
25. The major sources for this period, apart from official archives, are the Stanford Private Papers (Jagger Library, University of Cape Town), the Hargreaves Private Papers (Methodist Book Room, Cape Town), and J. W. Macquarrie, ed., *The Reminiscences of Sir Walter Stanford* (2 vols., Cape Town 1958 and 1962). It is discussed

in *D.S.A.B.* I, 350: P. Hargreaves; 722: Sigcawu; 766: W. E. M. Stanford; Cragg, Amampondo and Colonial Authorities, ch. 14; C.C. Saunders, The Annexation of the Transkeian Territories, 1872–1895 (D.Phil. Oxford 1972) ch. VII.
26. Encl. in Torrens to Stanhope, 15.12.1886, *Br. Parl. Papers 1887, LXI (C 5022).*
27. *Cape Parl. Papers,* G 59, 1894.
28. C. H. Tredgold and W. P. Buchanan, *Decisions of the Supreme Court, Cape of Good Hope,* XII (1895): Sigcau vs The Queen, 30.7.1895, and the Queen vs Sigcau, 8.8.1895.
29. G.H. 1/102: Judgement of Privy Council in case of Prime Minister (Cape of Good Hope) vs Sigcau (Cape Archives).

7

NATAL AND THE TRANSKEI, TO 1879

B. A. le Cordeur

ONE of the most striking features of white-ruled Natal in the nineteenth century was its spirit of extraordinarily aggressive expansionism. Unlike the sister colony, the Cape, which was often a "reluctant imperialist", Natal seldom flagged in its enthusiasm for expansion. Like the Cape, on the other hand, Natal's expansionist drive was all-pervasive. The Natalians struck out in all directions: northward across the Tukela, north-westward beyond the Drakensberg, and southward across the Mzimkuku (or even, in their wilder dreams, across the Mzimvubu).

Sir Keith Hancock has drawn attention to the fact that white expansionism in southern Africa has occurred on many different levels and through a great variety of often conflicting agents: hunters, traders, missionaries, farmers, soldiers, speculators and administrators.[1] Although substantial fundamental research has been done on several aspects of Natal's expansionist drives to the south, this has only revealed the extent of the gaps which remain in our knowledge and understanding of the expansionist process in general in that area. The purpose of this chapter is to synthesise the main findings of the research that has so far been completed,[2] and to attempt to identify some of the major areas where systematic research could well contribute to the understanding of Transkeian history in general in the period until about 1879.

Causes of Natal's expansionism in the south

The reasons for Natal's expansionism towards the south were as varied and even contradictory as were the agents who were responsible for it. At first the search for colonial security was probably the dominant motive. Not merely was Natal almost surrounded by black peoples at various stages of political integration and military power, but her European settlers constituted the first white community in the history of southern Africa to live side by side with an overwhelmingly preponderant African population within its own territory.

It was in no small measure this search for security within and outside the colony which inspired various schemes to "dump" many of Natal's so-called "surplus" Africans beyond the southern border of the white settlement: the resolution of the Volksraad in August 1841 to remove all those Africans not in the employ of whites to a tract of land beyond the Mthamvuna River, and to create a buffer state between the Republic and the tribes of the south; the scheme of Sir Harry Smith in 1848 to acquire all of Pondoland; and Theophilus Shepstone's enthusiastic support of the idea, in 1849, 1850, 1851, 1852 and, in a less ambitious form, in 1854.[3]

But even within the first few years of formal white settlement in Natal, the interplay of motives prompting southward expansion was evident: one of the most powerful was the land hunger of the whites. The Boers of the Republic of Natal had had a voracious appetite for land, and in subsequent years the evidence given before successive official commissions reflected the widespread frustration of Natal's whites at their inability to secure what they regarded as adequate land.[4] The evidence of one of the witnesses to the 1848 Land Commission was typical of the way in which this need was rationalised: he complained that there was far too little land in Natal for "the settlement of a population of Europeans sufficiently numerous to protect themselves and to exercise over the natives a predominating influence towards effecting their civilisation."[5] Like their counterparts on the Eastern Cape frontier, many of them, in the words of Professor Galbraith, too easily "identified land-grabbing with the will of God."[6] It is, indeed, difficult to imagine that even if a completely stable frontier and colony had been attained, expansionism would have ceased. By 1848, there was virtually no land available in Natal for Africans or for immigrants or even for importunate landless whites: on the other hand, only partially occupied, fertile land which would probably not be difficult to obtain, lay temptingly within reach immediately beyond the southern border.[7]

Shepstone himself realised that the land and security problems were in many ways interdependent. He approached the problem not only as it related to the question of colonial security, but also as an administrator, charged with keeping the peace, as were all servants of the imperial and colonial governments in this period, merely by the exercise of influence.[8] Asked to comment on Smith's scheme, Shepstone welcomed the fact that its implementation would contribute to the elimination of one of the most serious problems from which Natal suffered – the existence of numerous petty and independent tribes on the borders of the colony. "I have experienced more disobedience and serious opposition to the government from the few tribes in contact with them," he stressed, "than from the whole of the native population in Natal put together."[9] Shepstone genuinely believed that to remove the Africans beyond the southern border would be in the interests of the Africans as well as of the whites.[10] He recommended that the area be placed under the sovereignty of the Crown, and that a British Resident or Commissioner be appointed to govern it "as connected with the district of Natal."[11] By April 1850, when Faku in desperation ceded all the country between the Mzimkulu and Mthamvuna Rivers to the Natal Government, it looked as though Natal had at last made a significant breakthrough.[12] But the scheme was not ratified by the High Commissioner, and in 1854, Shepstone, after negotiations with Faku, acquired free access to the Mzimvubu River and complete control, short of actual possession, of the port.[13]

By the end of the 1850s, no success had yet been achieved in implementing any of these schemes. As the restlessness on and beyond their southern border increased, the Natalians protested vociferously that the interminable disputes between the tribes in and outside of Nomansland were very adversely affecting the Africans within the borders of Natal itself. They were given permission by the Secretary of State to annex the area between the Mzimkulu and the Mthamvuna claimed by Natal by virtue of the Harding cession of 1850, although after Sir George Grey and Sir Philip Wodehouse had tried to ensure that the Griqua and other landless peoples would be accommodated, Natal was actually able to annex only the coastal section. Sir John Robinson, the first premier of Natal, was later to comment that the annexation of this County of Alfred in 1866 might have added only about 170 000 hectares and about 40 kilometres of coastline to Natal, but it excluded any other power "from obtruding itself there", and it was "a distinct contribution" to the Natalians' "self-importance."[14]

By the 1870s, the problem of security still existed. The Natalians were by then concerned with two areas in particular: Nomansland and Pondoland. In the later 1860s, Wodehouse had put even more Africans under Griqua rule in Nomansland.[15] At the same time, remnants of tribes filtered in and settled at will: landless Basotho from the Caledon River valley; peoples from the overcrowded Wittebergen reserve in the Cape Colony and, not least, remnants of chiefdoms outlawed by Natal itself. Adam Kok, in an ambitious bid at "empire-building", hoped to bring all the peoples from the Gatberg to the Natal border under his jurisdiction.[16] His expansionist ambitions brought him into conflict not only with the Bhaca and Nehemiah Moshweshwe, but also with the Mpondo and the Natal authorities. Shepstone, for his part, hoped to make a last bid to obtain his "new Zululand" in the Transkei before responsible government was inaugurated at the Cape. He and Keate suggested that Grey's scheme for Griqualand should be completed by the appointment of a British Resident Magistrate.[17] Instead, Barkly appointed a Commission to report on the situation.[18] Kok admitted to the Commission that the Griqua had been responsible for frequent violations of the Natal border. The Commission was so shocked at the extent to which relations between the Griqua and their neighbours had deteriorated that it recommended that Griqualand East should be incorporated into Natal.[19] But again Natal was to be disappointed.

Finally, Natal strove to acquire Pondoland, or, failing that, at least the mouth of the Mzimvubu (St Johns River). Here, as in the case of Nomansland, economic considerations probably figured more prominently in the calculations of Natal's expansionists; but even here they were not the decisive factor. The mineral resources of the areas to the south excited interest among not a few Natalians. Shepstone himself investigated the rumours of the alleged mineral wealth in the Mpondo country in 1854–55; but this was only after he had decided that he needed the territory for Natal's "surplus" Africans.[20] Floundering in the throes of the depression of the 1860s, the colony must inevitably have hoped to be able to benefit from the copper, nickel and coal deposits which had been discovered in Griqualand and Pondoland by Natal's Surveyor-General and numbers of prospectors from about 1865.[21] In 1867, the Umzimvubu Prospecting Company of Natal sent an expedition to investigate the deposits.[22] Shepstone's Cape rivals observed that he had taken two wagon loads of ore back to Natal for testing, and he reported officially to the Natal Government on the discoveries.[23] In the following decades, Natal concessionaires continued to evince considerable interest in the possibility of Natal's control of the area.[24] It was a great blow to them when, in 1873, Joseph

Orpen of the Cape was appointed as Magistrate with the chiefdoms in the St Johns area and agent in Nomansland; for some of these Natal concessionaires hoped to revive claims to mining rights which they had bought in the past and which had lapsed. Orpen warned John X. Merriman that the Natal Company wished "to get the territory for *Natal,* and then to work up their case in their own little colony and get their rights recognised."[25] But, so far as could be ascertained at the time, the mineral deposits were unimpressive in extent. Moreover, when the pitch of excitement reached too high a level in the Cape Parliament, the Treasurer-General felt obliged to warn members "that the Government will feel it their duty to act with great caution in any dealing with the native tribes in connection with this matter."[26] Although the Natal Government might have been less inclined to exercise such restraint, no evidence can be found that either of the colonial governments ever attached sufficient weight to the reports to induce it to take positive steps to attempt to incorporate any territory on that score.[27]

Nor were the purely commercial pressures of traders strong enough to lead to governmental action. By the mid-sixties, it is true, Natal traders were selling significant quantities of hoes, picks, ploughs and wagons to the Mpondo, and exporting cattle and timber via Port St Johns, and by the mid-seventies, there were an estimated fifty to sixty traders in Pondoland alone.[28] But George Cato, the most prosperous trader at Port Natal from the late thirties and for several decades a man with probably as great a personal stake as any in the trade with Port St Johns, expressed great disgust and indignation at the suggestion that the possession of the mouth of the Mzimvubu was commercially so important that the Mpondo should be coerced into ceding it to Natal.[29] In 1873, similarly, Sir Henry Barkly reported officially that both the amount of trade done through the port and the facilities for doing so had been greatly overrated.[30]

Whatever individual traders or even officials might think,

the colonial authorities in general became increasingly sensitive about the extent to which colonial customs dues were evaded or blows struck at colonial trade itself by the smuggling of goods into the colonies, as well as into the Transkei, through the Mzimvubu River mouth and other points along the lengthy coast of South-East Africa.[31] In 1876, the Secretary of State for the Colonies himself, though not prepared to antagonise the Mpondo by actual annexation of the port, acknowledged that the colonial governments had real grounds for concern.[32] Commercial expansion of Natal was obviously occurring in this part. But even after the Cape had taken possession of the port, Natal merchants continued to control the trade, and as late as 1894 the Colonial Office could still remind the Natal authorities that it was not necessary formally to take possession of territory in order to promote trade relations with its peoples.[33]

The branch of commerce which raised special issues and created special problems was the trade in arms and ammunition. Were the Natalians so anxious about the military and political, let alone the economic, implications of the duty-free importation of arms through the "back door" to the highly inflammable colonial frontier areas and even into the colonies themselves, that they demanded control over the Transkeian coast? It is true that when Barkly visited the area at the height of the gun-running controversy in 1873, he reported that firearms had not been brought in via the Mzimvubu River mouth in any appreciable quantities in recent months.[34] Moreover, the Governor's Commission of 1872 reported at about the same time that much of the gun-running into the Transkei that did take place originated in Natal itself.[35]

But many people in high official positions in both colonies, in addition to private individuals, expressed concern throughout the period at the need to control the importation of arms and ammunition through Port St Johns. In 1864, a Select Committee of the Natal Legislative Council claimed that one-fourth of the Mpondo had guns.[36]

J. C. Warner, who reported in "strictly private" notes periodically to Richard Southey, the Cape Colonial Secretary, called Southey's attention in 1867 to the fact that the smuggling of arms and ammunition was taking place through the Mzimvubu River mouth to "a very serious extent", the main culprit being a coasting vessel, the *Little Bess,* which, after taking in stores at Port Elizabeth, met a vessel up the coast, "which has come from England or elsewhere", from which arms were transferred to the *Little Bess* and landed at the port.[37] Thomas Jenkins, the missionary with Faku, was sufficiently concerned about the trade in guns and liquor through the port to favour British control of Pondoland.[38]

Although from the second half of the 1860s certain economic factors operated more potently than before in Natal's expansionism in regard to Pondoland, there were really bigger issues at stake than the economic, and they were still concerned essentially with the security of the colonies. Within Pondoland itself, Mqikela, Faku's successor, did not wield the authority of his father. Boundary or tribal disputes between the Mpondo and their neighbours, the Mpondomise, the Bhaca, the Xesibe and, not least, the Griqua, invariably affected the attitude of Natal's own African population or led to the flight of refugees and therefore to diplomatic crises of one kind or another.[39] Walter Currie was genuinely concerned about the need to prevent Moshweshwe and Adam Kok from combining in a drive towards Port St Johns.[40] By 1864–65, Adam Kok himself was far more concerned at reports that Nehemiah Moshweshwe and Mqikela were plotting to attack the Griqua simultaneously from the north and the south, and to drive them from the country.[41] Wodehouse was so perturbed – indeed unnecessarily so – at the possibility of Free State expansion through Lesotho towards the port, that on at least three occasions he tried to buy the port from Faku and his successor.[42] The most aggressive expansionists in both colonies, on the other hand, looked upon the establishment of a customs house at the mouth of the Mzimvubu as merely the first step towards acquisition of the surrounding territory as well, and the Natalians began to talk about their "natural and proper boundary" being the Mzimvubu River.[43]

But it proved increasingly difficult to penetrate the preserves of the Mpondo chiefs. The Magistrate of Alfred, Henrique Shepstone, co-operated with his father in continuing to settle some of the inter-tribal quarrels about which Natal was so sensitive.[44] Theophilus Shepstone himself, to the annoyance of the High Commissioner, went to Pondoland, to attempt to stop Mpondo and Griqua raiding parties from traversing Natal soil and drawing the colony's Africans into their disputes.[45] In 1872, Barkly's commission reported that it would not be possible to persuade the suspicious Mqikela, Faku's heir, to accept a British Magistrate on Mpondo soil; and in 1873, the High Commissioner himself was again unsuccessful in trying to obtain Mpondo permission even to construct a colonial customs house at the port.[46] The Cape Government meanwhile extended its influence in Pondoland by various devices, not least of which was the appointment of Joseph Orpen as Magistrate with the tribes in the St Johns area and agent in Nomansland.[47] Finally, Barkly's successor as High Commissioner, Frere, suddenly seized the port in 1878, and the Cape was prevailed upon to take it over in 1884.

Finally, there was the possibility that Natal's expansion into the Transkei, like white expansion into other parts of Africa, could have been encouraged by the chiefs or tribes of the Transkei themselves. It was a common phenomenon, in contacts between white colonial societies and neighbouring African chiefdoms, for tribes in trouble or which expected to reap advantages of one kind or another to request to be "taken over" by the Crown or even by one of the neighbouring white states. The Natal Government did receive requests from chiefdoms to the north and to the south to be "taken over" or recognised.[48] The tribes settled in the territory ceded to Natal by Faku in 1850 had in several cases, for example, requested to be taken under the wing of the Natal Government.[49] When Shepstone was negotiating with Faku in Pondoland in 1854, he informed Cato in a private letter that he had been "obliged to refuse overtures of allegiance from tribes residing" as far distant as the territory south of the Mthatha River.[50] Indeed, Shepstone, the foremost Natal expansionist, had very early shown how readily Natal's urge to expansion could be rationalised in terms of a "mission" to her less fortunate black neighbours. Within two years of the appointment of most of the leading officials of the British colony of Natal, he assured the General Secretary of the African Institute in Paris: "Natal is the key to the black nations of South Africa. It is surrounded by numberless tribes of natives, multitudes of whom, seeing the difference of enlightened from savage government have fixed their eyes upon it as the bright ultimatum of their hopes whenever they shall become emancipated from the thraldom of their present barbarous governments."[51]

But African invitations to be taken over by Natal did not exactly flood in; more frequently, the peoples to the south of Natal appealed to the High Commissioner or even the Cape Government to save them from Natal's grasp. Adam Kok successfully resisted the imposition of Natal rule or even the extension of Natal's influence. When Orpen visited Kokstad in 1874, for example, Kok made it clear that although he would be reluctant to come under the direct rule of Britain or the Cape, he would not even consider being placed under the control of the Natal Government.[52] Faku agreed to the cession of 1850 only as a last resort, and thereafter steadfastly resisted all efforts by all whites to buy, let alone annex, his port. If the Natal Government did ally itself with any of the lesser chiefs, this does not appear to have assisted its expansionism at all. The subject of black–white interaction at the diplomatic and political level is one of the areas in which research now most needs to be concentrated.

In short, many of Natal's colonists might be interested in land-grabbing and some of her merchants in commercial expansion. But it was not they who made policy. The decision-making was done by officials, and although Shepstone and others might have had inflated ambitions for an enlarged Natal, in general the authorities could see no alternative to the extension southward of their control or at least influence in some form or another. There was, firstly, the possibility that independent African or Griqua rule could continue in those areas, but there were, as we have seen, countless objections to that in the eyes of the Natalians. Secondly, the areas could be allowed to come under Cape rule; but the Natalians did not believe that the Cape authorities could be relied on to keep the peace; moreover they regarded themselves as having a far stronger claim than the Cape to control the areas adjacent to their border. Thirdly, the protective wing of the Imperial power could have been spread over the area. This the Natalians might have found more acceptable than the other alternatives, but they knew that there was less and less likelihood that it would occur. Natal's attempted expansion was therefore causally linked not merely with developments within and on and across her southern border, but also with the attitudes and policies of the Imperial authorities and of her Cape rival, and with the less tangible though no less real factors of personal vision, prestige and self-interest.

Failure of Natal's expansionism in the south
There were several main reasons for the almost uniform failure of Natal's expansionist endeavours in the south. In some cases, it was because of the resistance of African and other chiefs. It is true that on many occasions when the whites believed that there were really compelling reasons for assuming control over any African-ruled territory, they rode rough-shod over the most determined African opposition. For example, when, by the mid-sixties, the Natal, Cape and Imperial authorities had reached agreement among themselves that Natal should be allowed to have the territory which eventually became Alfred, Faku's most vociferous protests were simply ignored, as were those of the leading chief of the area, Xolo. Similarly, in 1872, when Barkly's commission drew a border-line between the Mpondo and their neighbours, it dismissed the Mpondo ob-

jections to what was proposed.[53] In 1878, too, when Frere was convinced of the necessity to have possession of Port St Johns, the port was seized in the face of Mqikela's indignant remonstrances. But it would have been far more difficult for Natal to have carried off such a coup on her own. Both Faku and Adam Kok had particularly strong reasons to be suspicious of the intentions of the Natalians. Shepstone himself reported in dismay to the Colonial Secretary of Natal during his negotiations with Faku in 1854 that "Faku himself frequently declared to me that truth resided at Graham's Town and the Cape, but not at Natal."[54] The Griqua, like Natal and the Mpondo, aimed at establishing suzerainty over the Eastern part of the Transkei. Adam Kok put up a particularly spirited resistance to any suggestion that he should sacrifice any land or power to Natal; in 1867, he refused to negotiate even a boundary adjustment with Natal, declaring suspiciously to Shepstone, "Let the High Commissioner come himself and say where the boundary between us is to be."[55] Faku, similarly, defiantly refused, on one occasion after another, to sell Port St Johns to either of the colonial authorities; this contributed to the fact that the Cape, not Natal, eventually acquired it at the hands of a High Commissioner who had reasons of his own for desiring such an arrangement.[56]

The failure of Natal expansionism owed something, too, to the actions of the missionaries, who were usually primarily concerned about frontier peace and the welfare of the tribesmen.[57] Although as late as 1866 there were only some 15 missionaries in the area between the Kei and Natal, some of them occupied positions which were of crucial political significance. Jenkins was always alert to the attempts of Natal to seize Mpondo land.[58] The protests of Shaw against the 1850 Faku cession to Natal played a key role in the sequence of events which led the High Commissioner to refuse to sanction the cession. By denouncing the "robbery" in unequivocal terms and bringing pressure to bear upon Smith, the missionaries had probably prevented Pondoland from being incorporated into Natal and being divided among European settlers.[59] In Griqualand and Pondoland the missionaries were by no means the willing agents of expansionist white capitalism portrayed in the conventional image of African polemicists.[60]

Cape expansionism and rivalry was another not inconsiderable obstacle to Natal's drive southwards. Successive Cape governments were by no means as single-minded about the virtues of expansion into the Transkei as were the Natal authorities; but at times the leading members of Cape ministries could be moved to eloquence or even intrigue in regard to expansion across the Kei. In May 1867, for example, Warner, writing to the arch-expansionist Southey about Port St Johns, confided that the appointment of an official by the Cape Government "to take charge of the port . . . would, of course, involve an expense of some 300£ p.a.; but it would be after all a cheap way of getting in the 'thin edge of the wedge' at the St Johns River, and prevent other parties from getting possession of that port. And, moreover, would be in entire accordance with your policy of making our influence felt in those parts."[61] Not a few people at the Cape were afraid, too, that Adam Kok might be induced by the Natalians to part with his land, as the Griqua had so long been selling theirs to the Free State. Later, the Cape authorities became anxious about the complications which could arise when the already elderly and infirm Adam Kok died without a direct male heir. It was decided to attempt to bring the Griqua under colonial rule as speedily as possible. Before setting out on his tour to Natal at the end of 1874, Barkly had promised to do his best, in his capacity as High Commissioner, to set such negotiations afoot. When he arrived at Kokstad, he found the position of the government so bad that it was clear that "if the Cape Government was to assume the responsibility of governing the country at all, it ought to do so promptly and without an interregnum." After some haggling with Kok, two representatives of his government and one of the Magistrates for Griqualand arrived in Cape Town, and detailed arrangements for the assumption of authority over the territory by the Cape Government were completed.[62]

A similar blow was struck in the 1870s at Natal's pretensions in Pondoland. After the High Commissioner had prevailed upon the Natalians to restrain themselves for the moment in regard to their claims to Pondoland and Port St Johns, Lieutenant-Governor Bulwer of Natal discovered that this had merely played into the hands of Natal's rivals at the Cape. "Your Lordship will, I am sure," complained Bulwer to the Secretary of State, Lord Carnarvon, "not blame me if I speak frankly to you, and if I tell you that it is the belief here that the action taken by the Cape Government towards the Amapondos is in pursuance of the ulterior policy that that government has in view – namely the annexation to the Cape of the whole Pondo country."[63]

When the Cape was in such an "annexationist" mood, there was little that the smaller and less important colony of Natal could do to compete with her. The main reason for this was that the High Commissioners had the real initiative, resources and prestige for taking action, and they tended to do so through and on behalf of the Cape Colony rather than of Natal. Their High Commission gave them control over the external relations of Natal, and few of them hesitated to use the power.[64] In 1850, for example, Smith had refused to ratify the Faku cession to Natal, because the Natal authorities had demanded cattle without consulting him, and because he had been persuaded that the raids into Natal had not even been committed by people settled in Faku's territory.[65] In 1854, Grey effectively destroyed Shepstone's "removal" scheme, largely because it clashed with his own "grand design" for the Transkei.[66] In the 1860s, Grey and Wodehouse asserted their authority so vigorously that they were able to prevent Natal from acquiring most of the territory that it had been given permission by the Secretary of State himself to annex in Nomansland.[67] The actions of Barkly, in 1874–75, though not a premeditated blow at Natal, certainly did have the effect of enabling the Cape Government to act swiftly in setting the scene for the annexation of Griqualand East. The Natal press boiled with indignation at the "territory ... filched from us" and the land "recently rifled from us by Sir Henry Barkly for the Cape Government."[68] Probably the most dramatic example of the decisive use of the High Commissioner's powers in favour of the Cape was Frere's seizure in 1878 of Port St Johns, for which Natal had been striving for so long. Even the Secretary of State thought that Natal had been unjustly treated.[69] But Frere, anxious to achieve his "final solution" to the problem of the Transkei as an important preliminary to his confederation of southern African states, took advantage of the Secretary's recent appointment and lack of familiarity with the local situation.[70] He made it clear that it was quite out of the question to consider the annexation of the port to Natal or even for Natal to share the customs revenues with the Cape – as had been proposed in 1874.[71]

There were a number of reasons why the High Commissioners did so little to assist Natal and so much more on behalf of the Cape. Most important, perhaps, was the fact that from the time of the institution of the office, the High Commission had been held by the officer who was also Governor of the Cape. In the days before responsible government, he had depended for advice and support upon the Executive Council, many of whose members had wide local experience; after responsible government had been inaugurated, High Commissioners like Barkly tended to be very cautious about taking any actions (even those which rightly were exercised in their capacities as High Commissioners) without the advice of what Barkly repeatedly called "my responsible advisers." Conversely, the Cape Ministry virtually had the High Commission at its disposal. There was, too, the fact that Shepstone's obvious objective of a "Greater Natal" and his ambition to head a "native empire" and be supreme chief of all South-East Africa, continually threatened to obstruct or undermine the often diametrically opposed plans of successive High Commissioners: Grey, Wodehouse and Frere were all firm believers in the superiority of Cape magisterial rule and, by contrast, the potential dangers of Shepstonism;[72] nor did they favour the idea of Shepstone's extending his power base into the surrounding independent African territories. Imperial belief that Natal could not be trusted to administer African affairs wisely was greatly enhanced by the Langalibalele rebellion; nor did it seem wise to allow Natal's small white population, which was already governing an overwhelmingly large African population, to attempt to govern any more blacks.[73]

Significance of Natal's expansionist attempts in the south
Natal's expansionist endeavours and failures in the south were significant in several ways. Natal obtained a small amount of not very useful territory, the County of Alfred; but, on the other hand, the Cape acquired a much larger and more valuable area on the borders of Natal itself. The irony of this was soon amply demonstrated. When rebellion broke out in Griqualand East only two years after the arrival of Capt. Blyth as first Magistrate at Kokstad, Blyth immediately telegraphed to Natal for assistance.[74] Similarly, after Cape authority had been entrenched at Port St Johns, General Thesiger wrote to Shepstone from Pietermaritzburg: " . . . I am off in a week's time to the St Johns River to superintend the disembarkation of the detachment which is to garrison our new acquisition . . . Should the northern Pondos give trouble, there is a sufficient force at this place to put them down. In fact, any operations against Umqikela must necessarily be carried on from the Natal colony as a base . . ."[75] In the 1880s and after, trade between Griqualand East and Natal was ruined when the Cape Government erected a customs post on the Mzimkulu. The question as to whether Griqualand East belongs to Natal or to the Cape has remained a bone of contention to this day.

When Natal's ambitions were thwarted in the south, the Natalians became even more determined that they should not lose Zululand as they had lost Lesotho and most of the Transkei; they pursued their drive into Zululand with even greater energy. Much now needs to be discovered about the dynamics of this expansionism in all directions. The expansionists need to be identified and their careers studied in relation to the much wider issue of the power and pressure groups in Natal life at that time. The related question of the interaction between the various African peoples within Natal and those on and beyond her borders – about which the Natal Government complained so persistently – needs to be investigated in depth. The frustration of many of Natal's objectives in the Transkei contributed further to the general apathy (if not aversion) with which Natal and the Cape viewed each other; the cause of closer relations in southern Africa received yet another blow.

The Cape, on the other hand, was sometimes spurred on by the expansionist pressures of her more restless sister colony. One of the factors which finally precipitated the Cape into the annexation of Pondoland in 1894, for example, was the reflection that if the Cape did not take it, Natal might well succeed in doing so.[76] Indeed, one of the absorbing features of colonial expansionism is how it could be fuelled not only by long-term (and often continuing) factors, but also by opportunities which were created by the process of expansion itself. A revealing example of this phenomenon is to be found in one of the many letters in which Southey, with somewhat brutal frankness, unburdened his mind to his counterpart, the Colonial Secretary of Natal, Major Erskine. It affords an illuminating glimpse of what might be termed "the sub-imperialist mind" in action, showing how expansion could in some instances ultimately acquire a purpose and a momentum of its own. Referring to the impending incorporation of Lesotho by Natal at the beginning of 1868, Southey confided in Erskine: "... Some people down here [i.e. at the Cape] think we are awfully slow that we do not annex Moselikatzi's land at once, and as you are going to take over the Basuto, don't you think we might as well go in for Waterboer, Mahura and Moselikatzi. When you have got Basutoland, Natal and this colony will meet or very nearly so, and if it doesn't quite, we can easily annex a little more to make it so on our Northern and your Southern border, and then if we run round the Free State and Transvaal and join you again about the sources of the Vaal river, we should become doubly united..."[77]

So far as the significance of Natal's expansionist endeavours for the Transkei is concerned, this is most difficult of all to assess. Professor Monica Wilson's classic study deals with the impact of the white presence and white over-rule upon Mpondo society in the long term.[78] More recently, Professor Hammond-Tooke has published important historical surveys of some of the individual chiefdoms of the area.[79] What is now needed is an historical study of the immediate, as opposed to the long-term impact of the coming of whites in all their different capacities. Factional politics of the main tribes of the area in the period before the arrival of the whites will require intensive research, as will an investigation of the same phenomena in the years immediately after white penetration had begun. The relation of the internal politics to the external relations of the individual tribes demands systematic analysis. Historians will doubtless seek to discover how far the whites deliberately exploited political disaffection within individual chiefdoms and how far their coming led to the segmentation or re-grouping of chiefdoms. Changes in external trade and the effects of this upon internal politics will demand attention, as will the economic importance, service functions and political impact of the missionaries. In the post-confrontation phase, historians will have to probe far more deeply the complexities of settlement and interpenetration of groups and individuals on the land; the position in Griqualand East should be of particular interest and importance in this respect. The interaction of official and unofficial elements in the expansionist process will also need to be explored. As for the sources, none of the different types of evidence has yet been exhaustively investigated, and many have not even been touched.

FOOTNOTES

1 W. K. Hancock, *Survey of British Commonwealth Affairs* (3 vols.) (London 1937-42) *passim*.

2 In particular B. A. le Cordeur, The Relations between the Cape and Natal, 1846-79 (*AYB* 1965 part 1); D. G. L. Cragg, The Relations of the Amampondo and the Colonial Authorities (1830-86), with special reference to the role of the Wesleyan Missionaries (D.Phil. Oxford 1959); Waldemar B. Campbell, The South African Frontier, 1865-1885: a Study in Expansion (*AYB* 1959 part 1); and C. C. Saunders, The Annexation of the Transkeian Territories (1872-1895), with special reference to British and Cape Policy (D.Phil. Oxford 1972).

3 A. J. du Plessis, Die Republiek Natalia (*AYB* 1942 part 1) pp. 158-9; Cragg, Relations of Amampondo and Colonial Authorities, pp. 139-41, 207-10; *Proceedings of the Commission Appointed to Inquire into the Past and Present State of the Kafirs in the district of Natal*... (Pietermaritzburg 1852) Part 1, pp. 71-78; Shepstone to Cato, 28 March 1854, Shepstone Papers (Natal Archives).

4 J. A. I. Agar-Hamilton, *The Native Policy of the Voortrekkers (1836-58)* (Cape Town 1928) p. 29; E. H. Brookes and C. de B. Webb, *A History of Natal* (Pietermaritzburg 1965) pp. 50-53; *South African Archival Records, Natal No. II* (Cape Town 1960) pp. 258-9; *cf. Proceedings and Report of the Commission appointed to inquire into the Past and Present State of the Kafirs in the district of Natal*... (Pietermaritzburg 1852-53) *passim*.

5 *S.A. Arch. Recs., Natal No. II*, p. 258.

6 J. S. Galbraith, *Reluctant empire: British policy on the South African frontier, 1834-1854* (Berkeley 1963) p. 43.

7 See especially the report of Smith's own Land Commission in April 1848: S.G.O. IV/1/1, pp. 44-8 (Natal Archives). *Cf.* A. F. Hattersley (ed.), *John Shedden Dobie: South African Journal, 1862-66* (Cape Town 1945), pp. 150, 153.

8 Campbell, South African Frontier, pp. 49-50.

9 *S.A. Arch. Recs., Natal No. III* (Cape Town 1962) p. 79.

10 Brookes and Webb, *History of Natal*, p. 58; Agar-Hamilton, *Native Policy of Voortrekkers*, p. 38.

11 *S. A. Arch. Recs., Natal No. III*, p. 79.

12 E. C. 1 *passim* (Natal Archives); Cragg, Amampondo and Colonial Authorities, p. 127 sqq.

13 J. Garvock to Fynn, 2 November 1850, Fynn Papers; Shepstone to Cato, 28 July 1854, Shepstone Papers (Natal Archives); Cragg, Amampondo and Colonial Authorities, pp. 149-50, 155-156, 217.

14 Sir John Robinson, *A Life Time in South Africa* (London 1900) p. 266; *cf.* Le Cordeur, Relations between Cape and Natal, pp. 94-104.

15 Frank Brownlee, *The Transkeian Native Territories: Historical Records* (Lovedale 1923) p. 46.

16 See chapter 5.

17 Keate to Barkly, 10 August 1871, G. H. 637/17 (Natal Archives).

18 T. J. N. Knoll, The Griquas of Griqualand East until about 1878 (M.A. University of Cape Town 1935) p. 66.

19 T. Botma, The Griquas of Griqualand East: their relations with the

colonial authorities, 1872–78 (B.A. Hons. University of Cape Town 1966), p. 19; *cf.* Saunders, Annexation of Transkeian Territories, p. 82.
20 Shepstone to Cato, 21 May 1854 (private), Shepstone Papers (Natal Archives); *cf.* Le Cordeur, Relations between Cape and Natal, pp. 73–75.
21 See, e.g. *Natal Mercury,* 9 May 1867.
22 Part of their journal is reproduced in A. F. Hattersley's *Later Annals of Natal* (London 1938) pp. 20–33.
23 J. C. Warner to Southey, 30 March 1867, Southey Papers (Cape Archives); Shepstone to Colonial Secretary of Natal, 15 April 1867, G. H. 340 (Natal Archives).
24 Saunders, Annexation of Transkeian Territories, p. 409.
25 J. M. Orpen to J. X. Merriman, 14 September 1874, Merriman Papers (South African Library).
26 *Votes and Proceedings: Cape Leg. Co.,* 28 June 1867.
27 *Cf.* Saunders, Annexation of Transkeian Territories, pp. 385, 409.
28 Campbell, South African Frontier, pp. 35, 70.
29 Cato to Henrique Shepstone, 20 March 1872, Shepstone Papers (Natal Archives).
30 Barkly to Pine, 11 December 1873, G.H. 333/87 (Natal Archives); *cf.* also *Natal Statistical Book* for annual trade statistics.
31 See e.g. Scott to Newcastle, 31 May 1862, G.H. 274/157; Scott to Newcastle, 21 November 1863, G.H. 275/132; Wodehouse to Administrator of Government, Natal, 21 August 1865, G.H. 332/19 (Natal Archives); Erskine to Southey, 18 July 1866, 10 August 1866 etc., Southey Papers (Cape Archives); Bisset to Wodehouse, 4 August 1866, G.H. 636/222; Barkly to Carnarvon, 5 July 1876, G.H. 23/33 (Cape Archives).
32 Carnarvon to Bulwer, 20 May 1876, G.H. 24 (Natal Archives).
33 Saunders, Annexation of Transkeian Territories, pp. 261 sqq., 426.
34 Barkly to Pine, 11 December 1873, G.H. 333/87 (Natal Archives).
35 *Cape Parl. Papers:*A.12, 1873.
36 Natal Legislative Council Debates, 10 August 1864 *(Natal Mercury,* 23 August 1864); *Natal Courier,* 24 August 1864, 31 August 1864. *Cf.* also Scott to Newcastle, 21 November 1863, G.H. 275/132 (Natal Archives).
37 Warner to Southey, 28 June 1867, Southey Papers (Cape Archives).
38 Campbell, South African Frontier, p. 71
39 Cragg, Amampondo and Colonial Authorities, Chap. XI; *Natal Mercury,* 22 December 1870.
40 Currie to Southey, 14 September 1862, Southey Papers (Cape Archives).
41 Botma, Griquas of Griqualand East, pp. 11–12.
42 Le Cordeur, Relations between Cape and Natal, pp. 106, 109.
43 See, e.g., *Natal Mercury,* 30 October 1863, 1 April 1864; Warner to Southey, 22 May 1867, Southey Papers (Cape Archives); Bulwer to Carnarvon, 19 August 1875, G.H. 280 (Natal Archives).

44 Shepstone to Henrique Shepstone, 31 August, 30 September and 23 November 1871, 24 October 1872, Shepstone Papers; Barkly to Musgrave, 1 November 1872, G.H. 333/59 (Natal Archives).
45 Keate to Barkly, 5 December 1871, G.H. 637/47 (Natal Archives).
46 Le Cordeur, Relations between Cape and Natal, p. 210; Barkly to Pine, 11 December 1873, G.H. 333/87 (Natal Archives).
47 Barkly to Kimberley, 14 November 1873, G.H. 23/32 (Cape Archives).
48 See, e.g., Bisset to Carnarvon, 16 January 1867, G.H. 276; Keate to Granville, 20 August 1870, G.H. 278; Keate to Kimberley, 23 September 1870, G.H. 278; Shepstone to Henrique Shepstone, 11 November 1871, Shepstone Papers (Natal Archives).
49 E.C. 7, pages 28–35 (Natal Archives).
50 Shepstone to Cato, 21 May 1854 (private), Shepstone Papers (Natal Archives).
51 Shepstone to General Secretary, African Institute, Paris, 10 November 1847, Shepstone Papers (Natal Archives).
52 *Cape Parl. Papers:* G.27, 1874, p. 105.
53 Saunders, Annexation of Transkeian Territories, pp. 68–9, 81.
54 Shepstone's report to Natal Government, 16 August 1854, S.N.A. 1/8/5, pages 278–85 (Natal Archives); *cf.* also Warner to Southey, 1 March 1867, Southey Papers (Cape Archives).
55 Shepstone to Colonial Secretary of Natal, 30 March 1867, G.H. 340; Bisset to Wodehouse, 4 May 1867, G.H. 636/250 (Natal Archives); *cf.* also chapter 5.
56 See *infra* p. 177.
57 Campbell, South African Frontier, p. 69; Cragg, Amampondo and Colonial Authorities, p. vi.
58 Campbell, South African Frontier, pp. 28, 65.
59 M. B. Shaw to Jenkins, 18 December 1850, Jenkins Papers (Gubbins Library, University of the Witwatersrand); *cf.* Cragg, Amampondo and Colonial Authorities, pp. 44, 155–166.
60 Cragg, Amampondo and Colonial Authorities, *passim.*
61 Warner to Southey, 22 May 1867, Southey Papers (Cape Archives).
62 Recounted in Barkly to Carnarvon, 12 March 1875, G.H. 23/32 (Cape Archives). *Cf.* Campbell, South African Frontier, pp. 65–66. *Cf.* Natal's attitude reflected in *Times of Natal,* 24 October 1874.
63 Bulwer to Carnarvon, 26 November 1877 (private and confidential), G.H. 649/7 (Natal Archives).
64 This theme is very thoroughly explored in J. A. Benyon, Basutoland and the High Commission with particular reference to the years 1868–84; the changing nature of the Imperial Government's 'Special Responsibility' for the Territory (D.Phil. Oxford 1969). *Cf.* Campbell, South African Frontier, p. 4.
65 See *S.A. Arch. Recs., Natal, No. III*, pp. 260 sqq.
66 Le Cordeur, Relations between Cape and Natal, pp. 74–76.
67 Ibid., pp. 95–109.
68 Natal Legislative Council Debates, 5 November 1874 *(Natal Mercury,* 10 November 1874); *Natal Mercury,* 29 April 1875; *Natal Witness,*

15 June 1875, 2 March 1877.
69 W. B. Worsfold, *Sir Bartle Frere* (London 1923) p. 103: Hicks Beach to Frere, 2 October 1878 (private).
70 Benyon, Basutoland and the High Commission, pp. 333–357; Saunders, Annexation of Transkeian Territories, p. 195.
71 Frere to Hicks Beach, 26 August 1878, 3 September 1878, G.H. 23/24 (Cape Archives); Cragg, Amampondo and Colonial Authorities, p. 366.
72 Ruth E. Gordon, *Shepstone: the role of the family in the history of South Africa, 1820–1900* (Cape Town 1968) p. 174; Leonard Thompson ed., *African Societies in Southern Africa* (London 1969) p. 289; Benyon, Basutoland and the High Commission, p. 155; Saunders, Annexation of Transkeian Territories, pp. 28, 196, 446.
73 Campbell, South African Frontier, p. 4.
74 *Times of Natal*, 17 April 1878, 13 May 1878, 24 June 1878.
75 Thesiger to Shepstone, 16 August 1878, Shepstone Papers (Natal Archives).
76 Saunders, Annexation of Transkeian Territories, p. 422.
77 Southey to Erskine, 18 February 1868, Southey Papers (Cape Archives).
78 M. Wilson, *Reaction to Conquest* (London 1936).
79 e.g. W. D. Hammond-Tooke, *The Tribes of Mount Frere District* (Pretoria 1956); *The Tribes of Willowvale District* (Pretoria 1956-7); *The Tribes of Umtata District* (Pretoria 1957); *Bhaca Society* (Cape Town 1962).

8

THE ANNEXATION OF THE TRANSKEI

C. C. Saunders

THE bald facts about the annexation of the Transkei by the Cape are well-known. Most histories mention how in 1854 Sir George Grey, the Cape Governor and High Commissioner, urged that the whole area across the Kei River right through to Natal should be brought under white rule; how at the beginning of the 1870s the perhaps half a million people between the Kei and Mthamvuna rivers still lived in independent African chiefdoms and a Griqua state; and how after 1872, and the grant of responsible government to the Cape, that colony moved to bring within its bounds what had by then become an enclave between its eastern districts, Lesotho, Natal and the Indian Ocean. The stages by which the territories east of the Kei were annexed to the Cape have often been set out: first Fingoland, the Idutywa and Griqualand East in 1879, then Port St. Johns in 1884, Thembuland, Gcalekaland and Bomvanaland in 1885, the Xesibe country in 1886, the Rhode in 1887 and finally Pondoland in 1894, the annexation of which completed the process of incorporation and made the north-east boundary of the Cape and the southern boundary of Natal one.

Such is the outline of the story, but by themselves these facts tell us little. Only when we begin to answer the host of questions they pose will we approach an understanding of the meaning of this annexation. Why did it happen as it did? What was the relation between advancing white control and the extension of formal legal jurisdiction east of the Kei? What form did annexation take, and what was its impact on the people of the Transkei? What was its significance for the Cape as a whole? This chapter has been written in the belief that these problems have been ignored too long and that a start should be made to investigating them.[1]

Extension of control and annexation

Given the geographical situation of the Transkei, and that the 1870s, 80s and 90s were the great age of scramble and conquest in southern Africa, it was hardly possible that the territories east of the Kei could have escaped coming under white rule. If the destination was inevitable, however, the route travelled to get there was not. One particularly striking fact about the annexation is how long it took – over two decades – to be completed. When the Cape's first responsible ministry decided in 1873 that the self-governing colony should expand across the Kei there were a considerable number of important independent African states within what was in 1910 to become united South Africa; by 1894 Pondoland was the only such state in that area to have survived. To ask why the annexation of the Transkeian territories was so long drawn-out a process will shed light on why the annexation occurred in the way it did.

It is, however, important first to distinguish between the extension of Cape control east of the Kei and the formal incorporation of territory there within the colony's bounds. The first meant the introduction of magistrates, and change "on the ground"; the latter was a legal step which made the territory part of the Cape. Elsewhere in Africa annexation on occasion preceded the extension of control;[2] in the Transkei extension of control always came first. The Cape Parliament would not have consented to annex territories not yet "pacified", or which did not promise to pay for their administration.

Extension of control east of the Kei proceeded fairly rapidly after 1872, faster than the first Cape ministry anticipated when it first accepted responsibilities in that area. It was not pushed into a policy of expanding there by domestic pressure-groups, either of missionaries (though some missionaries did press for Cape rule in the Transkei, believing it would aid their work), or of traders interested in the expansion of commerce, or of farmers wanting more land or labour. What the Molteno ministry was chiefly interested in was stability on the eastern frontier of the colony; the speeches, memoranda and private correspondence of Charles Brownlee, who became the Cape's first Secretary for Native Affairs in December 1872, make this clear beyond doubt.[3] Brownlee and his colleagues believed that conflicts between African groups east of the Kei threatened to involve the colony itself in war. Stability, therefore, demanded control. But, if that were so, this very reason for advance across the Kei suggested that advance be cautious. Too rapid an attempt to tame the turbulent frontier might produce the very instability which extension of Cape control was meant to bring to an end.

Though the Cape Government began to advance cautiously in 1873, Joseph Orpen, the agent it appointed east of the Kei in July of that year, was an ardent expansionist who soon carried the government forward into Griqualand East more quickly than it had intended to go. Two months after Orpen's appointment Brownlee accepted that the Mpondomise chiefs Mditshwa and Mhlontlo should be accepted as "British subjects" and brought under white rule.[4] In October 1874 independent Griqua rule came to an end east of the Drakensberg. The following year Brownlee "took over" Thembuland when the difficulties of the Thembu ruler, Ngangeliswe, gave the Cape the opportunity to extend "protection" and introduce magisterial rule. The war which broke out between Cape forces in the Transkei and the Gcaleka in September 1877 took the colonial ministry by surprise but enabled the colony to seize Gcalekaland, the territory of the enemy, and Bomvanaland as well. In the aftermath of the war, Sir Bartle Frere, the High Commissioner, was instrumental in preparing the way for Cape officials to be stationed in Xesibe country and at Port St Johns.

By the end of 1878, then, all of the Transkei except Pondoland had been brought under Cape magisterial rule. Yet the first annexations did not take place until September 1879,[5] and much of the territory ruled by Cape magistrates in 1878 was not annexed until 1885. The Cape Government had expected that extension of control would be followed by annexation almost at once. Without formal annexation Cape magisterial rule had no legal validity, though the vaguely-defined powers of the High Commission were used so as at least partially to obscure this.[6] In the case of Pondoland annexation did follow hard on the heels of the end of African rule: in March 1894 Cape troops were moved up to the Pondoland border and chief Sigcawu submitted to white rule; by the end of September an Annexation Act had been passed by the Cape Parliament and Pondoland had become part of the Cape.[7] The question why annexation east of the Kei took so long to be completed must therefore be broken down. We must ask why it took so long for Pondoland to be brought under Cape rule, but first let us ask why in the other cases annexation did not take place until long after the extension of Cape control.

Why annexation was delayed
By the time Pondoland was annexed in 1894 the annexation procedure was well-tried and the various steps involved could be taken speedily. In the mid-1870s there was no certainty as to how the responsible colony should go about annexing territory beyond its borders. Much time was spent waiting for one move to be completed before the next was begun. Both the Colonial and the Imperial Government took time feeling their way from step to step. The Cape Government had first to persuade Parliament to pass a resolution approving the expediency of the annexation of the area concerned. This resolution then went to England, where Letters Patent were issued approving the annexation

of that territory. After these had been received at the Cape, the Colonial Government could then introduce annexation legislation into Parliament. Once passed, the Annexation Act had to be approved by the Imperial Government or its agent in South Africa. The actual annexation followed when a proclamation was issued in terms of the Act. This cumbersome procedure was gradually streamlined, but in the 1870s it allowed much opportunity for delay. Unforeseen developments frequently brought the movement towards annexation to a temporary halt and set back the planned timetable, sometimes by years.

Britain was at times responsible for delaying the course of annexation. The Cape, as a colony, had to obtain British permission before it could annex, and this gave the Imperial Government a lever which it could use to try to get the Cape to act on some other matter. In 1876 Britain refused to allow the annexation of Thembuland unless the Cape first agreed to take over Griqualand West;[8] in 1879 it made it a condition of the annexation of Thembuland, Gcalekaland and Bomvanaland that the Cape first declare itself in favour of a South African confederation.[9] Towards the end of 1879 Britain decided that the question of the annexation of Thembuland, Gcalekaland and Bomvanaland should no longer be tied to quite other issues,[10] but then turned round and demanded that it supervise the way the territories to be annexed were to be governed once within the colony.[11] In imposing this new requirement, the British Government was influenced in part by a strong humanitarian lobby in London anxious to lessen what it saw to be the injustices of Cape African policy. But the chief reason for requiring supervision was that the British Government had become concerned that left to themselves the Cape colonists would provoke an African uprising and that Britain would then have to come to the rescue by sending in imperial troops. The new condition was a way of demonstrating imperial concern at the direction Cape African policy was taking under the Sprigg ministry. The Cape refused to surrender any of its freedom to determine its own African policy, and it was not until 1882, when circumstances had changed, that Britain dropped its demand for supervision.[12]

Ironically, the Cape had by then temporarily lost interest in annexation. Its initial enthusiasm for empire east of the Kei did not last into the 1880s. In 1873 the colony's first responsible ministry under Molteno had assumed the task of African administration on the eastern frontier with confidence, but a decade later war and rebellion east of the Kei and in Lesotho had shattered that confidence and for most of the 1880s the Cape was a reluctant imperialist, afraid to assume additional responsibilities, especially if they seemed likely to involve the risk of war. The people of the Transkei, for their part, through their response to the white intrusion, themselves helped shape the pattern of annexation. The Cape-Xhosa war of 1877–78 carried Cape troops and magistrates into Gcalekaland and Bomvanaland, but it also helped delay the course of annexation, especially when followed within three years by another armed attempt to reverse the incoming tide of white control. To the Cape the Transkeian rebellion of 1880–81, coming on top of the war of 1877–78, served as a warning that to rule east of the Kei might involve endless trouble. The Cape might find it difficult, if not impossible, to deal with a succession of rebellions. Revenue from the territories the Cape was ruling did not meet the cost of their administration, and there was as yet no solution to the problem of how to integrate the Transkei with the rest of the colony in such a way that the whites' dominant position in the colony as a whole was not jeopardised. Better then, many began to argue at the Cape, that the colony retreat behind the Kei.

Alternative solutions
The Transkeian rebellion not only held up annexation of the territories east of the Kei to the Cape, but also helped promote the cause of an alternative to Cape rule there. That the whole area should be allowed to revert to independent African rule was not seen as a realistic alternative, for that was thought to mean "anarchy" on the Cape borders.[13] Nor would the Cape admit Natal rule of any of the Transkei to be an alternative. The reasons why Natal's gaze had been

drawn southwards for decades are analysed elsewhere in this book.[14] The long-standing rivalry between the two colonies, more a matter of prestige than economic competition,[15] prevented any Cape Government from considering allowing the northern colony to absorb even the smallest piece of the Transkei. The arguments Natal presented in support of its case for obtaining a slice of the Transkeian cake, some of which made good sense,[16] were brushed aside with contempt. But, though both the idea of returning to independent African rule in the territories already brought under white control and the proposal that Natal should expand south of the Mthamvuna were anathema to Cape politicians, the Cape Government was persuaded in the early 1880s of the merits of another solution: direct imperial rule of the territories east of the Kei by the British Colonial Office.

Britain never expressed any desire or willingness to rule the Transkei itself. Responsible government was granted the Cape as a means of shifting the burden of expansion in South Africa onto the self-governing colony. On the one occasion when it seemed in London that Britain's strategic interests in the sub-continent might be set at risk by what happened in the territories east of the Kei, those interests were swiftly safeguarded by the declaration of a purely nominal protectorate over the Pondoland coast in January 1885, the only purpose of which was to keep Germany out of the region.[17] Pressure for direct imperial rule for the territories was chiefly applied, not in London, but at the Cape itself. Saul Solomon and other colonists of a humanitarian persuasion were among the first to campaign for British rule east of the Kei. Support for their position on the future of the territories grew until in 1883 the Cape Government itself came out openly in favour of it.[18] By that year the Scanlen Government had become persuaded that if it transferred the military and financial burdens of empire east of the Kei to Britain, the Cape would have as great an assurance of stability in that area as if it ruled there itself. Of secondary importance was the fact that, for reasons which will be mentioned below,[19] there seemed no likelihood of any sizeable amount of Transkeian land becoming available for white settlement.

Had the Scanlen Government formally requested the Colonial Office in London to relieve it of the responsibility of ruling the territories – as it had Lesotho, which Britain agreed to take over from the Cape in 1883 – it is at least possible that the Transkeian territories might then have remained outside the Union when it was constituted in 1910 and been led to independence in the 1960s with the other "High Commission territories". In the event, however, the opposition to Scanlen in the colonial election of early 1884 rejected the idea of an imperial presence east of the Kei and Scanlen's departure from office following the election meant the end of the movement for the "retrocession" of the Transkeian territories to Britain.

Upington, Sprigg and Rhodes, Scanlen's three successors, firmly believed that the Cape should eventually rule all the Transkei and that when the time was ripe Pondoland too should be annexed. Pondoland remained under African rule until 1894 chiefly because the Cape was not sufficiently anxious to impose its rule there to risk having to suppress possible armed resistance by the Mpondo. Rhodes finally acted when it seemed that if he continued to refuse to act Natal might step in and obtain at least some of Pondoland. By the time the northern colony received responsible government in 1893, the Cape had in effect been told by the Imperial Government that it might take over Pondoland whenever it wished to do so, whether that involved the use of force or not.[20] After civil war erupted on Natal's southern border in late 1893, the High Commissioner hinted that unless the Cape intervened to control the Pondoland situation, the promise that it might have *carte blanche* there might be jeopardised.[21] Rhodes was then quick to intervene and end African rule in Pondoland, leaving Natal with empty hands.

Some consequences of annexation
From the first annexation of Fingoland and Griqualand

East in 1879, the Transkeian territories, instead of being fully incorporated into the Cape's political, legal and administrative systems, as British Kaffraria was in 1866, were kept separate from "the colony proper" and governed in a distinctive way. The basic reason for this special status accorded the Transkei was that the great bulk of the Transkeian population was black, and that these blacks lived, not on white farms, but on their own land. In the South African context remarkably little Transkeian land fell to whites. This was partly because of the delay over annexation: legal title to land could not be granted before formal annexation had been completed. But annexation came eventually and yet little land was set aside for whites. In part this was because there was no land to set aside. As whites seized land in the more westerly sections of the Cape eastern frontier zone, Africans had continually been pushed back into "independent Kaffraria", where there was presumed to be room for them. But there was nowhere for Africans to be pushed to beyond the Transkei. Given the type of agriculture practised there, the Transkei was densely populated by the end of the 1870s. Pressure of population on the land was made worse by the fact that the Cape Government as deliberate policy forced many groups of Africans from the Ciskei across the Kei in the 1870s and 80s.[22] One answer to the question why more land did not fall to whites in the Transkei is that it fell to whites in the Ciskei instead, the Transkei being used as a "dumping ground" for unwanted Africans.

Another part of the answer is that in the 1880s and 90s Cape governments feared that to take large sections of land from Africans east of the Kei might provoke another revolt, and no government was prepared to risk that. Some land that had belonged to the rebels of 1880–81 was sold to whites, but in 1882–83 the Cape Government of the day checked an influx of white squatters into the western districts of the Transkei. As already mentioned, the Cape did not absorb Pondoland until 1894 not because it was forbidden to do so by the Imperial Government but because it feared the Mpondo might resist with arms an attempt to end their independence and that a Mpondo war might set the rest of the Transkei aflame. It was almost a decade after the Lesotho fiasco that the Cape recovered its earlier confidence in its ability to rule large numbers of Africans. There was not a second Transkeian rebellion – after 1881 African resistance to the pressures of white rule moved into other channels, such as the independent church movement[23] – but the possibility that there might be another rebellion made the Cape cautious in its administration east of the Kei and prevented more land being taken into white hands.

That a part of the Cape might be ruled separately from the rest ran across the deeply-rooted belief in identity held by most Cape politicians in the middle decades of the century. It was only in the 1880s and 90s that the idea that a sizeable part of the colony might be administered indefinitely as a separate African area gained wide-spread acceptance. The leading Cape administrators serving in the Transkei in these decades – Stanford, Elliot and Blyth – were convinced of the need for a separate status for the Transkei. As a "black man's country" they believed it should be ruled more autocratically than the rest of the colony. Gradually Cape politicians came to argue that it was in the interests of the Transkeians that the area be a "reserve", protecting the African population from the inroads of white farmers and exposure to the disruptive effects of the ordinary Cape law. Less frequently mentioned was the fact that giving the Transkei a separate status would make it easier to turn it into a labour pool.

Treating the Transkei differently was in the interests of white control, not only in the Transkei itself, but also in the enlarged colony as a whole. The Cape's white minority did not view the addition of the Transkei's large black population to the colony without considerable concern. In the mid-1870s one third of the colonial population (excluding Lesotho, which, as it turned out, was only temporarily part of the Cape) was white.[24] When the third general colonial census was taken in 1891, it was estimated that had the boundaries of the colony remained as in 1875 the percentage of whites would have increased slightly in the intervening period. But instead of being over one third of the total in 1891, the white population was under one quarter. This was because the African share had shot up to 55 per cent.[25] By the time the next colonial census was held, a decade after the annexation of Pondoland, Africans constituted 60 per cent of the total population of the Cape. Commenting on this, the 1904 census report remarked: "Successive annexations of territory in which there is an enormous preponderance of coloured inhabitants are chiefly responsible for the adverse [sic] ratio."[26] The white community at the Cape, then, found itself becoming more and more of a minority in a society in which the number of Africans increased by leaps and bounds. The result was that the white race attitudes of the frontier, the belief in racial difference and the idea of the African as enemy, far from weakening in the era of stability following the end of the initial resistance to the extension of white control east of the Kei, instead hardened and helped shape government policy. As the colony's African population increased, talk of assimilating it faded and fewer made mention of the colony's "civilising mission". The white governing class came to fear that the Africans of the Transkei, instead of becoming "civilised" by being brought within the colony, might "barbarise" the colony. Barriers went up to prevent this happening. "Owing to the smallness of the white population", Rhodes told the Cape Parliament in 1894, "they [the whites] must do everything to maintain their supremacy."[27]

By reducing the proportion of whites in the total colonial population, the annexation of the Transkeian territories highlighted the elitist nature of "self-government" at the Cape. Though the incorporation of the Transkei posed no immediate threat to white control of the political system in the enlarged colony, the Cape's white minority nevertheless took advantage of the occasion to entrench its position of dominance. At the same time as the colonial franchise was extended across the Kei in 1887, it was made more

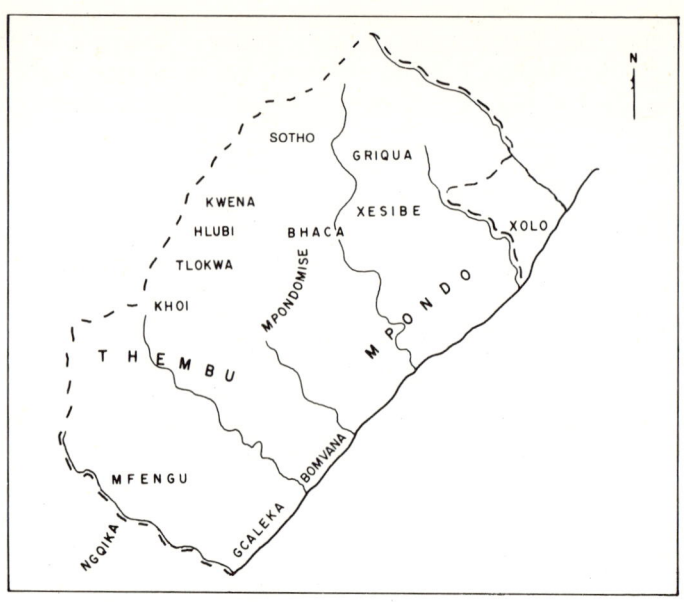

▲ The Transkeian Territories: *Peoples (c. 1872).*

▼ The Transkeian Territories: *Political divisions (1880's) and the main road through the territories.*

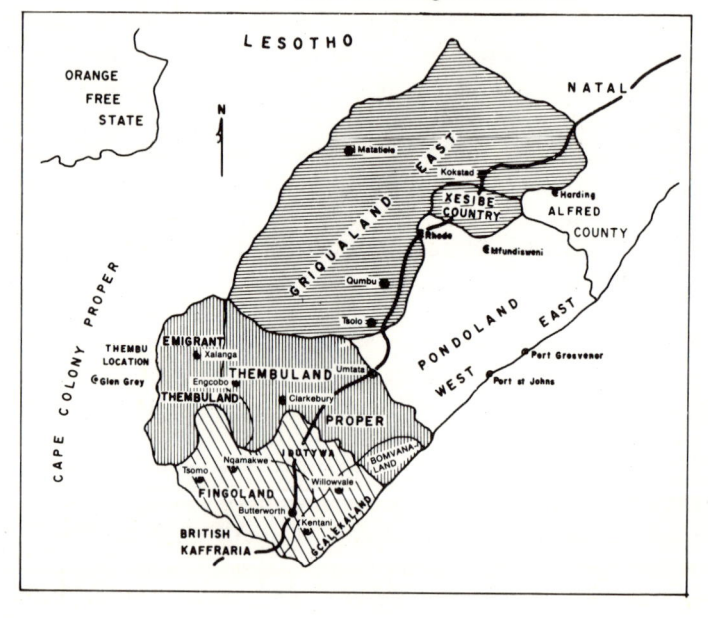

difficult for Africans to obtain the vote in the colony as a whole. The Parliamentary Voters Registration Act of 1887 and the Franchise Act of 1892 both restricted African participation in Cape politics.[28] In approving them the Imperial Government in effect accepted that the Cape's white minority might do what it wished to secure itself in power. In this way, then, it may be said that the annexation of the territories east of the Kei to the Cape helped make clear what had only been implied in the grant of responsible government to the colony in 1872: that self-government in the form of responsible government had transferred to the Cape's white minority the power to determine its place in the community of which it formed part, a community which by the end of 1894 included all the people of the Transkei.

FOOTNOTES

1. In this chapter I draw upon my unpublished thesis, The Annexation of the Transkeian Territories, 1872–1895 (Oxford D.Phil. 1972), which examines the evidence on which many of the following arguments are based.
2. Northern Nigeria is a good example.
3. See, e.g. Brownlee's report to the Cape Colonial Secretary, 2 May 1873, in N.A. 840 (Cape Archives) (part of this report was printed as *Cape Parl. Papers,* A 10, 1873).
4. Brownlee's memo of 27 Sept. 1873, N.A. 159 (1873 folder) (Cape Archives).
5. Proclamations 110 of 15 Sept. 1879 and 112 of 17 Sept. 1879, given in A.N. Macfayden, ed., *Statutes, Proclamations and Government Notices in force in the Native Territories of the Colony of the Cape of Good Hope, on the 30th June 1907* (Cape Town 1907) pp. 4–38.
6. On this see J. Benyon, Basutoland and the High Commission with particular reference to the years 1868–1884: The Changing Nature of the Imperial Government's "Special Responsibility" for the Territory (Oxford D.Phil. 1969).
7. Act 5 of 1894 and proclamations 339 and 340 of 1894 (Macfayden, ed., *Statutes,* pp. 236–8).
8. Herbert to Molteno, 6 Sept. 1876, C.O. 879/10, Confidential Print African 105, p. 158 (P.R.O.).
9. Hicks Beach to Frere, 12 June 1879, C.O. 879/16, Confidential Print 203, p. 157 (P.R.O.).
10. V. Hicks Beach, *Life of Sir Michael Hicks Beach,* I (London 1932) p. 164: Hicks Beach to Frere, 20 Nov. 1879.
11. Frere to Hicks Beach, 26 Jan. 1880, C.O. 48/493 (P.R.O.).

12. Saunders, Annexation of Transkeian Territories, ch. IV.
13. E.g. *Cape Argus,* 14 August 1879, speech by Sprigg in Cape Assembly, 12 August.
14. Ch. 7.
15. B. le Cordeur, The Relations between the Cape and Natal, 1846–1879, *AYB* 1965 part 1.
16. For example, after Natal's southern boundary was fixed at the Mthamvuna River in 1866, the main road from Harding, the administrative centre of the new county of Alfred, to Pietermaritzburg ran for a stretch through Cape territory, an anomaly which called for at least an adjustment of the border that would give Natal control of the road. No such adjustment was ever made.
17. *Cape Gov. Gazette,* 5 Jan. 1885: Proclamation by the High Commissioner, 5 Jan. 1885.
18. Saunders, Annexation of the Transkeian Territories, ch. V.
19. Below, pp. 193–4.
20. Saunders, Annexation of the Transkeian Territories, pp. 413–8.
21. *Cape Parl. Papers,* G 59, 1894, p. 12: High Commissioner to Cape ministers, 5 Feb. 1894.
22. The expulsion of the Ngqika in 1878 is only the most striking example of this.
23. Cf. C. Saunders, Tile and the Thembu Church, *JAH,* XI (4) 1970.
24. *Cape Parl. Papers,* G 42, 1876, p. 11.
25. *Cape Parl. Papers,* G 6, 1892, pp. xvii–xviii.
26. *Cape Parl. Papers,* G 19, 1905, p. xxix.
27. *Cape Times,* 13 August 1894.
28. Figures on the growing number of Africans registering to vote before the 1887 Act are given in J. L. McCracken, *The Cape Parliament 1854–1910* (Oxford 1967) p. 80 note 1. The Acts of 1887 and 1892 are analysed in S. Trapido, White Conflict and Non-white Participation in the Politics of the Cape of Good Hope, 1853-1910 (London Ph.D. 1970) ch. VII and Saunders, Annexation of the Transkeian Territories, ch. VI.

9

AFRICAN EDUCATION AND SOCIETY IN THE NINETEENTH CENTURY EASTERN CAPE

Michael Ashley

THIS chapter examines the definitions of the rôle of western-type education for Africans held by whites and blacks in the eastern Cape in the nineteenth century. The society which formed the *milieu* in which these definitions developed was one in which a strong element of conflict was present. In these circumstances it was natural that European and African definitions of what education for Africans should comprise should differ. This paper attempts an analysis of these differences.

Taking a broad view, the Europeans can be seen as the initiating agents in the modernisation of South African society.[1] Although tenuous to begin with, their control became more and more complete as the century progressed and one of the functions of this control was to try to keep a grip on the process by which the Africans entered into the developing society. African education was crucial to this process and the European definitions of it varied according to the different phases of the process. Definitions also differed somewhat as between missionaries and government, but they were together concerned progressively with evangelisation, cultural conversion and pacification, economic requirements and social control. African reactions to modernisation, and the education which accompanied it, changed from an initial rejection to a growing acceptance and enthusiasm. Rejection sprang from their realisation of the threat European education posed to their traditions and identity, acceptance developed with the breakdown of intact traditional societies and the realisation that education was the road to mobility, to the achievement of aspirations, in the new society that they were entering.

In the first quarter of the nineteenth century, African society formed what was for the most part a cohesive and intact social order. The chiefs' power ensured the continuance of custom and tradition. Even at that stage, however, marginal groups, the Mfengu and Gqunukhwebe, existed outside the mainstream of Cape Nguni life. Although exhibiting Cape Nguni language and customs, they did not possess the same degree of social cohesion, in the case of the Mfengu because of the Mfecane, in the case of the Gqunukhwebe on account of the Khoi presence and links with the colony and Europeans.

The missionaries found these people the most receptive to their endeavours, and many of their early claims of success refer to converts to Christianity who came from Mfengu or Gqunukhwebe society.[2] The missionaries were an important force from the 1820s onwards. They came from England and Scotland as a result of the Evangelical Revival with a desire to convert people who were living in what they regarded as a fallen state to a belief in God and in Jesus Christ, His only Son. These early missionaries accepted that all men belonged to one family. Nevertheless, their view was of "benighted" rather than "noble" savages, whose salvation lay not only in a belief in God but also in the adoption of a "civilised" way of life, in their eyes the European culture of the period. Africans were seen as "a fine race of people and nothing but religion and civilisation are wanting to exalt them in the scale of being – to raise them in true dignity of human nature".[3]

The slow progress the missionaries made in their work of

conversion, even among the Mfengu,[4] taught them that adoption of Christianity and "civilisation" went hand in hand, thus indicating that the real problem they faced was one of cultural conversion.

Education was seen as indispensable to the work of conversion. Schools were necessary to teach Africans to read the Bible. Thus functional literacy both in the vernacular, as translations became available, and English, was the initial aim. As the cultural obstacle to conversion became apparent, education was to be a means whereby pupils were weaned away from the tribal way of life. Outstation education was confined to functional literacy, while at the mission stations proper the curriculum was broadened to include English reading and writing, arithmetic and geography. The missionaries were aware, however, that schools could do more than impart knowledge and skills. They could also effect a change in values and habits. In his Draft Memorandum on the Increase of the Native Agency of 1831, William Ritchie Thomson outlined some of the indirect benefits resulting from regular schooling, including the habit of attending regular meetings and the "disciplining of the disposition".[5] The role of education was thus defined as part of the attack on tribal culture. After the war of 1835, the desire to expand their system of education was so strong that the missionaries created an important role for "Native Agents", Africans who enjoyed a higher level of education than was currently available and who could thus play a useful auxiliary role in mission work. It led the Scots to establish Lovedale and the Wesleyans the Watson Institute in Grahamstown.

While the early missionaries may have acknowledged a common brotherhood with the aboriginal inhabitants, they did not demonstrate a similar respect for the traditional culture. They attacked "ancestor worship", witchcraft and magic, polygamy, the *lobola* custom, initiation and styles of dress. Pressure was brought to bear on children at school to abandon these practices, and the wearing of clothes was a crucial issue. The "School – Red" division dates from this time.[6] Schools were focal points for the missionary pressure on those aspects of traditional culture which were seen to be obstructing the advance of Christian civilisation.

The Cape Nguni rejected the education that was offered. It was rejected as part of the attempt to change their way of life, their national customs and their identity. To become a "school" person was to lose a way of life, a culture. It was to accept an education which involved the idea that many of the traditional customs and rites were obnoxious to Christianity. In addition, chiefs found school people unamenable to their authority, and boys were diverted from their herding duties, thus interfering with economic life. The result was that mission educational effort, for the first half of the century, was directed largely towards the Mfengu, the Gqunukhwebe and refugees from tribal society such as people accused of witchcraft.

Various sanctions were employed against anyone attending school, and the late 1830s and early 1840s were marked by extremely low school attendance. Describing the period immediately before the war of 1846, Williams says that the situation in the area served by the Scottish missions "appears to have been one which almost smacked of national hysteria", with a boycotting of church and school on a wide scale.[7] There is also evidence that Cape Nguni leaders took aggressive action to assert their traditional identity. There are mission accounts of traditional ceremonies being held within sight of the missions, particularly on the Sabbath, in defiance of the missionaries and as reminders to their own people.[8]

After the war of 1847 and the subsequent annexation of British Kaffraria, government interest in education became very strong. There was now the problem of administering intransigent tribesmen who had previously lived outside the colonial borders, and government saw education as an instrument for the pacification and incorporation of the tribesmen into colonial society. As African political and military resistance sprang from an intact tribal structure, the aim became one of "civilisation". Missionary activities fitted well into this programme, as shown by Sir Harry Smith's 1848 circular asking their advice on how best to achieve this aim. Among the recommendations was one for expansion of education, particularly through the increase of native schoolmasters.[9] Small government moneys were made available to the missionaries for educational purposes.

The linking of the "cultural conversion" or "civilising" role of education of the missionaries to government programmes for pacification and social control was greatly strengthened by the arrival of Sir George Grey as Governor in the 1850s. After experience in Australia and New Zealand in the "pacification" of the aboriginal inhabitants, he was an enthusiastic supporter of the programme of industrial education. The purpose of this industrial education was to "civilise races emerging from barbarism" by turning them into a settled and industrious peasantry, ready to work on their own land or that of European farmers. Government financial support and encouragement led to the establishment of industrial departments or institutions at Lovedale, Healdtown, Salem, Lesseyton, D'Urban, Shiloh and Goshen. Education was fitted into an overall policy aimed at undermining the power of chiefs, encouragement of African peasant agriculture and mixed patchwork landholding in the Ciskei. The combined effect of these policies, the war of 1850–3, and the disastrous cattle-killing of 1857 was the serious disruption of tribal society. Numbers of individuals became detached from the tribal social matrices and ready to enter into new relationships.

This process was accelerated by the decisive economic changes resulting from the discovery of diamonds and, later, gold. Africans were sucked into the developing economy and racial inter-dependence became characteristic of South African economic life everywhere. The idea grew that education was to be viewed, not as the enemy of traditional society but as the key to the new conditions with which the Africans found themselves faced.

White over black
Davis describes the irony in the situation that now arose.[10] Whereas the missionary and government aim had hitherto been the cultural conversion of Africans, now that the latter were ready for change Europeans no longer wanted it, at least along the lines worked for by the early missionaries. Growing racial competition in South African society was one important factor, and the society that was emerging saw Europeans stressing the subordinate position of Africans. Davis stresses, too, the importance of changes in racial thought in Europe and Great Britain, arising from the influence of Charles Darwin's theory of evolution.[11] These changes identified the racial group as a unit of development[12] and applied the concept of the survival of the fittest to inter-racial struggles. Africans, according to this view, were emerging from barbarism, were racially handicapped and faced a long evolutionary growth before they could aspire to parity with Europeans.

Missionaries and government showed the influence of these new considerations. Whereas the older generation of missionaries were conscious of cultural superiority they did not employ racial and evolutionary categories in their thinking. Thus Tiyo Soga, the first African to be ordained in the Presbyterian Church, was taken to Scotland, educated there and married to a Scottish woman, and was clearly not considered to suffer from any inherent disability due to his race.[13]

The change in Scottish missionary attitudes can be seen in the dispute between the first principal of Lovedale, William Govan, and his successor, James Stewart.[14] Stewart joined the staff of the institution in 1867, bearing a set of instructions from the Foreign Mission Committee of the Free Church in Scotland. Whereas Govan had run Lovedale as a European institution, Stewart and the Mission Committee, representing the new views, saw it as needing to more fully adjust itself to its African conditions.

Govan, catering both for the children of European missionaries and Africans, aimed for European standards and curricula, providing what the Rev. H. Calderwood described as "a very superior English classical and mathematical education" at the higher levels.[15] Although there were very few Africans in the upper levels of the institution, Govan saw their numbers increasing. He saw the African future in an integrated society and maintained that they needed the highest form of European education they could cope with.

> It is desirable that Natives should be enabled to take their place alongside of Europeans, not only in the office of the ministry, but also in the various positions of society, secular as well as ecclesiastical.[16]

Thus Africans, following the Tiyo Soga model, were to be given a European education which would assimilate them fully into European society. There were no considerations of a racial nature in the matter of the individual's achievement of status.

The Foreign Mission Committee, however, wished to stop the teaching of Latin and Greek to Africans, having English as the only "classical" language. The stress was to be on producing Native Agents who would fill the roles of readers and catechists. At this stage, African educational efforts should be directed towards the general uplift of the race, rather than upon the education of a restricted number of elites and their full assimilation into colonial society. Stewart backed the new policy and soon became principal of Lovedale. Education for Africans was now to be different from education for Europeans. Stewart clarified his position in an address to the Lovedale Literary Society in June 1884. He told his audience that they should not aspire to an education of the same kind as enjoyed by Europeans, which in those days was largely mathematical and classical at its higher levels. This was because aspirations must not be personally channelled, but should be bound up with the general progress of the race.[17] Thus Latin and Greek were actually closed to Africans, except those doing the theology course.[18] There was no point, said Stewart, in teaching the dead languages "to a race as yet intellectually dormant and far behind in the race of nations".[19] This in effect cut Africans off from the core of Victorian education, as the study of the dead languages was seen as preparing the whole person for a higher life of fine taste and judgement.

The education Stewart planned was broad and practical and designed to begin the long task of general uplift, also of fitting Africans for the realities of colonial society. Thus Lovedale should turn out men who had had a practical education and who would work industriously, under European supervision if necessary. Teachers were trained for native schools, also as catechists and preachers, and young men were apprenticed and trained in the trades of printing, wagonmaking, blacksmithing, carpentering, bookbinding, general agricultural work and telegraphy. It must, however, be noted that Stewart did not permanently exclude Africans from higher education. In 1878 he had declared that Lovedale or some other place should eventually become a university for Africans. By 1903-4 he was strongly advocating the establishment of a Native College for South Africa.[20]

Stewart found an echo in the evidence given by the Rev. Charles Taberer of St. Matthew's before the 1879 Education Commission.
> Many children attend the schools for a few years and the only after-results are that they are able to read Kaffir fairly, English imperfectly and to write a very imperfect letter. And then, as a consequence of their superior knowledge, they look upon the positions of ordinary servants and labourers as beneath them. Not being fitted at the same time for any other, they become idlers at home and a burden to society in general.[21]

Mission attitudes correspond to those held by government at the same time. European definitions of the role of education were crystallised in the Education Act of 1865, which regularised government support for education. There were to be three categories of schools, one primarily for whites, one for poor whites and coloureds, and one for aborigines. The third aimed only at elementary education. In his Report of 1868, Sir Langham Dale accepted that standards of instruction would for a long time remain low in these schools because the intellectual power among the Africans was "dormant".[22] There must be a basic education for the many, higher education serving only to create a class whose "very advantages have made a wide breach between themselves and their heathen kindred and have been at the same time inoperative or inadequate to open them a way into higher social intercourse".[23] The need was for industrial education which would provide trained labour, prevent Africans becoming "educated idlers" and make for general security. Dale further supported the view that European education must always be the colony's first concern.

The 1880s saw the beginning of an extremely high level of European hostility towards African education of any kind at all. In July 1887, for example, the Hon. Mr van Rhyn moved in the Legislative Council that "the time has now arrived that the Government should henceforth discontinue all grants for the instruction of Natives".[24] Some of this hostility arose from fear of African competition in the skilled trades.[25] There was also fierce criticism of the "bookish" education offered by the missions and the type of African who emerged from them. The latter they saw as being potentially disruptive to society as their ambitions could clearly not be satisfied in the tribal context or in a subordinate social position. Education was believed to be creating "an aggressive spirit ... which renders them less docile and less disposed to be contented with the position for which nature and circumstances have fitted them."[26]

So James Stewart and Langham Dale, both committed to the cause of elementary and industrial education, found themselves forced to use the defence that education was a positive, not a negative force in ensuring the stability of the existing social order. *Lovedale Past and Present,* a review of past and present pupils published in 1887, was compiled by Stewart as an answer to his critics. In the introduction he emphasised that Lovedale pupils did receive a practical education preparing them to work usefully, and that educated people were preferable to uneducated as they were less liable to steal cattle or commit other anti-social acts. Lovedale was particularly upset by the accusation that one of its ex-students had died in the war of 1877 fighting on the side of the rebels. In his Report of 1883, Dale asserted that education was a firm ally of peace as educated natives had all to lose and nothing to gain by war.[27] In spite of these efforts there were severe cut-backs on expenditure on African education by the Cape Parliament in 1888, a time of general economic depression.[28]

Africans demand education
During this time, while Europeans were defining the role of African education in terms of fitting Africans for subordinate roles in society, teaching them to work industriously in trades and agriculture, and making them amenable members of the society of the time, African demand for education was steadily growing. The breaking-down of tribal society had led to the growth of a small but active African elite, many the children of parents who had been among the first to be educated and to move away from the tribal world. They saw education as the key to social mobility in the new society which was emerging, the *sine qua non* for personal advancement and for the growth of an educated elite to provide leadership for the Africans of the colony. To them education was the agency which would enable them to enter fully, and on equal terms, into the new society. There appears also to have been growing support for education among tribal elites. One can cite the example of initiative leading to the formation of Blythswood. There was, from the 1860s onwards, a steady growth in the number of African schools qualifying for aid in terms of the 1865 Act.[29]

The modernising elites formed the Native Educational Association in 1879, with the Rev. Elijah Makiwane as president. This was a pressure group working for better facilities, particularly at higher levels. The need for it sprang from the fact that Lovedale was the only school in the colony where Africans could get an organised secondary education. Apart from men like Makiwane, Bokwe and Mzimba who pursued theological studies at higher levels at Lovedale, the first African matriculant, S. P. Sihlali, passed the examination in 1880, followed by J. T. Jabavu in 1883, and the next five all passed in the 1890s.[30] Jabavu was an outstanding example of this new elite. After he had qualified as a teacher at Lovedale, he taught at Somerset East. At the same time he apprenticed himself to the local newspaper to learn about printing and also studied under a Gill College professor, Greek and Latin being his favourite subjects.[31]

It is in the context of elite aspirations that the African demand for a classical education, very noticeable from a reading of the columns of the *Christian Express* in the 1880s, must be viewed. To take one example, Joseph Moss, an interpreter in the High Court in Kimberley and a Lovedale product himself, gave an address in the Kimberley Town Hall in which he expressed the dissatisfaction of the elite with the education available. He made the point very strongly that many of the objections raised against educating Africans only had weight because the education they received was half an education. It needed to be the finest European education available, which included the classics, before adequate judgment could be made.[32] At a more mundane level, the frequent complaints made by European educationists of the African obsession with examination results, which exposed them to the criticism that they did not appreciate what education was really all about, constitute further evidence of an attitude which regarded education as the key to social mobility.

The separatist churches provided another source of initiative in the provision of schools. The African Methodist

Episcopal Church's schools included one in Cape Town (the Bethel Institute); schools established by the Ethiopians and African Presbyterians received government aid. It was in the campaign for higher education, however, that the separatists and the A.M.E. Church made the greatest impact. They sent a large number of students, over 100 at least, to Negro Colleges in the United States, notably Lincoln, Howard, Wilberforce and Tuskegee.[33] Seboni speaks of "an unparalleled exodus of non-European students to Great Britain and the Continent in search of higher education" in the last years of the 19th century.[34] J. T. Jabavu sent his son to the United Kingdom when he failed to gain admittance to Dale College, Kingwilliamstown. Fear of the consequences for South African society of foreign influences to which the students were exposed, particularly in America, was a strong factor leading the South African Native Affairs Commission to recommend the establishment of a South African Native College for higher education. This was eventually founded in 1916.

Thus the nineteenth century closed with strong African demands for the adequate provision of a Western education which would equip Africans to compete in a South Africa offering increasing economic and social opportunities. This demand met strong resistance from the entrenched whites who feared the consequences of anything other than a carefully controlled expansion of African education. The pattern which persists to the present had been set.

FOOTNOTES

1. When I use the term "modernisation" I have in mind the broad definition offered by S. N. Eisenstadt: "Historically, modernisation is the process of change towards those types of social, economic and political systems that have developed in Western Europe and North America from the 17th to the 19th centuries and have then spread to other European countries and in the 19th and 20th centuries to the South American, Asian and African continents" (*Modernisation: Protest and Change* (Engelwood Cliffs 1966) p. 1).

2. D. Williams, Missionaries on the Eastern Frontier of the Cape Colony (Ph.D. University of the Witwatersrand 1959) ch. 7.
3. *Glasgow Mission Society Annual Report,* 1823, p. 21. Quoted in D. Williams, Missionaries, p. 172.
4. D. Williams, Missionaries, ch. 8.
5. See D. Williams, Missionaries, pp. 205–7.
6. M. Wilson and L. Thompson, eds., *Oxford History of South Africa* I (Oxford 1969) p. 265.
7. D. Williams, Missionaries, p. 342.
8. D. Williams, Missionaries, p. 338.
9. A. E. du Toit, *Earliest South African Documents on the Education and Civilisation of the Bantu* (Pretoria 1963) p. 17.
10. R. H. Davis, Nineteenth Century African Education in the Cape Colony: A Historical Analysis (Ph.D. Wisconsin 1969) p. 289.
11. Davis, Nineteenth Century Education, p. 173.
12. M. Banton, *Race Relations* (London 1970) ch. 3.
13. J. Chalmers, *Tiyo Soga* (Edinburgh 1877).
14. R. H. W. Shepherd, *Lovedale, South Africa: The Story of a Century 1841–1941.* (Lovedale 1940) pp. 152–67.
15. Shepherd, *Lovedale,* p. 147.
16. Shepherd, *Lovedale,* p. 156.
17. *Christian Express,* 2 June 1884, p. 91.
18. Shepherd, *Lovedale,* p. 173.
19. *Christian Express,* 2 June 1884, p. 90.
20. Shepherd, *Lovedale,* pp. 260–1.
21. Cape of Good Hope, *Education Commission* 1879, p. 151.
22. Cape of Good Hope, *Report of the Superintendent-General of Education* 1868, p. 8.
23. Cape, *Report of SGE,* 868, p. 7.
24. Shepherd, *Lovedale,* p. 222.
25. Shepherd, *Lovedale,* p. 223.
26. *South African Native Affairs Commission,* 1905 I, p. 66.
27. Cape, *Report of SGE* 1883, p. 6.
28. Davis, Nineteenth Century Education, p. 274.
29. Davis, *ibid,* p. 246.
30. D. D. T. Jabavu, *The Life of John Tengo Jabavu* (Lovedale 1922) p. 14.
31. Jabavu, *Life of Jabavu,* p. 13.
32. *Christian Express,* 1 Oct. 1884, pp. 155–158.
33. Evidence of Bishop Coppin in *South African Native Affairs Commission* 1905 II; M. Seboni asserts (The South African Native College, Fort Hare, 1903–54 (D.Ed. University of South Africa 1954)) that over 200 Non-Europeans went to the United States for higher education.
34. Seboni, The South African Native College, p. 7.

10

SOME FIELDS FOR RESEARCH

Monica Wilson

THE conference at which most of the material in this book was presented demonstrated the value of cross-disciplinary studies. The first two chapters of the book underline this. Mr Derricourt has considerably extended our knowledge of early settlement in the Ciskei and Transkei, proving the richness of material available, confirming the interaction of hunting people and stock owners, and indicating that cattle-owners lived in the Keiskamma valley from the eleventh century A.D. He has shown a conflict between archaeological evidence and oral tradition, since in the foothills of the Drakensberg only evidence of hunting peoples has so far been found, whereas oral tradition (as recorded before 1883) points to a movement of pastoral peoples – Thembu, Mpondomise, Xhosa – from the upper reaches of the Mzimvubu towards the coast.[1] Further intensive archaeological work is clearly needed to trace the movements of people. Did the "sources of the Mzimvubu" of oral tradition mean no more than the middle belt of the Transkei as opposed to the coast? Ancient game-crossings over the Drakensberg might prove particularly valuable points for study, for game-crossings persist in time and have been the haunt of hunters elsewhere, through centuries. Fortunately, a study by a zoologist, Mr C. J. Skead, on the mammals of the Ciskei, showing their distribution and certain migration routes, is nearing completion.

Professor Opland, an English language scholar, shows the value of traditional praise poems for understanding past political relationships and contributes appreciably by demonstrating the *combination* of memorized and improvised phrases. The praises also illuminate contemporary relationships and are adapted to the audiences to which they are recited, as Dr Mafeje showed in his analysis of the scalding phrases used in the praises of a Thembu chief on a visit to Langa in 1961, and those recited by the bard *(imbongi)* of the senior Thembu chief, Sabata, in the Transkei, between 1959 and 1963[2]. The political implications of the poems are reflected in the violent disagreement between Xhosa-speakers of different political parties on the reputations of living bards.

In a valuable paper presented at the conference, but not included in this volume since it dealt with Zululand, Professor Colin Webb showed a connection in Natal between access to a variety of resources in types of grazing and agricultural land and the growth of kingdoms. Alberti mentioned in 1810[3] the importance of differences in sour, sweet, and mixed veld to the Xhosa, the advantages of change in pasture, and the burning of sour-veld, and there can be no doubt that the movement of cattle-owners in the Transkei and Ciskei was related to types of grazing.[4] Various "great places" of Xhosa chiefs were in sweet-veld areas, but some used the sour-veld of the Mathole – "the mountains of the calves" – for early summer grazing, and Mpondo chiefs had cattle-posts on the sour-veld of the coast. Van der Kemp mentioned that the Xhosa "prefer a woody situation"[5], and there is ample evidence that the Nguni people generally selected forest or bush land for cultivation, and fertilized the soil by burning the bush. This continues on the edges of forest country even where open grassveld is available for cultivation, for the good reason that yields are much higher where woodash has fallen. The hunting people preferred an "open situation"[6] and drier country, since their bows were useless in wet weather. Many of the rock-shelters known to have been occupied were indeed in rain-shadow.

There is a great need for detailed local histories with maps, showing altitude, rainfall, soils, veld-types, forest or bush, reed beds, clay and ore deposits, rock shelters, settlements as now existing, as remembered in oral tradition, and as proved by artifacts and middens. Footpaths and boundaries marked by stone cairns *(izivivane)* are also pointers to ancient lines of communication and boundaries. Even changes in veld types can sometimes be documented from oral history, written record, or botanical evidence. Acocks' maps of *Veld Types in South Africa* provide a basis, and it is conspicuous that his projection for the year 1400 shows no sour-veld for the Transkei or Ciskei but forest or bush country, joining sweet-veld in the mountains. A small area of mixed grassveld around Matatiele is the one exception.

Changing land use can also be recorded by local historians who take the trouble to collect, collate, and sift oral tradition. For example, where were the cattle posts and hunting areas of 19th century chiefdoms: where did men go to hunt when mourning the death of this or that chief? And when and where were compact villages established on communal land? What were the compulsions to move? The change in the distribution of homesteads within my own memory in the Tyhume valley is conspicuous, and is linked to increasing density of population but also to government pressure. There is evidence that among the Bhaca the valley bottoms – the straths – were once reserved for grazing, being the richest land available, and only later used for fields.[7] Was this a general pattern? And before the concentration of homesteads under government pressure were the chosen sites indeed *always* along ridges or high on their slopes? The "great places" and burial places of at least some chiefs can be identified and appropriately marked. And what has been the shift in crops grown, and at what dates?

There are tantalizing references to trade routes along which tobacco, dagga, and metal passed; then ivory and cattle in exchange for beads and blankets. There is reference in written records to a track passing the modern Fort Brown, to the fair at Fort Willshire and the Keiskamma crossing nearby; to elephant hunters steering by "Cafferlandsberg", which was almost certainly Intaba ka Ndoda near Debe Nek. Were the Kei, Mbashe, Mthatha, and Mzimvubu crossings for traders single or many?

Work on place names, their corruption, derivation and diversity, reflecting a succession of locally spoken languages, has been done by a number of scholars,[8] but many local names are still unrecorded on maps or in written records, and these also are important for historical understanding, for place names throw light on history. So also do local differences in dialect. These are modified by schools, by literacy, by radio, and by working away from home, and dialect differences need to be recorded quickly.

The work on crafts, on artifacts, on styles in dress such as is being done by Mr Gitywa of Fort Hare, Miss Shaw of Cape Town and Dr van Warmelo of Pretoria[9] reflect the rapidly changing material culture of the region. The point of greatest interest to the historian and anthropologist is when and why certain changes occurred. For example, Chief Poto recorded that the general use of red clay as a cosmetic was dropped in the Nyandeni during the mourning for his father, Bokleni – a period when no one might use cosmetics – but it was not resumed when the country came out of mourning. A generation later, Western Pondoland took instead to using reckets-blue for blueing blankets and cloths. This was after 1933 and before 1954; exactly when and why has not been recorded. It was, however, a fashion that took hold also among the Nyakyusa of Tanzania during the 1940s or early 1950s, and is likely to have spread from the goldmines of the Reef or of the Orange Free State where both Mpondo and Nyakyusa worked, and sometimes fought. Who were the fashion leaders and who initiated this change? Drums were not made or played traditionally in the Transkei or Ciskei, and they began to be heard in the Tyhume valley of the Ciskei in the early 1960s, played by or for Zionist leaders.

For most historians political history is nearer the centre of interest than ecological change or changes in artifacts, music, and styles. But in political history, also, local histories are badly needed with details of oral tradition of the royal line, of lineages (identified by *iziduko*) clustering in the area, of the proportions of each, of cleavages existing and how these have persisted and changed through time. Reading of clashes occurring and recurring in some districts, the outsider asks what are the root causes of these: conflict over grazing, or arable land between local groups? Conflict over leadership? Conflict between conservative and radical? Are "school people" and "reds" distinguishable? Do they co-operate or does opposition between them still exist? Do alignments persist through generations or do they change? And what are the occasions of conflict? Fights obviously flare up at beer drinks, particularly at the Christmas or New Year festivities, and the indications are that, in some areas at least, the lines of cleavage have remained constant through generations, and reflect primarily competition for land. It remains to be demonstrated how widely such a hypothesis holds.

Some ancient conflicts are resuscitated and used by party politicians for their own purposes: this happens in all racial groups in South Africa. But some conflicts disappear, and it is relevant for the historian and anthropologist to consider *why* some conflicts persist and others do not. Conflict between highland and lowland in Scotland, and on the Scottish-English border has largely disappeared, but it has not between Protestant and Catholic in Northern Ireland. Will ambitious politicians succeed in reviving the conflict between Rarabe and Bhele in the Ciskei, which emerged 140 years ago but which had largely healed? To ask such a question is not to exacerbate the conflict but to bring it into the open.

A number of papers in this volume deal with the struggle for land and power. These are themes long interpreted in partisan terms from the white side. Several of the papers here – notably that by Dr Saunders – provide a new interpretation, but the need for examination and interpretation of archival material by black South African historians is pressing, for the questions asked are inevitably modified in some degree by the viewpoint of the investigator.[10] One paper reflecting this was presented at the conference by Mr R. Makalima but unfortunately it was not offered for publication. The need for further economic analysis is also plain.

Histories of some missions and schools have appeared but we know very little about the reasons why some flourished and others did not; why some Independent Church leaders attracted a large following and their organizations survived, while other groups disappeared. The histories of particular families, those of innovators like Ntsikana, Soga, Jabavu, Makiwane, Bokwe, Mzimba, and those of conservatives like Njajula the diviner (mentioned by J. P. Fitzgerald, the first medical officer at Grey Hospital, King William's Town), whose descendants still practise near Debe Nek, would throw light on the process of change. Noni Jabavu has written of her Jabavu and Makiwane forebears, and there have been books or articles on some of the others,[11] but very many family histories remain to be recorded. The Xhosa chief, Maqoma, "the greatest politician and best warrior in Kaffraria", awaits a biographer worthy of him, one capable of delving deep in oral tradition as well as combing the archives. And the contradictory assessments of his contemporary, Charles Brownlee, also await examination.

It is unlikely that more than one or two local areas, or one or two of these topics, will be studied by professional research workers – historians or others – and the accumulation of material for local histories will inevitably depend upon the interest of amateurs. The greatest contribution to local histories is likely to come from school-masters, lawyers, government officials, clergy, retired men and women – black and white – living in country areas and interested in the history of their own home districts. The business of universities, editors of professional journals, and presses, is to provide advice and encouragement. There was a flowering of chronicles of "tribal" or clan traditions in the thirty years between 1900 and 1930, many of them published from Lovedale.[12] It is time for local histories of another sort, particularly those bringing together evidence from several disciplines, to emerge.

The struggle for land and power is one aspect of history, but there are many others, and a widening of historical interest to include other themes in the Ciskei and Transkei is long overdue. The proposals made here are slanted towards fieldwork as opposed to library research. This is not merely the predilection of an anthropologist but the advice of a great historian, R. H. Tawney: "What historians need is not more documents but stronger boots".

FOOTNOTES

1. *Reports and Proceedings of the Government Commission on Native Laws and Customs* (Cape Town 1883) pp. 403, 405. Sketch map of Natal before 1812.
   J. H. Soga, *The South-Eastern Bantu* (Johannesburg 1930) p. 91.
2. Archie Mafeje, A Chief Visits Town, *Journal of Local Administration Overseas,* London 2 (2) (1963);
   The Rôle of the Bard in a Contemporary African Community, *Journal of African Languages* 6 (3) 1967.
3. L. Alberti, *Description physique et historique des Caffres,* (Amsterdam 1911), pp. 22-4;
   Monica Wilson, *The Thousand Years Before van Riebeeck,* Raymond Dart Lecture (Johannesburg 1970) pp. 5-6.
4. Monica Wilson, The Early History of the Transkei and Ciskei, *African Studies* 18 (1959) p. 172.
5. J. T. Vanderkemp, Report, *Transactions of the Missionary Society,* (London 1804-13) 1, 437.
6. *Ibid.*
7. W. D. Hammond-Tooke, *Bhaca Society* (London 1962).

8. A. Kropf, *A Kaffir-English Dictionary* (Lovedale 1899), second edition edited by R. Godfrey (Lovedale 1915) Appendix I;
   Basil Holt, *Place Names in the Transkeian Territories* (Johannesburg 1959).
9. V. Z. Gitywa, *The Arts and Crafts of the Xhosa in the Ciskei,* Fort Hare Papers 5 (2) (Fort Hare 1971);
   E. M. Shaw and N. J. van Warmelo, *The Material Culture of the Cape Nguni,* (Annals of the South African Museum, Cape Town 1972).
10. G. Myrdal, *An American Dilemma,* (New York 1944) appendices 1 and 2.
11. J. A. Chalmers, *Tiyo Soga* (Edinburgh 1877);
    J. K. Bokwe, *Ntsikana* (Lovedale 1914);
    Noni Jabavu, *Drawn in Colour* (London 1960); *The Ochre People* (London 1963);
    F. Wilson and D. Perrot, editors, *Outlook on a Century* (Lovedale 1972), pp. 50, 173, 177, 182, 537, 550, 557.
12. W. B. Rubusana, *Zemkinkomo Magwalandini* (London 1906);
    W. D. Cingo, *I-Bali labaTembu* (Palmerton 1927);
    R. T. Kawa, *Ibali lama Mfengu* (Lovedale 1929);
    Victor Poto Ndamase, *AmaMpondo, Ibali ne-Ntlalo* (Lovedale n.d.);
    A. Z. Ngani, *Ibali LamaGqunukwebe* (Lovedale n.d.);
    T. B. Soga, *Intlalo ka Xosa* (Lovedale n.d.);
    J. H. Soga, *The South-Eastern Bantu* (Johannesburg 1930).

INDEX

Abonzai (people), 65
Acocks, J., 215
African Methodist Episcopal Church, 209–210
Afrikaners, 85–6, 128, 164, *see also* Voortrekkers
Alberti, L., 42–3, 88–9, 214
Alfred (county), 133, 166, 178, 196
Amalinde (battle), 21
Amathole (mountains), 49, 58, 64
Archaeology, xii, 40–1, 48, 50, 51, 53–6, 213, pl. 4–6
Arundel, Earl of, 151
Ashley, M., xiv–xv, 199–211
Ayliff, J., 108–9, 118, 121, 124–5

Babbelaan, (chief), 52
Barkly, Sir H., 167–9, 171, 173, 175–7
Barrow, J., 42
Bashee, see Mbashe
Batavian regime, 83–99
Batua (people), 48, 62
Bethel Institute, 210
Beutler, Ensign, 41, 52, 62–3
Bhaca (people), 50, 129–131, 136–9, 145, 149, 167, 170
Bhele (people), 217
Bhuti, M. A., 25, pl. 1
Bikitsha, V., 122, 133
Billie, 23–4
Blyth, M., 194
Blythswood, 208
Boers, *see* Afrikaaners
Bokleni (chief), 216

Bokwe, John Knox, 44, 209, 218
Bomva (chief), 59
Bomvana (people), 39, 59, 64
Bomvanaland, 45, 185, 187, 189–190
Boundaries, *see* frontiers
Bowker, J. M., 110
Boyce, W. B., 146, 158
Brazil, 92
British army, *see* frontier wars
Brownlee, C., 29, 60, 187, pl. 9
Brownlee, J., 44, 51, 218
Bruintjies-Hoogte, 63
Buffalo (river), 51, 57–8, 62–3
Bulwer, Lt. Governor, 176
Bumazi (chief), 60
Buntingville, 146
Burns-Ncamashe, S. M., 10–11, 21–3
Bushmans (river), 51, 63
Bushmen, *see* San
Butterworth, 109

Cabe (chief), 60
Calderwood, Sir H., 205
Cape Colony, xiv, 40, 84–5, 90–2, 120, 141, 147–8, 150–1, 168, 177–9, 185–198, and *passim*
Cape Mounted Rifles, 117
Cape Nguni, *passim*
Cathcart, Sir G., 120
Cato, G., 168
Cattle killing, *see* Nongqause
Centaurus (ship), 41
Chalumna (river), 57
Christian Express, 209

221

Cijisiwe (chief), 136–7
Cira (chief), 60
Ciskei, *passim*
Clapham (ship), 41
Clarkebury (mission), 147
Cobb, Captain, 118
Collins, Colonel, 41–3, 49, 64
Coloured (people), 131, 134, *see also* Khoi/coloured
Commission on Native Laws and Customs, 44, 54, 60
Congo (chief), *see* Cungwe
Cook, P. A. W., 3, 59
Cradock, 113
Cragg, D. G. L., xiv, 145–162
Cumgce, 57
Cungwe (chief), 52, 58
Currie, Sir W., 155, 170

Dabe, *see* Ndabe
Dale, Sir L., 207–8
Dale College, 210
Dalindyebo, Chief Sabatha, 11–17, 20, 214
Davis, R. H., 204
Dawabe, 59
Dedesi, (stream), 54–5, 57, 59-60
Dema, W., 118
de Kiewiet, C. W., x, 86
Derricourt, R. M., ix–xvi, 39–82, 213
de Villiers, H., 159–160
Difaqane, *see* Mfecane
Dower, W., 138
Drakensberg (mountains), 39, 49, 50, 53–5, 61, 128–9, 163, 213
Dubandlela (chief), 59
Durban (town), 149, 168
D'Urban, 203
D'Urban, Governor, 105, 108–110
Dutch East India Company, 91–2

Dwangwano, 60

Eastern Cape, *passim*
East Griqualand, xiv, 50, 54–5, 61, 127–144, 155, 157, 166–7, 175–6, 178, 185, 192–3, 196
education, xiv–xv, 199–211
Elliot, H., 194
Erskine, Major, 179
Ethiopian Church, 210

Faku (chief), 50, 129–130, 133 145–156, 165–6
Farmerfield, 113
Fingo, *see* Mfengu
Fingoland, 185, 192–3, 196
Fish (river), 42, 49, 51–3, 57–8, 62–4, 71, 88, 115
Fodo (chief), 130–1, 136
Foreign Mission Committee, 205
Fort Beaufort, 113, 118, 150
Fort Brown, 113, 216
Fort Peddie, *see* Peddie
Fort Thompson, 113
Fort Willshire, 40, 216
Frere, Sir B., 157, 171, 174, 177, 187–8
Freund, W. M., 83–99
frontiers, 40, 52–3, 61–5, 83–99, 148–154, 185–198
frontier wars, 64, 101–126, 153, 187, 190
Fynn, H., 152–3

Gaika, *see* Ngqika
Gambushe (chief), 59, 64
Gamtoos (river), 41, 53
Gando, 58
Gatberg, 131, 134
Gcaleka (chief), 43, 58
Gcaleka (people), 63–4, 93, 107–9, 116, 185, 187,

189–190, *see also* Hintsa
Gcalekaland, *see* Gcaleka
Gconde (chief), 57–8
genealogies, 8, 43–8, 53, 80, 93
Germany, 191
Gitywa, V. Z., 216
Gonaqua (people), 44, 51–3, 57, 62–3, 71–2
Goshen, 203
Govan, W., 204–5
Gqunukhwebe (people), 52, 58, 62, 93, 111–2, 146, 200
Graaff-Reinet, 89
Grahamstown, 113, 115, 146, 201
Great Fish River, *see* Fish
Great Trek, 84–6, 96
Grey, Sir G., 30–1, 106, 121, 128–9, 155–6, 166–7, 176–7, 185, 202–3
Griqua (people), xiv, 50, 127–144, 167, 171, 187, *see also* Kok
Griqualand East, *see* East Griqualand
Griqualand West, 189
Grosvenor (ship), 43, 50, 64–5, 71

Hammond-Tooke, W. D., 92, 180
Hancock, Sir K., 163
Harding, W., 152, 166
Hargreaves, P., 147, 158–160
Harinck, G., 60, 93
Healdtown, 203
Hercules (ship), 42
Herschel (district), 137
Hlangweni (people), 130–1, 136
Hintsa (chief), 5, 42, 59, 108
Hintsati, 58
Hlubi (people), 4, 108, 116, 138

Hole-in-the-Wall, 61
Hottentots, *see* Khoi
Hoza, 23–4
Hubberley, W., 65
Hubner, H., 58, 62
hunter-gatherers, *see* San

Idutywa (district), 185
imbongi, 11–37, pl. 1–2
Ingeli (mountains), 134
Iron Age, *see* archaeology
Ityala lamaWele, *see* Mqhayi
Izele, 58
izibongo, 11–37
iziduko, 17

Jabavu, J. T., 209–210, 218
Jabavu, N., 218
Janssens, Governor J. W., 42
Jenkins, T., 143, 146, 148, 152–7, 170, 174
Jeramba, 63
'Joobie' (chief), 64
Jordan, A. C., 28–9
Joyi (chief), 119
July, J., 134–5
'Justus', 44

Kaffraria, *passim*
Kat (river), 64, 117
Kat River rising, 95
Kei (river), xv, 42, 49, 57–9, 62–5, 119, 185–8
Keiskamma (river), 40, 42, 51–2, 58–9, 63, 213, 216
Kentani (district), 6
Khamile, M., 24
Khawuta (chief), 58
Khoi (people), xv, 40, 51–3, 57, 62, 65, 85, 88–95, 200, pl. 7, *see also* Gonaqua
Khoi/coloured (people), 103–4, 116–7, 131, pl. 8
Kinira (river), 60

Klipplaat (river), 49
Koba, 63
Kobonqaba (river), 65
Kohla (chief), 51
Kok, Adam, 130, 133, 138, 167, 170, 172, 175, pl. 12
Kok, J. M., 90
Kokstad, 159
Kowie (river), 64
Kreli, see Sarili
Kropf, A., 55, 57
Kubusi (river), 64
Kusane (chief), see Kwane
Kwane (chief), 52
Kwenera (river), 63

Land Commission (1848), 164–5
Langalibalele, 178
Late Stone Age, see archaeology
Lebenga, 138
le Cordeur, B., xiv, 163–184
Le Fleur, 130
Legassick, M., 85
Lehana (chief), 131–2, 137
Lesotho, 131, 178, 183, 192
Lesseyton, 203
Letele (chief), 131
Le Vaillant, F., 42, 63
Lichtenstein, H., 42–3, 89
linguistics, 40, 52, 55
Little Bess (ship), 170
Lipheana, M., (chief), 137, 140
London Missionary Society, see Van der Kemp
Lotana, 59
'Love' (chief), 64
Lovedale Institution, 24, 40, 201, 203–9, pl. 10
Lungu (people), 48, 64
Luzipo (chief), 116

Mabacqua (people), 64

Mabunu, N., 8–9, 24, pl. 2
Mada'kane, 49
Madura, 49
Madusi, 60
Magamma (chief), 58
Magwai, 137
Maitland, Sir. P., 115, 148–151
Majolo (chief), 60
Makalima, R. K. S., 218
Makanaena (people), 48
Makaula (chief), 130, 138–9
Makiwane, Rev. E., 209, 218
Malangana (chief), 56, 59
Manisi, D. Y., 9–10, 20–1, 29–33
Maqomo (chief), 218
Matanzima, Chief Kaiser, 20, 25
Matatiele (district), 137
Matola, 49
Matomela (people), 111
Matroos, H., 118
Mbashe (river), 50, 58–9, 61–2, 64–5, 108
Mbo (people), 45, 62–5
Mbutuma, M., 11–17, 20, pl. 1
Mdangi, 58
Mditywa (chief), 187
Mdlangaso (chief), 159
Mdutyana (chief), 130–1, 136
Merriman, J. X., 168
methodists, see Wesleyans
Mfecane, xiii, 39, 108, 130, 145, 200
Mfengu (people), xiii, 5, 39, 43, 101–126, 138, 200–2
Mfundisweni (mission), 146
Mgabisi, 60, 64
Mgazana (river), 64
Mgazi (river), 59, 64–5
Mgcambi (chief), 60
Mhlambiso (chief), 110
Mhlontlo (chief), 187
minerals, 167, 215

missionaries, 40, 43, 95, 112, 174–5, 199–211, *see also* Wesleyans
Mkulu, 59
Mlanga (chief), 59
Molteno, Sir J., 187, 190
Moore, A. K., 87
Morosi, L., 137
Moshweshwe (chief), 120
Moshweshwe, Nehemiah, 131–2, 137, 167, 170
Moss, J., 209
Mount Fletcher (district), 134
Mount Frere (district), 130
Moyer, R. A., xiii, 101–126
Mpondo (people), xiv, 39, 44, 50, 56, 60, 62, 119, 129, 132–3, 145–162, 170–4, 178, 193, 214, *see also* Faku
Mpondomise (people), 39, 40, 44, 54, 59–60, 62, 64, 129, 132, 138, 143, 170, 187
Mqhayi, S. E. K., 5–6, 17–37
Mqikela (chief), 154, 156–8, 170–1, 178
Msana, 59
Msiza (chief), 60
Mtakatyi (river), 64
Mtentu, 59
Mthamvuna (river), 60, 149, 152, 164–6, 185, 191, 198
Mthatha (river), 57–8, 60, 62, 64–5, 150, 155, 172
Myeki (chief), 59–60
Mzimba, 209, 218
Mzimkulu (river), 61, 130–1, 148–152, 155, 165
Mzimvubu (river), 50, 52, 54, 57, 60–2, 65, 72, 145–6, 149, 155, 166–171

Nadibi (chief), 63
Napier, Sir G., 148–151
Natal, xiv, 56, 60, 62, 98, 129, 132–7, 141, 145–6, 149–156, 163–184, 190–2
Native Educational Association, 209
Ncamashe, S. M. B., *see* Burns-Ncamashe
Ncaphayi (chief), 129, 149
Ncindisi (chief), 60
Ncocora, 57
Ncukana, 138
Ncwana, K. K., 5
Ncwini (chief), 59
Ndabe (chief), 59, 63
Ndamase (chief), 155
Ndawo, H. M., 1–2
Ndlambe (chief), 53, 88
Ndlambe (people), 112
Newtondale, 111
Ngangeliswe (chief), 187
Ngani, A., 25
Ngcwangaba forest, 58
Ngcwangu (chief), 57
Ngqika (chief), 42, 63, 70, 93
Ngqika (people), 43, 64, 93, 198
Ngqunguba (chief), 60
Ngwane (people), 108, 112, 124
Nicholson, B., 44
Njajula, 218
Njilo (chief), 59
Njokweni (people), 111
Nkanga, 59
Nomansland, *see* East Griqualand
Nomotis (people), 63
Nomtsheketshe (chief), 136
Nondabula, 136
Nongqause, 29–30, 154
Noord (ship), 41
North America, 84, 87, 97
Nossa Senhora de Belem (ship), 62
Ntabankulu, 57

Ntinde (people), 58, 93
Ntose (chief), 59
Ntsikana, 218
Nxego (chief), 59
Nyakyusa (people), 216

Oakleigh farm, 48
Ongeluks Nek, 128
Opland, J., xiii, 1–37, 214
oral data, x–xi, xiii, 1–37, 43–8
Orange (river), 89–128
Orange Free State, 128, 158, 170
O'Reilly, P., 140
Orpen, J., 168, 171, 187
Oxland, J. O., 157

Palmerton, 153
Palo (Mpondomise chief), 60
Palo (Xhosa chief), *see* Phalo
Paravicini di Capelli, W. B. E., 42
pastoralists, *see* Khoi
Paterson, W., 42, 63
Pearce, R. H., 87
Pearcetown, 131
Peddie, 109–113, 119
Phalo (chief), 43, 52, 56–9, 62
Phato (chief), 111
Philip, J., 95–6
Philippolis, 128
Pine, B., 152–3
place names, xv, 52, 216
Pommer, S., 131, 136
Pondo, *see* Mpondo
Pondoland, 50, 137, 166–176, 185, 188, 191–2, 195–6, *see also* Mpondo
Pondomise, *see* Mpondomise
Port Elizabeth, 113, 170
Port Natal, *see* Durban
Port St Johns, 155–7, 167–171, 174–8, 185, 188
Portuguese, 41

Poshuli, 132
praise poems, 1–36, 214, pl. 1–2
Presbyterian Church, 204, 210, *see also* Lovedale
Pretorius, M. W., 128

Qanga, 60
Qokana, 57
Qora (river), 41, 62–3, 65
Quakeni, 146
Queen Adelaide Province, 109
Qwabe (people), 130

Rarabe (chief), 58–9, 64
Rarabe (people), 24, 53, 59, 64, 93, 122, 217, *see also* Ngqika, Sandile
Read jr., J., 117–8
Rhode, 59, 185
Riligwa (people), 62
Rhodes, C., 159, 192, 195
Robinson, Sir. J., 166
rock art, 48, 50, pl. 4–6
Ross, R., xiv, 127–144
Rubusana, W. B., 1–2, 4–6, 17, 24–7, 29–32
Ruyter, 53

Sacramento (ship), 62
Salem, 113, 203
San, 48–51, 63–4, 85, 129, 215, pl. 4–6
Sandile (chief), 122
Sandile, Chief Archie, 10–11, 17–24
Santo Alberto (ship), 61, 70
São Bento (ship), 61
São João (ship), 61
São João Baptista (ship), 48, 51, 62
Sarili (chief), 119, 121
Saunders, C. C., ix–xvi, 185–198, 218

Scanlen, T. C., 191–2
schools, *see* education
Scott, J. H., 159
Seacow (river), 49
Seboni, M. M., 210
'Sembo' (people), 62
Seyolo (chief), 110
Shaka (chief), 145
Shaw, E. M., 216
Shaw, W., 146–156
Shepstone, H., 171
Shepstone, Sir T., 110–1, 125, 129, 164–7, 171–2, 177–8
Shepstone, W., 44
Shiloh, 113, 117, 203
Sidoi (chief), 130–1, 136
Sigcawu (chief), 158–9, 188
Sihlali, S. P., 209
Sikomo (chief), 57
Skead, C. J., 213–4
Smith, Sir H., 109, 118, 120, 151–3, 164–5, 174, 176, 203
Somerset, Sir C., 40
Sontlo (chief), 60
Soga, J. H., 45–8, 52, 54, 58–9
Soga, T., 45, 204–5, 218, pl. 11
Solomon, S., 191
Somerset, H., 113
Sotho (people), 50, 128, 131–2, 134–5, 137–8, 179, *see also* Lesotho
sources, xii–xiii, xvi, 40–8, 79–80, 161–2, 181, 218–9
South African Native College, 206, 210
Southey, R., 170, 179
Sparrman, A., 41–2, 49
Sprigg, G., 192
Stanford, W., 50, 158–9, 194
Stavenisse (ship), 41, 51, 58, 60, 62
Stewart, J., 204–8, pl. 10
Stockenström, A., 89, 92, 109–110

stone age, *see* archaeology
Strachan, D., 135
Stuurman, D., 94
Sundays (river), 57
Suurveld, 65
Swazi, 3

Tabankulu, *see* Ntabankulu
Taberer, C., 206
Tahle (chief), 60
Talo (chief), 59
Tawney, R. H., 219
Tembu, *see* Thembu
Thackwray, J., 111, 113
Theal, G. M., 45, 54, 61–2
Thembu (people), 11–17, 39, 40, 49, 50, 59, 62–5, 119, 214
Thembuland, 41, 185, 187, 189, 196
Theopolis, 117
Thesiger, General, 178
Thiba (chief), 136–7
Thlaping (people), 128
Thomson, W. R., 201
Thunberg, C. R., 41
Tina (river), 60, 138
Tlokwa (people), 132, 137
Togu (chief), 43, 51, 54, 56–7
trade, 40–1, 51, 69, 90, 145–6, 168–170, 178, 216
traditions, *see* oral data
Transkei, *passim*
Transorangia, 85, 128
Tshiwo (chief), 51–2, 58
Tsholomnqa, *see* Chalumna
Tshomane (people), 48, 64
Tshomane (place), 58
Tsitsa (river), 60
Tsitsikamma, 113
Tsolo (district), 50, 60, 62
Tsomo (river), 49, 59, 63–4
Tswana (people), 128
Tyhume (river), 40, 215, 217
Tzeba (chief), 63

Uitenhage, 88, 113
Umngazana, *see* Mgazana
Umtamvuna, *see* Mthamvuna
Umtata, *see* Mthatha
Umte (chief), 60
Umyeki, *see* Myeki
Umzimkulu (river), *see* Mzimkulu
Umzimkulu (district), 135–6
Umzimvubu, *see* Mzimvubu
Umzimvubu Prospecting Company, 167
Upington, 192

van der Kemp, J., 42, 70–1, 95–6, 214
van Plettenberg, J., 42, 63
van Reenen, D. G., 42, 49
van Reenen, J., 43, 64
van Rhyn, Hon. Mr., 207
van Warmelo, N. J., 216
Velile, *see* Sandile, Chief A.
Vereenigde Nederlandsche Ge-Octroyeerde Oost-Indische Compagnie, 91–2
Voortrekkers, 86, 131, 148–151, *see also* Great Trek

Warner, J. C., 170, 175
Watson Institute, 201
Webb, C., 214
Wesleyans (Methodists), xiv, 145–162, 201, *see also* W. Shaw, Jenkins
White, C., 138
Williams, D., 202
Wilson, M., xv, 32, 54, 86–8, 180, 213–220
Wodehouse, Sir. P., 137, 156, 166, 170, 176

Xesibe (people), 60, 129, 133, 170, 185, 188, 196
Xhosa (people), 2, 4–11, 17–32, 39–59, 62–78, 88–126, 185–8, 213–6, *see also* Cape Nguni
Xolo (chief), 173

Yako, St. John Page, 25
Yali-Manisi, D., *see* Manisi
Young, Lt. Governor H., 115

Zanzolo, *see* Hintsa
Zibi (chief), 138
Zondwa (chief), 59
Zulu (language), 55
Zulu (people), 1–4, 21–3, 27, 39, 55, 145
Zululand, 178, 214

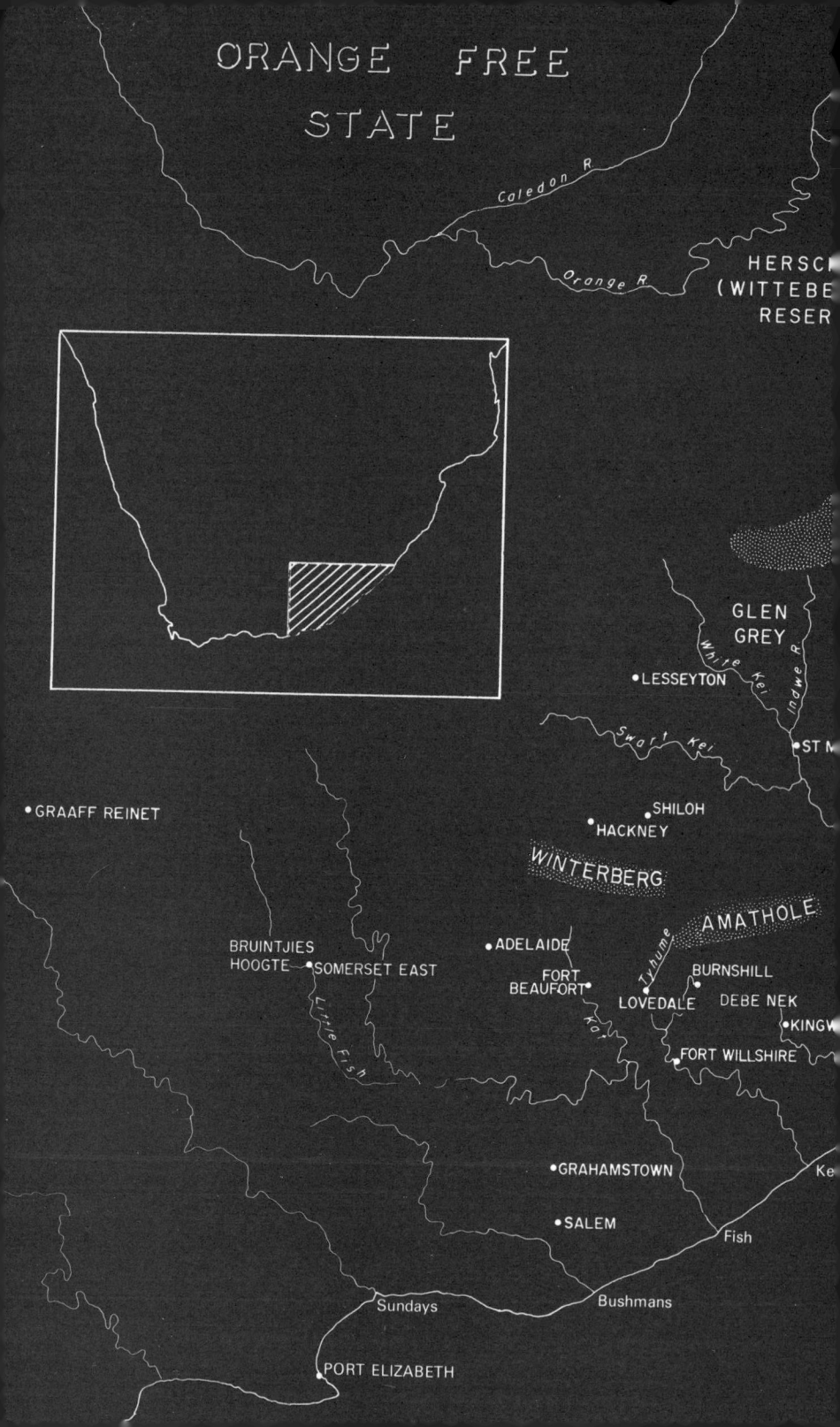